HOW THE OTHER HALF LIVED

How the Other Half Lived

A PEOPLE'S GUIDE TO AMERICAN HISTORIC SITES

Philip Burnham

ff

Faber and Faber

Boston · London

Library of Congress Cataloging-in-Publication Data
Burnham, Philip.
    How the other half lived : a people's guide to American historic sites / Philip Burnham.
        p.   cm.
    Includes bibliographical references.
    ISBN 0-571-19862-7 (cloth)
    1. Historic sites—United States.   2. Historical museums—United States. 3. Minorities—United States—History.   4. Women—United States— History. I. Title.
    E159.B92   1995
    973'.074—dc20   94-49318
                                                           CIP

Interior photographs by Philip Burnham
Jacket design by Adrian Morgan at Red Letter Design
Jacket photographs courtesy of the Bettman Archives

Printed in the United States of America

For Robbi, whom I met at the beginning;
for Beth, who died along the way;
and for my family, who has always been there.

Contents

Introduction

A FEW YEARS AGO I was visiting George Washington's home in Mount Vernon, Virginia, when I overheard a couple as they peered into the doorway of a rebuilt slave quarter. "They didn't have it so bad," one of them said, surprised at the rather elaborate spread before them. The bunk beds were covered with quilts, the woodwork had fine details, the copper kitchen utensils would have probably fetched good money on the antique market. That they didn't have it so bad seemed to be the desired impression, in fact. A sign near the doorway noted, however, that most of the slaves would have lived in "structures that were considerably less substantial than these."

The sign seemed to be admitting something about the state of historic preservation, at least at Mount Vernon. After all, the shacks where the field hands had lived were nowhere to be seen. Yet I knew that imagining how most slaves lived by looking in the "fancy" domestic quarters wasn't much better than taking a tour of the Washington house to get an inkling of living conditions experienced by the average dirt farmer. What do our public sites tell us about those who built and maintained the plantations, I wondered—not just those who lived in the Big House.

So it is that a small observation has grown into a book about public history: the monuments, road signs, landmarks, and museums that memorialize our past. Although a statue to Confederate soldiers in a small Alabama town may be the result of popular sentiment, it's my belief that most public-history sites are the legacy of well-organized

special interests. We think of landmarks as having a self-evident purpose: "It happened here, so let's mark it." But what historic sites most
often recall is less dictated by munificent motives than by agendas of
political expedience. Public history is a mixture of research, hardball
politics, and public relations, infused with a generous dose of ancestor
worship to give it the appropriate air of respectability.

What's seductive about historic preservation is that it has a way of
disguising itself as philanthropy. Monuments to soldiers stand in
shady public parks. Highway markers and picnic tables provide rest
for the road-weary. The National Park Service charges no admission
for many of its historic sites. Of course, taxpayers ultimately foot the
bill, but the beauty of public history is that, as part of the public
domain, it's simply there to be enjoyed. As such, preservation seems
—on the face of it—aloof from the reach of money and influence
peddling.

In fact, so much of our public history is "free" that it's tempting to
believe it has to be "true" as a result—like assuming it's OK to breathe
the air because you don't have to pay for it. Most of us don't like to
imagine the authorities hiding embarrassing truths or controversial
questions—especially about events that transpired so long ago. Yet so
much of our public history is passed down either anonymously or by
committee that dissent becomes difficult. Who's going to argue with
the Commonwealth of Virginia, the Veterans of Foreign Wars, or the
Daughters of the Utah Pioneers, especially if they're performing a
"public service"?

Of course, not all our history *is* free. Many private—and some public—sites charge an admission fee high enough to dent the pocket-
book of any middle-class family. But even then, the dignified status of
"private nonprofit" exudes a wholesome spirit of disinterestedness.
What's more, some of the most popular private sites were founded by
families whose names still connote a tradition of public service:
Henry Ford (Greenfield Village); John Rockefeller Jr. (Williamsburg);
Henry Francis and Arthur Du Pont (Winterthur, Nemours). Even the
heftiest admission fee may be dimly perceived as part of our philanthropic heritage. As I once heard a guide incomparably put it, "Isn't it
nice of the Du Ponts to have restored this mansion for us?"

Whether a site is maintained by taxes, admission fees, or corporate grants, it's hard to escape the feeling that it must be administered
fairly. Such is the aura of "historic preservation," a phrase that im-

plies a permanent, unshifting sense of values informed by the most dignified of motives. In such a realm, history is a shrine or relic to be saved from the ravages of commercial development. Given this attitude, it's not surprising that we tend to take history as it's dished out to us at public sites. While the occasional controversy does occur, it usually erupts as the result of a small, vocal, well-organized minority.

In the 1960s, the New History proposed that our telling of America's past had left many people out of the story. The study of manual laborers, women, and people of color began to cast the upbeat narrative of America in a different light, using the perspective of social history to look at the nation from "the bottom up." The recent multiculturalism movement, in large part, has been an outgrowth of this alternative. Such trends inspired the basic questions of this book: How have our monuments, museums, and historic sites responded to changes in historical thinking? Have our public sites accommodated to change, proposed a viable alternative, or remained untouched? In short, open to today's public, are historic sites open to interpreting the public of the past as well? If ever there was a subject ripe for social history, it is the monuments that we purport to share in common.

I've taken as my overall theme the interaction between racial and ethnic groups. Given the vast number of American minorities, I chose ones that have been reevaluated in recent years, particularly those who paid a steep price in the process of nation-building: Native Americans, African Americans, and Hispanics. Because they often found themselves in an adversarial role with the majority culture or the federal government, I was anxious to see how their stories—significantly revised in the New History—have been reconsidered at public sites.

The chapters are tied to popular themes. The Indian battle (Chapter 1) has a practically mythical status in American culture. The plantation and the mission (Chapters 2 and 3) dominate public history in the Southeast and Southwest respectively, and have shaped the way we think about people of African and Spanish heritage. Of course, not all Native Americans entered into violent conflict with Europeans, not all African Americans were plantation slaves, and not all Hispanics worked to convert the natives to Catholicism. As a result, I offer alternative visions of each group along the way. But the landscape of public history (essentially battlefields and monumental architecture) is such that these themes are impossible to ignore when considering the history of American minorities.

These groups are less monolithic than we commonly imagine. One of the unfortunate by-products of multiculturalism has been to think of minorities as self-contained groups when in fact they were permeable and overlapping. So the mixture of identity in the American grain is a major theme of the book. As the New History has also reexamined the role of women, I take up their case separately (Chapter 4), since that has been the tendency of so much feminist scholarship. Because gender cuts across divisions such as race and class, however, women's stories are found in different places throughout.

Finally, before the Conclusion of Chapter 6, I attempt a synthesis (Chapter 5) that looks at all of these groups in the context of a national vision. The vehicle for this synthesis is the railroad, an industry that provided entry-level employment for immigrants, native peoples, ex-slaves, and women in a way that no previous endeavor had. The Iron Horse is a story not only about the melting pot, but also about labor strikes, blacklisting, industrial accidents, and the forgotten role of America's unskilled labor. Here I consider the Chinese as a case study in the double-edged legacy of the railroad.

It would have taken me a lifetime to visit every museum and go to every site. Thus this book includes what I consider to be a representative sample of preserved historic places. Using both the *American Guide* series produced by the Federal Writers' Project in the 1930s and the recent *Smithsonian Guides to Historic America,* I selected places according to several criteria: 1) that they be open to, and interpreted for, the public; 2) that they have a broad geographical distribution; 3) that they be owned and administered by a variety of interests—federal, state, and municipal governments; private/ non-profit and commercial corporations; and 4) that they either be popular with the public or engage an important element of recent scholarship.

Clearly this is not Fodor's. Although I mention Williamsburg only in passing, Women's Rights National Historic Park, which has relatively few visitors, merited an entire section because it is one of the few sites where the new feminist scholarship is considered at all. What's more, my visits focus on the more permanent aspects of preservation—printed literature, orientation films, official tours, and physical layout. The vast majority of my visits are to places where something of historical importance actually occurred, rather than "site-neutral" museums or exhibits. Similarly, an analysis of annual historic reenactments—an important genre of public history I refer to on occasion—is beyond the scope of this work.

Other boundaries are more arbitrary: I take 1492 and the encounter between native and European cultures as a chronological starting point. For an ending, the close of the nineteenth century seemed less artificial than most. By 1900, the country was radically different from the way it had been even thirty years before: immigration from southern and eastern Europe was changing the ethnic makeup of the country; the government had declared the frontier officially closed; and in 1898, the Spanish-American War ushered in an era when America's wars would henceforth be fought comfortably far from home.

So I set off. I've spent a good part of the past two years pulling over and reading signs, holding up traffic on two-lane highways to find a way back to that pull-off for the historic marker. The attraction of "what happened here" became almost as strong an incentive to pull over as the common pit stop. But the signs that really pointed the way were found in a curator's anecdote or a voice buried in a book of history. How the other half lived, I discovered, didn't turn out to be a matter of public record after all.

HOW THE OTHER HALF LIVED

The Indian Battle

THE STRONG OF FAITH are welcome at the National Shrine of the North American Martyrs in Auriesville, New York—but let the weak at heart be warned. Visitors will find a museum, dining hall, retreat center, and a coliseum for special events that can hold up to ten thousand people. But the history of the Martyrs' Shrine is much more than the sum of its buildings. My guide, Father John Doolan, consents to show me the site of the former Mohawk village of Ossernenon, where the head of Isaac Jogues was impaled on a palisade after his martyrdom in 1646. A Jesuit like Father Doolan, Jogues was captured in an Iroquois ambush in 1642, beaten, made a slave, and forced to endure an unspeakable litany of tortures before the Mohawk (a branch of the Iroquois) murdered him, his head put on public display and his corpse thrown in the river.

A marble statue on the grounds depicts Jogues carving the name of Jesus on a tree. Sensing that I don't quite get it, the father tells me to look more closely. Jogues is missing parts of two fingers, chewed off by the Iroquois, he explains, "[who] figured they would get strong by sucking his blood." So begins my tour of the Shrine, owned by the New York Province of the Society of Jesus, whose six hundred acres have welcomed as many as a quarter million pilgrims in a single year.

We follow the path overlooking the Mohawk Valley. Father Doolan pauses by a park bench. "This is the Hill of Torture," he reveals, where French and Huron prisoners were made to run the gauntlet. "[The Iroquois] pummeled them," he explains. "They tortured them. They

*Near the Hill of Torture: the statue of Isaac
Jogues, National Shrine of the North American
Martyrs, Auriesville, New York*

tied them up . . . stripped them, and taught the children how to throw
hot coals on them." Three of the martyrs (including Jogues) are remembered with giant wooden crosses at the shrine entrance. "[One
captive] was seen praying through this," the father says glumly, "so
they cut off his lips." The first pilgrimage by Catholic communicants
to Auriesville occurred in 1885; the martyrs were canonized in 1930.
When a tour bus of senior citizens pulls up, the father excuses himself

to attend to official duties, and I'm left to reflect alone on the fate of the Jesuit fathers in New York.

The unsuspecting tourist who follows the highway two hours west of Auriesville to a place called Ganondagan is likely to be confused. There the Iroquois and French clashed again forty years after Jogues's ordeal, and a different memory of their encounter is preserved. A New York state historic site that was opened in 1987, Ganondagan commemorates the place where French forces under the Marquis de Denonville (led by Christian Mohawk scouts) laid several Seneca villages to waste in 1687 in a bid to control the fur trade— burning, looting homes, and desecrating graves. Three interpreted trails and an orientation video in the visitors' center, says site manager Peter Jemison, offer "an objective view of what happened when a European army was directed at a civilian population." A descendant of Mary Jemison, a white captive adopted by the Iroquois, Jemison is proud that Ganondagan tells about the "other" Indian battle: when the victims were native people, not priests or pioneers. Ossernenon/Ganondagan: a pair of Iroquois names that mark a puzzling public dilemma.

The tale of how America was claimed from native peoples by immigrants from a faraway land is as deceptively simple as any founding myth. The images of the Indian battle haunt us still: scalping, captivity, torture, massacre, and extermination. Each side has detailed the other's atrocities. From Jesuits to Puritans, from Kentucky woodsmen to Oregon Trail emigrants, the battle symbolized a test of faith and the hope of a better life. For most native people, however, it was an act of unprincipled theft; some have gone so far as to call it genocide. What was apparently settled by force of arms in the last century is still being disputed by politicians, lawyers, and public historians in this one.

Everyone seems to know what an Indian battle looked like. A wagon train or troop of soldiers is on its way to a faraway fort when someone suddenly gets an arrow through the heart. They circle their wagons or retreat to an outcrop of rocks, all the while firing at a group of painted warriors who whoop and yell and take tremendous losses before riding over the horizon to regroup for tomorrow's attack at dawn. Hollywood may have made this a stock formula, but it hardly invented the idea. Since before the Civil War, our public monuments were documenting the horrors of Indian warfare, just in case anyone was inclined to forget.

The Indian Wars (so named because the sheer number of install-ments defied human memory) achieved a resolution through brutal guerrilla tactics on both sides. Although racial enmity may explain this in part, the strategy of battle also reflected more mundane facts. Most tribes had to use ambush as a tactic because of their small num-bers and the enemy's withering firepower. For their part, Europeans learned from experience that the only way to engage an elusive enemy was by surprise. The results were bound to be profoundly bitter.

The Indian battle was fierce and often unannounced. Women and children made up a high proportion of casualties. Often there were few or no survivors among the defeated—and little cultivates group hatred like the rumor of annihilation. Whether the victims were in-habitants of a small British settlement like Deerfield or of the native Pequot village at Mystic Fort, public memory hasn't always recalled them with the same enthusiasm. How we memorialize the battle says much about who we think paid the greater price for building a na-tion—and even who deserves the land that the battle disputed from the start.

TURF BATTLE AT THE LITTLE BIGHORN

In the foothills of the Rocky Mountains, the land begins to tell stories. After a fall rain in eastern Wyoming, the short-grass prairie is dressed in mustard and red. The faraway hills, rounded hummocks in the dis-tance, look like a huge prairie-dog town. For the weary observer, they could be a distant encampment of tepees, the West being a sinkhole of traveler's mirages. The hills seem to have been cut and clawed dur-ing a primeval American Dream Time.

At closer range, the land is more homely. What seemed smooth from a distance is hairy and thorny up close. Along the thistled coulees and ravines, the sienna grass washes to a dry brown. The rocks have crags; the hills, shadows. The land, windswept and tree-less, seems vacant. For dreamers there's more to see in the sky than in the land, where at least the clouds run on in a succession of chang-ing shapes. The sun is starting to go down over the mountains. You wouldn't know it from a postcard bought in nearby Sheridan, but this is the gateway to the West that I call Massacre Alley.

The Bighorn Mountains are home to a string of memorials to beleaguered men in blue. Set like a tombstone on a swell near Highway 87, the Fetterman Monument commemorates Captain William Fetterman, who, with eighty men on a supply escort mission for Fort Phil Kearny, was wiped out by a contingent of Sioux warriors nearby in 1866. It was a dress rehearsal for the famous Custer battle—my state tourist map even calls it "Massacre Hill." The next year the Wagon Box Fight took place, "one of the famous battles of history," brags a twelve-foot-high memorial a few miles from where Fetterman fell. The names of the soldiers—Hoover, Baker, Barton, Black, Buzzard, Gross, and others—are listed, some thirty in all, on a shaft erected by the Civilian Conservation Corps (1936) for the Sheridan Chamber of Commerce. One gets the impression that white men in the Bighorns were often surrounded by overwhelming numbers.

These are only opening acts for the main event in Montana. Seventy miles north on Interstate 90 are signs leading to the site of the most infamous of all Indian battles, said to have given rise to more artistic renditions than any other event in American history. Little Bighorn Battlefield National Monument attracts about a quarter of a million tourists a year to see the national cemetery (where Fetterman is buried) and the ravine that General George Armstrong Custer descended one fateful June day in 1876. Rife in the popular imagination with overtones of martyrdom and misplaced glory, the battle is America's version of "The Charge of the Light Brigade": "Into the valley of Death/ Rode the six hundred" . . . or almost. In a few hours of fighting, over 260 soldiers and attached personnel—Crow and Arikara scouts included—were surprised and killed by a much larger group of Sioux and Cheyenne, declared renegades by Washington for their refusal to settle on assigned reservations.

The battle's importance has always been exaggerated. If numbers are any index, many other Indian engagements had more total casualties. More important, historians agree that the battle had almost no strategic significance—after all, the losers of the Indian Wars emerged from the Little Bighorn triumphant. The appeal of the Custer defeat is emotional, not rational, a fact recognized by William "Buffalo Bill" Cody when he made it the climactic scene of his touring Wild West show. "The battle endures because the disaster to Custer's command, like the annihilation of the Texans at the Alamo, left no white survivor to tell the story"—so begins the official Park Service handbook. The flash point, then, is that a group of men (almost all white) were exterminated. Little Bighorn commemorates what began as a battle but has endured as a metaphor for the threat to civilization by menacing, darker elements.

The Park Service, which inherited the site from the War Department in 1940, has attempted to mute its tribute to Custer, responding to criticism from the Indian community. "Custer Battlefield" was dropped as the designation in favor of a neutral name that would glorify neither side. The last two superintendents have been Native Americans; park interpreters now include members of the Crow tribe, who once had little to do with the battlefield. Pressure from Native Americans continues for construction of a monument to the fallen Sioux and Cheyenne—one to match the memorial to Custer's contingent that was erected in 1881. *Last Stand at Little Bighorn,* a video narrated by Kiowa writer N. Scott Momaday, greets park visitors with a forty-minute overview that probes the more gaping holes in the traditional Custer myth of guns and glory.

But the layout of the park lends itself to more conventional hero worship. The visitors' center is a few steps removed from the spot where Custer fell. A plaque on the coulee road marks the site where he was last seen by his men before riding to disaster. The loop road for the auto tour leads south to the position taken by Major Marcus Reno's men—dispatched by Custer to reconnoiter before the battle, an order that would save many of them from destruction—a monument noting where the soldiers "were besieged by the Sioux Indians." This, then, is the fateful route taken by the bluecoats. The layout of the tour traces a sense of growing paranoia among the trapped band of soldiers who comprised the Seventh Cavalry. What was an offensive campaign (Custer had ridden hundreds of miles from Fort Abraham Lincoln before sighting the Indian village on the Little Bighorn River) is thus perceived by visitors as a desperate, defensive action against all odds. Our tendency is to sympathize with an embattled underdog, and the battlefield park expertly plays to that emotion.

How Little Bighorn Monument came to be preserved at all is a telling story about the politics of preservation. The current 760 acres didn't become "public" with a magic wave of the wand, but they might as well have. In 1886, President Grover Cleveland signed an executive order creating a national cemetery one mile square, a chunk of earth to be carved from the middle of the Crow reservation on which the battle had been fought. More than forty years later, Congress got around to approving compensation for the land—seized by executive fiat—that would become the heart of the battlefield site. In 1930, a sum of $3,045, established by Congress as a current going price, was authorized to the tribe. "The price of the land as it was [in 1886] would be very much smaller," Congressman Leavitt said before the House with a hint of pride, "because it was simply wild, open land." The Fort Laramie treaty of 1868 had not called it "wild," but land reserved "for the absolute and undisturbed use and occupation of the Indians herein named." As Crow tribal historian Joseph Medicine Crow told me, it was, to his way of thinking, a "nominal fee."

The battlefield experienced more growing pains. In 1926, Congress, in a burst of fiftieth anniversary enthusiasm, authorized the acquisition of 162 more acres—about the size of a yeoman homestead—to preserve the site five miles to the southeast where the troops under Reno and Captain Frederick Benteen staved off an attack in the aftermath of the Custer defeat. Compensation was provided the Crow landowners in 1928, and two years later the park superintendent took over. The "acquisition" of Custer battlefield, then, was a familiar American story: the government deemed the land desirable; Washington declared its possession to be in the national interest; compensation—eventually—was paid the owners, who were either not consulted in the decision or forced to relinquish their turf on terms dictated by Washington. The Custer battlefield was "obtained" in the tradition of how the West was won.

Land acquisition at Little Bighorn didn't end there. Since the early 1980s, the Custer Battlefield Preservation Committee, a nonprofit organization based in Hardin, Montana, has purchased ownership or permanent easement rights for an additional 2,200 acres on the original battlefield, most of it obtained from members of the Crow tribe. Says Jim Court, a member of the committee board of directors, the land has been obtained "to protect it from adverse use" and keep it in as near pristine condition as possible, reflecting conditions of 1876. Park superintendent from 1978 to 1986, Court would like to see the battlefield area zoned by the tribe for preservation. "One fellow was ready to build a house down on Medicine Tail Coulee," Court remembered, "which would have meant junk cars, power lines, old trailers, all the usual things you see on the reservation. . . . We stopped that. He agreed to sell to us . . . at a fair price, I might add."

The committee raised a million and a half dollars to buy the land,

Court says. Much of the money came from the sale of battle memorabilia—books, prints, videos, cassette tapes, even replicas of the marble tombstones to U.S. cavalrymen that line the battlefield. The miniatures were twenty-five pounds by weight, one hundred dollars by price, and cut from spare stones donated by the Park Service itself. Eventually the service cut off the supply of marble, grouses Court, though not before the committee raised ten thousand dollars from its sale. There were more graphic incentives, too. "Every dollar buys fifty square feet," crowed one committee flyer. For a twenty-five-dollar donation the contributor earned a deed: a nice way, as the committee put it, "to own a piece of history."

Worried about an eroding land base, the Crow tribe passed a resolution in 1987 preventing further expansion of the battlefield. But the Park Service, having helped establish the committee and encouraged its efforts at acquisition, has operated for a decade with the understanding that committee-owned land will one day be donated as an extension of the national monument. The NPS, however, cannot accept area outside its boundaries without congressional approval, a turn of events that seems unlikely given the tribal resistance that might ensue. Still, the federal government is sanguine: possible compromises include having the land placed in trust, leased to the Park Service, or managed with tribal assistance—all of which would preserve it as a de facto extension of the battlefield. Meanwhile, the Crow tribe is considering its own nearby development: a privately financed "living history" tribal village about which the Park Service (and the Sioux and Cheyenne) have expressed serious doubts. Long a symbol of contested values, the Little Bighorn is a turf battle still.

"[The Park Service] got greedy like everyone else," says Lloyd Mickey Old Coyote, freelance writer and former teacher of Native American Studies at the reservation-based Little Bighorn College. Old Coyote insists that 1868 treaty provisions regarding land sales—such as majority approval by tribal adult males—have never been obtained by the government, much less by the Preservation Committee. He sees the battlefield site as a symbolic example of a much larger reservation "land grab." In this century, the Crow reservation borders have shrunk by a million acres; within the reservation, almost half the land today is owned or leased by non-Indians, the result of land-poor tribal members selling off assets for needed cash. "We see it happening all the time," he complains, saying the tribe is powerless to maintain a land base in the face of powerful ranching interests and government agencies. As some of the elders have remarked about Custer, Old Coyote adds, "The damn fool should have got himself killed somewhere else." The Crow, of course, rode *with* Custer, not against him.

Created as a division of the Department of Interior in 1916, the National Park Service administers over eighty million acres of public land. Committed by legislation to tell an uplifting version of the American past at hundreds of historic sites, the NPS isn't anxious to memorialize events that reflect poorly on the federal government—such explains the persistent tone of heroic sacrifice at the Little Bighorn site. Since its inception, the bureau has obtained historic properties through a variety of acquisition strategies, including donation, fair market purchase, executive order, and, in the face of resistance, the legal process of condemnation that leads to its sovereign exercise of eminent domain. Its official insignia an Indian arrowhead, the NPS administers more total acreage than that of all federal trust land on Indian reservations across the United States.

Little Bighorn battlefield, then, isn't only about interpreting the Indian Wars, it's about the priorities of preservation itself. Though a significant battle, the Custer defeat has a renown out of all proportion with its historical importance. Perhaps, after all, its outcome has given some people—the descendants of the victorious Sioux and Cheyenne—something to cheer about as a symbol of native resistance. But visitors to Little Bighorn today will be told more about the trappings of ethnic pride than the tactics of local land acquisition. Nowhere does the park guidebook mention that the battle was fought on the Crow reservation—not on disputed territory—that happens to be about a third the size today it was in 1876. The beauty of Little Bighorn is that we can stand on the ground where the battle was fought and replay the event in our minds. But our preoccupation with a site can blind us to the circumstances in which historic ground is obtained in the first place.

THE MOTHER OF ALL INDIAN BATTLES

You wouldn't know it from their design of the Luxor Pyramid theater in Las Vegas, but Ordway/Kousoulas architects are shaping the way we look at one of the bloodiest Indian battles in our history. Based in

Bethesda, Maryland, the architectural design firm has worked at Park Service sites ranging from the White House visitors' center to the basement exhibit of the Lincoln Memorial. Not all its subjects have been quite so lofty, however. In 1992 the firm was contracted by the Park Service to take part in what was about to become an interpretive tug-of-war at a little-known military park in eastern Alabama.

Horseshoe Bend, as the park is called, doesn't have the resonance of Little Bighorn. Annual visitation at the visitors' center, about twenty-five thousand people, is small by Park Service standards. But the battle played a more crucial role in American history than the Custer debacle did. At a bend of the Tallapoosa River, a faction of Creek Indians popularly known as Red Sticks erected a fortification to defend against the U.S. infantry and Tennessee militia, hot in pursuit under the command of General Andrew Jackson. On 27 March 1814 Jackson attacked and overwhelmed the Indian position twelve miles north of present-day Dadeville, a critical step in the public career of the up-and-coming lawyer from Tennessee.

Hired to research and design a new historical exhibit for the park museum, Ordway/Kousoulas had its work cut out. "When we started," remembers principal partner Fred Ordway, "I was quite struck by the fact that here is a national military park . . . that commemorates a battle, not of a foreign intruder or an aggressor, but of the indigenous peoples in this country." It didn't fit his image about what was worth celebrating in American history. "It's not like the Revolutionary War where we were right and they were wrong," he explains of his ambivalence. The expansionist theme of Horseshoe Bend, riding as it did on the shoulders of a hero Ordway felt skeptical about from the start, made him cast a critical glance at the exhibit he'd been hired to replace.

It was a typical Park Service design from the early 1960s—light on historical detail, heavy on pastels and military maps, aimed at a general audience with a junior-high-school education. The exhibit was essentially a pedestal for Jackson, vaunting his prowess as brave soldier, generous conqueror, and future president who opened the way for cotton cultivation on "some of the best unsettled country in America." To say that the land was "unsettled" simply ignored the people who had long resided there, but Horseshoe Bend wasn't in the business of questioning the assumptions of Manifest Destiny.

Accustomed to the precision of blueprints and design documents,

Ordway couldn't escape the message contained in the battle's raw numbers. Casualties for Jackson's army and Cherokee auxiliaries amounted to 49 dead, 154 wounded—costly, but not extreme. Creek deaths, on the other hand, were conservatively estimated at eight hundred—the most any tribe ever lost in a single engagement with the United States Army. Park personnel explain the vast difference in casualties by referring the army's superior numbers and weaponry. Even revising army deaths upward to account for the mortally wounded, the disparity—to a layman—was still staggering. "The thing that really got me," remembers Ordway, "was that there was not any tempering of the sense that this was a real victory for Jackson."

"Jackson had three thousand soldiers," he continues. "There were a thousand Red Sticks with their families. And Jackson also had the Cherokees coming in from behind," he says of the pincer movement that surrounded the Creeks. Outflanked, outnumbered, outprovisioned, at Horseshoe Bend it was the "other side" that circled its wagons in the face of overwhelming odds. In the end, virtually no male Creek prisoners were taken. Looking a little sheepish under the track lights of his Bethesda conference room, Ordway, stressing his personal—not professional—opinions, mutters, "That's annihilation; that's not victory."

Interpretation and design of the exhibit was meant to be negotiated step by step with the Park Service, a process in which Washington wielded ultimate approval. By subcontracting research on the battle to an independent historian, the firm attempted to get a contemporary reading of Horseshoe Bend. Ordway notes the Park Service was receptive to most of their proposed changes. For example, several nineteenth-century prints in the new display will offer a reminder that, even in his own time, Old Hickory had plenty of enemies. A contemporary caricature, "Jackson the Great Father," satirizes his "compassion" for Indians, showing him seated in an armchair throne with a couple of small but full-grown Native Americans in his arms while several more stand at his feet. It was Jackson who approved removal of the Civilized Tribes across the Mississippi in 1830, supposedly for their own good; it was also Jackson who, in the tradition of the "great white father," adopted an Indian child captured during the Creek campaign and raised him as his own on his Tennessee estate.

While the park slide show alleges that "the sun was going down and had set on the ruins of the Creek nation," Ordway and his team wanted to avoid the misconception that the Creeks simply disappeared after 1814. They "were a people of their own making," he says, and the firm set out to fashion a cultural narrative that wouldn't just begin and end with the battle. A section called "The Fate of the Creeks" includes photos of tribal chiefs from the late nineteenth century—many with obvious African American blood—even as Ordway acknowledges the lack of extant images of women, whose absence in the photographic record he came to regret.

Park superintendent James David likes the new exhibit, calling the old one "dated" and "bland." But there were limits to what he could accept in the new one. An early proposal from Ordway included an 1828 caricature showing Jackson's face composed of writhing, naked bodies—an allusion to his bloody campaign against the Seminole Indians—that was rejected by the bureau as too strong. "You have to be careful rewriting history," David cautions, adding that although Jackson was unfair to Native Americans, "for his time period he was very popular."

"I don't think we were as successful as I would have liked," Ordway says of the Creek section of the exhibit. The Park Service balked at an attempt to claim that the Creeks were descendants of the ancient Mound Building cultures of the Mississippi; even so, after consulting with Creek tribal leaders, they relented enough to permit a few cautious allusions to the Mound Builders, both in text and pictures, as a compromise. Ordway understands that the Park Service was looking for a presentation that would meet the expectations of its audience. "People coming to a military park really are not going to be expecting to learn about Indian life in 1680," he concedes. "We asked for more [space about the Creeks] and they said, 'Tone it down.' . . . We've made some gains as far as telling the story before Horseshoe Bend and the aftermath. At the same time, the battle is the biggest wall and the players in the battle are the big story."

Whatever Ordway's discomfort about the battle, some historians have claimed the Creeks had it coming. The immediate justification for Horseshoe Bend was provided by the August 1813 massacre at Fort Mims, Alabama. On that day, Creek warriors under Chief Red Eagle (William Weatherford) stormed the fort and killed several hundred soldiers and settlers, including women and children (an event reenacted every year by local enthusiasts). A Victorian print depicting the Indians breaching the fort walls had a high profile in the old museum; Ordway settled on a more subtle device, screening a different print of the battle with foregrounded images to give it less emphasis. But the real story of Mims, it turns out, was its inhabitants.

The Fort Mims tragedy, as the new exhibit makes clear, wasn't just a massacre of white people. In fact, the longer people look at the "Creek War," the more likely they are to succumb to a case of blurred vision. Many of the fort inhabitants were of mixed blood—Indian and white; others were Creeks who had acculturated to white ways; still more were black slaves. Red Eagle, the chief who led the attack, was himself a slaveholder and the son of a white trader, something the Ordway exhibit acknowledges. Some slaves, however, were killed in the battle and others were carried off, a few even returning to the white settlements—facts the new exhibit fails to mention. As Jackson wrote to his wife in 1814, "say to [the overseer]—that I have a number of Fort Meams Negroes, that will be necessarily on my hand for a short time—and with them he can regain in his crop what he has lost by the sickness of his hands." Even the most heroic avenger could take advantage of disaster—Jackson kept some of the slaves for four years.

Although Jackson needed little more than an afternoon to complete the rout at Horseshoe Bend, it's taken Ordway/Kousoulas and the Park Service a few years to retell it. Through all the stages—needs assessment survey, interpretive planning, design layout, submission of fabrication documents, installation (opened March 1995)—a cogent attempt at complexity has been made. "A book can be good and not provocative," says Ordway, "but I don't think an exhibit can. . . . To do a really good, lasting exhibit, I think you need to have more information than the regular visitor can comprehend in one trip." The problem, of course, is that most visitors won't return to Horseshoe Bend, if they ever get there in the first place. For most Americans, it doesn't have the cachet of Antietam or Shiloh; it doesn't even have the catchy ring of Tippecanoe.

"Times have changed," Ordway says. "The public really needs to see the other side." This time they will see more of it. But there will still be no mention, for example, of several hundred Creek women and children taken as prisoners of war after the battle. Some were awarded to the victorious Cherokee—who, the Park Service alleges, made slaves of them. Others were sent into military confinement and, it appears, later released by treaty. In one way, the before and after versions of Horseshoe Bend are similar: the fate of noncombatants is extraneous to the story, perhaps no surprise in a military park. "It's hard to believe there were no women and children among the casualties," admits David, referring to Jackson's passing admission that two or three had been accidentally killed.

Horseshoe Bend is "not well remembered" by the Creek people, says Alan Cook, historic preservation officer for the Creek Nation in Oklahoma. Such was the trauma of removal from the southeast in the 1830s, he explains, that many people "determined they would never look back." But Cook says the Park Service never consulted him about major issues touching on the new exhibit, although the preservation office, he admits, was only created in 1994. "History has been the domain of the non-Indian and not the Indian," he rues, adding that he would like the tribe to contract for a full interpretive role at historic sites in the future. What about the original struggle on the Tallapoosa? "It was," he says matter-of-factly, "a massacre."

The consequences of Horseshoe Bend were enormous. The victory opened twenty million acres of land to white settlement (three-fifths of Alabama and one-fifth of Georgia), much of it part of the fertile cotton belt that would drive the economy of the antebellum South. The Indian Wars preceded the conflict with the Creeks and continued after their defeat, but Horseshoe Bend broke the hold of a powerful Indian confederacy in the southeast. That the battle is hardly known to the public is a strange irony. During the most famous era of the Indian Wars—the quarter century from 1866 to 1891—the U.S. Army counted fewer than a thousand deaths among enlisted men and officers, a figure roughly comparable to Creek losses on a single day in March 1814.

MASSACRE ON MAIN STREET

Any back-roads traveler will find statues that commemorate the "virtuous" Native American. Sculptures of Red Jacket (Buffalo, New York); Chief Menominee (Plymouth, Indiana); and Massasoit, friend of the Pilgrim fathers (Plymouth, Massachusetts) remember acts of stoic courage or benevolence that Americans have long been fond of memorializing. But even the well-meaning testimonial can have a darker side. A massive bronze of an Indian erected by private subscription in St. Charles, Illinois, (1988), is inscribed "we owe the Pottawatomi of

*A typical massacre memorial: the sixty-foot-tall
Wyoming Monument, Wyoming, Pennsylvania*

the Fox River Valley our gratitude and respect," adding that Chief
Shabni warned the settlers of a coming attack under Sauk chief Black
Hawk and saved the settlements from destruction. Monuments to
"good" Indians often come hand in hand with memories of "bad" ones.

But for every site saluting an act of cooperation between Indian
and non-Indian, there are more recounting gruesome betrayals. The
Wyoming Massacre monument near Wilkes-Barre, Pennsylvania,
laments of a largely Indian force that "desolation and ruin marked his
savage and bloody footsteps through the valley." The Last Indian Raid
Museum in Oberlin, Kansas, touts the final native depredation in the

state with the display of an arrow that was found stuck in a cow after the attack. Massacre Rocks State Park, near American Falls, Idaho, recalls the wagon massacre of 1862 in which nine white people were killed. It's a pretty but stark place; a group of black boulders looms across the river from a small canyon, and the park is complete with outdoor theater and fire pit. In a nature preserve, an Indian massacre seems to be just a part of the natural order of things.

The memorial to the Indian menace is hardly a rural specialty. Scranton, Pennsylvania, marks the memory of its town founder, Isaac Tripp, who was killed by Indians. A plaque at Fort Nashborough in downtown Nashville, Tennessee, recalls that the city fathers fought off freezing weather, "pestilence and savage Indians" in their quest to found a settlement on the Cumberland River. At the corner of Michigan Avenue and Wacker Drive in Chicago, an inscription dating from 1928 remembers the inhabitants of Fort Dearborn, who "were brutally massacred by the Indians they will be cherished as martyrs in our early history."

One New England community has gone so far as to use the massacre as a founding story. Historic Deerfield, a nonprofit organization incorporated in 1952, has restored a Massachusetts town whose English roots date to the seventeenth century. A well-appointed village of some fifty buildings whose preservation recalls the hardy yeoman spirit of New England, Old Deerfield is run by a full-time staff of forty-five people, has an annual budget that tops $3 million, and attracts thirty-five thousand visitors a year. "Deerfield is a beautiful ghost," the official guidebook mysteriously begins, "haunted by the drama and violence of its early history."

That history is most remarkable for one event, an outbreak in the long-running struggle known as the French and Indian Wars. In the winter of 1704, the French, with Mohawk and Abenaki allies, burned and pillaged the town in a surprise attack, killing 48 settlers and marching off 111 more to captivity in Canada. The town was resettled in 1707, due in part to the efforts of Reverend John Williams, who lost a wife and two children in the raid and survived to write a narrative of his experience. "Ever since that time," intones the tourist video at the Hall Tavern, "the people of Deerfield have showed an extraordinary interest in local history and preservation." Indeed they have. A town that rose from its own ashes, Deerfield has turned the proverbial hatchet job into the foundation of a thriving tourist industry.

"We like to call it the greatest example of above-ground archeology in America," offers public relations officer Grace Friary, explaining that the site caters to bike riders, hikers, diners, and shoppers as well as the furniture and pewter crowd. Historic Deerfield is proud of its pedigree: many employees have been descendants of the massacre victims of 1704; people in nearby South Deerfield still trace their lineage back to them as well. Inhabited by some three hundred people—about the same number as when the town was attacked in 1704, the guidebook says—Historic Deerfield is an icon of the independent small town and its hard-won existence.

The backbone of the community is "the Street"—a collage of house museums that range from the early colonial era to the nineteenth century. Old Deerfield makes for a pleasant, if chronologically confused, ramble down memory lane. In some houses, different rooms are furnished to reflect different periods, suggesting more an upscale historical mall than a conventional restoration. But good taste predominates: trash cans are hidden inside stained wood containers; guides are dressed in period costumes, but don't assume antiquarian accents; weary travelers can take lunch or spend a night at the quaint Deerfield Inn (1884), which anchors the mile-long street. Visitors to Deerfield don't just take a step back in time, they make a leap of faith into several eras at once, an architectural smorgasbord of early Americana.

The Street has many treasures, but Deerfield's most famous is kept under glass on nearby Memorial Street. On display at Memorial Museum is the front door of the John Sheldon House (1698), a building razed in 1848, but only after its most precious relic from the famous raid was retrieved for posterity. About six feet tall, the Indian House Door has an iron knocker, is studded with nails, and features a gaping hole at its center large enough to put a hand through. That's just the point—the hole was cut by a tomahawk in 1704, and "its hatchet-hewn face still tells the tale of that fateful night," as a stone memorial on the Street puts it. Surrounded by Plexiglas and off limits to photography, the Door has been on display at the museum since 1880, one of New England's best-known historic attractions. It calls up what is an antique but still serviceable image for many Americans: this is what happens when you let a bunch of Indians on Main Street.

The Door couldn't be in better company. On a facing wall in the building are marble tablets dedicated to the Deerfield victims, the stones first displayed in 1882 by the Pocumtuck Valley Memorial Association, owner of the museum. Even today, the captions are sobering. "Sheldon, Hannah, wife of John, 39, shot through the old Indian house door"; "Mercy [Sheldon], 2, killed on the doorstone"; "Mary Field," reads another, "adopted by an Indian. . . . She married a savage and became one." In a display case below sits a more literal reminder of captivity, a single shoe worn by a Hatfield girl, captured by Indians and released in 1677. Beneath the somber tablets that speak of so much destruction, the once-ruby slipper of Sarah Coleman has turned a drab gray.

In the 1990s, when Deerfield's history started seeming a little one sided to the Association, the exhibits began to reflect more current sensibilities. So a new plaque near the Door recounts that Manifest Destiny was seen with different eyes by native peoples and colonists. In the adjoining Native American room, the taped voice of an Indian scholar laments misconceptions of indigenous people. White captives (including John Williams's daughter Eunice), we read elsewhere, sometimes returned to the settlements with Indian spouses to visit their old families. But the Indian crafts and artifacts on display seem more the province of art and archeology than history. Not so the Door—a massive historic presence—and the marble tablets that seem to derive from a source as sure as Moses. The Memorial and Native American rooms seem separate and hardly equal.

Museum curator Suzanne Flynt finds the tablets "racist" and "offensive," though she adds that they offer a window on nineteenth-century attitudes. Complaints by Abenaki Indians notwithstanding, the museum trustees will never allow the stones to come down, she believes. On arriving at the museum in 1981, she was appalled to find an Indian skeleton on display. She subsequently had it removed to storage and later reburied. She would like to move the Door elsewhere to play down its influence, an idea that has so far met with resistance in the association. Talking of their plans to acquire as many as three more buildings, she admits that the Native American room in the Memorial Museum "begs to expand."

For now, the New History remains contained on the museum's second floor, not allowed to filter into the rarefied air of Deerfield proper. Along the shady streets are boulders of New England stone inscribed with almost runic terseness. There's John Stebbins, whose house was burned in the attack and who, "with wife and six children . . . was carried captive to Canada," one inscription reads, only to conclude as a plaintive refrain: "He, his wife, and son John came back." In the old burying ground down Albany Road is a small, unpretentious mound, topped by a stone inscribed with Yankee restraint: "The dead of 1704." My guide says it was an Indian burying ground when the English arrived, but has no idea what happened to the original graves when the colonists began to put down their own.

Readers of the official guide, *Historic Deerfield: An Introduction,* will be relieved to learn that the English never meant any harm to the tribes of the region, an assertion that will make the massacre, for most people, even more inexplicable. Local natives, we read, died from nothing more than European diseases and attacks by other tribes. The English are congratulated for taking over the fields of the dying Pocumtuck—presumably just picking up where the locals left off. The fact that English and Indians fought two major wars in seventeenth-century New England over disputed land is barely mentioned. The massacre of 1704 was visited on the people of Deerfield as inexplicably as a flood or a plague of locusts.

The terror of Deerfield—and much of its fascination—is that so many people were carried into Indian captivity. But other kinds of bondage barely rate telling in the official story. "Some of the enemy who brought drink with them from the town fell to drinking," wrote Reverend Williams of his captivity, "and in their drunken fit they killed my Negro man." The guidebook notes that Williams lost his wife and two children in the raid—but not that his two slaves were also murdered. In 1729, the Reverend inventoried two more servants—Mesheck and Kedar—appraised at eighty pounds apiece. And as for Ensign Sheldon—deacon of the church, builder of the Indian House (fully reconstructed and open for tours), survivor of the massacre—he inventoried seven slaves in his estate of 1732. Strange as it may seem, the streets of Deerfield would have known the tread of such unsung inhabitants as Titus, Cato, Pompey, Blossom, and Romanoo; this was a town that knew slavery until after the Revolution. In several visits to Deerfield over the years I have never heard them mentioned.

Old Deerfield is a rare thing: a model town founded on a disaster. The massacre was the event that toughened the ancestors, made their descendants "determined never to forget their past." Complete with restored Main Street, post office, inn with twenty-three guest rooms, and the outline of the stockade pointed out by cheerful

Barely marked: Sand Creek "battleground," Sand Creek, Colorado

guides, Deerfield stands as a classic bastion, whether fortified against Abenaki Indians or the more mundane ravages of time. More for the candle mold and pewter crowd than the flintlock set, Deerfield is a gentrified cousin of "Remember the Alamo," even if the stockade walls have long since disappeared and the battle is only the beginning of an inspired lesson rather than its bloody climax.

Such tragedies happened—why shouldn't we remember them? But one has to look hard to find the converse of Historic Deerfield in the realm of public history. The simple roadside marker is the closest we come to recognition of conflicts that inspire less pride than embarrassment—and these are often belated. The Sand Creek Massacre (1864), in which over a hundred Cheyenne and Arapaho (most of them women and children) were killed by volunteer militia, wasn't marked by the state of Colorado until 1986. The site is accessible on a two-track dirt road lined with barbed wire, provided the visitor pays two dollars for egress to a local rancher. A marker on a rise of scrub above the dry creek bed describes it as a "battleground," a description that has more to do with wishful thinking than objectivity.

Near Preston, Idaho, a state marker of 1990 remembers the "Bear River Massacre," in which several hundred Shoshone were killed in a surprise attack by California volunteers in 1863. The sign is offered to counteract an obelisk below it crowned by a miniature tepee, erected in 1932 by the Daughters of the Utah Pioneers and the Boy Scouts of America. The obelisk, while noting that casualties on the Indian side were ten times those suffered by the army, adds righteously that many Indian women and children were combatants and that "175 horses and much stolen property were recovered."

I went a long way before finding a more striking memorial to Indian dead. In Gnadenhutten, Ohio, a monument some fifty feet high was erected in 1872 to the massacre of ninety Delaware Indians—men, women, and children—under the care of Moravian missionaries. The natives, the memorial reveals, "triumphed in death" after being killed by white settlers in 1782. Normally, an Indian version of Deerfield wouldn't be fit for such a reminder. But there were extenuating circumstances in Gnadenhutten that made the natives' plight poignant in the Victorian age: these Indians, the memorial makes clear, were Christian. A few feet from the stone a sign marks the "birthplace of the first white child born in Ohio," a reminder of the new order that had come to replace the Delaware.

FRANCES SLOCUM: NEVER CAME BACK

When the smoke had cleared, the Indian battle usually wasn't over. The worst fate, tradition had it, was reserved for some of the survivors. The image of white people carried into the wilderness as bound captives has inspired high emotion since the time of the first European settlements in North America. The Puritans used captivity as a warning of God's dissatisfaction with the congregations of New England. Literati such as James Fenimore Cooper and Charles Brockden Brown adapted the narrative to the purposes of American Gothic, and the dime novel in the nineteenth century used it as a lurid come-on for melodramatic tales of abduction and heroic rescue. White America has a long obsession with the fate of hostages—particularly women—dragged into the woods by howling savages.

By now, Indian captivity is just another roadside attraction. In Lancaster, Massachusetts, a sign recounts where hostage Mary Rowlandson camped with Indians after they burned the town in 1676. In Letchworth State Park (New York) is a statue of Mary Jemison, who "lived 78 years of her life as a captive and adopted member of the Senecas," dressed in buckskin with a bronze papoose on her back. Virginia's Hungry Mother State Park is named because of "a legend of an Indian raid in which a woman was carried off with her infant." In eastern Kentucky, Jenny Wiley State Resort Park remembers a woman captured by the Cherokee and Shawnee in 1787; Texas marks the spot where, in 1836, Cynthia Ann Parker was grabbed by Comanche. You don't have to drive far in America to find the roadside story of a white woman in distress.

Few survivors had as dramatic a story to tell as Frances Slocum, five years old when she was carried into captivity a few months after the Wyoming Massacre of 1778 near Wilkes-Barre, Pennsylvania. In the cemetery where Slocum is buried, near Peru, Indiana, a monument erected in 1900 notes that she married a Miami chief, bore two daughters who married clergymen, and "became a stranger to her mother tongue. She became a stranger to her brother, and an alien to her mother's children, through her captivity," (an allusion to the Psalms). A stern bit of Victorian moralizing it is, the epitaph leaning on the cautionary tale of the captive who never came back. As for the cemetery, it's one of those public monuments many locals are hard put to find, the site hidden on county road 900S, best found with a compass and county survey map.

Slocum didn't commit her story to paper because she never learned how to write. But this has hardly weakened the reputation of someone who's had more parks named for her than many an ardent conservationist. In Wilkes-Barre, near the place of her capture, is the Frances Slocum Playground, with swing-set and basketball court facing a long set of row houses; a few miles from town is the Frances Slocum State Park. In central Indiana is the Frances Slocum State Recreation Area—yet another preserve named for an Indian captive—providing camping and fishing for those anxious to have a wilderness weekend without experiencing the terror of the wilds.

Up the road at the county historical museum in Wabash, curator Jack Miller tells me they have a shawl and pair of moccasins made by Slocum—both of them prized possessions. "You can go and take a gander," he offers, but has launched into the tale of "the lost sister of the Wyoming" before I can even get out of my seat. It may be the best story that Wabash has, next to its claim to have been the first electrically lighted city in the world (1880) and the hometown of singer

Crystal Gayle. A lot of stories, I figure, have been floating around these halls where Miller has his office—a turreted building of Bedford limestone erected in 1899 to honor the area's Civil War veterans. "I love to hear it," Miller admits of the Slocum story, gazing out the window as though he'd forgotten I was even there, a pose he manages to hold for close to an hour. "I like to tell it, too."

Slocum lived for some seventy years with the Delaware and Miami, Miller tells me. After she was taken from her home (discovered because her feet protruded from beneath a closet door) she was prized as a captive for her red hair and adopted by a Delaware chief to replace a deceased daughter of the same age. She married twice and bore several children. Her first husband, a Delaware, treated her brutally; her second, much beloved, was a Miami named Shepoconah. As interesting as the facts of the bare outline are, we know them only because of a small but crucial betrayal.

Slocum might have remained in Indiana unknown to the rest of the world had it not been for a passing trapper in 1835 named George Ewing, fluent in the Miami language, to whom she confessed she had been born in the white settlements. At first Ewing was dubious: her red hair had turned gray; her bearing and language were Indian, not white; she couldn't even remember her Christian name. But when she took off her shawl and revealed to him a white arm, he was at last convinced she was telling the truth. She recalled that her father wore a big, broad-brimmed hat—evidence, Ewing thought, that he was Quaker. Fearing the story would cause a sensation if it ever went abroad, she made him swear he would tell no one until she had been laid in her grave.

If Ewing had been true to his word, the Slocum family would have been spared the ordeal that followed. Although sworn to secrecy, Miller says, the trapper wrote a letter about Slocum to the Quaker settlement in Lancaster, Pennsylvania. There the letter was somehow pigeonholed and forgotten. When a new postmaster stumbled upon it two years later, it was printed in *The Lancaster Intelligencer,* a local temperance sheet with a large circulation. Somehow it found its way to Wilkes-Barre, where a pastor recognized the tale and passed on word to the Slocum family. On the chance it might be their lost sister, Joseph and Isaac Slocum started for Indiana in 1837, soon to hire an interpreter and arrange a meeting with Frances in Peru.

When the time came, it's said that Frances received her brothers

coldly, not believing they could possibly be family. Joseph remembered she had lost part of a finger in a wood-chopping accident as a
child. As proof of their bond, he asked to see her hand. Sure enough,
the fingertip was missing. He called out "Frances!" and she replied
"Franka, Franka," repeating the name she hadn't heard for years. But
the emotion was visible on only one side. "She didn't break down,"
Miller says solemnly, evincing a touch of Hoosier pride, "because
she'd been brought up Indian." He pauses for a moment, adjusting his
ivory-tipped bolo tie. The chimes from the Christian church down
the street begin a sprightly version of "What a Friend We Have in
Jesus." I think it's about time to go see Slocum's shawl.

Before Miller can finish the story, we're joined by a special visitor.
Phyllis Miley is a resident of Wabash, a treasurer of the Miami Nation
of Indiana, and most important, Frances Slocum's great-great-granddaughter. She informs me that her Indian name is Maconaquah (Little
Bear Woman), the same name given to Frances. "I give all the credit to
my ancestors," she says at the start, a short, feisty woman with a mis-
chievous sense of humor. Her telephone recording has a passable imitation of John Wayne blustering, "Hold on there, pilgrim," advising
bashful callers not to hang up or "you're dead where you sit."

For schoolchildren and senior citizens, Miley is a small-town
celebrity, guiding tours to Slocum's grave while dressed in buckskin,
moccasins, and what she calls "my crown." Ever since she can remember, she's been known as Princess Maconaquah. Otherwise, she
isn't happy about what's happened to the eastern Miami, today 3,200
strong. The tribe has fallen on hard times, having failed for years to
gain federal recognition and the numerous benefits it confers. What's
more, the media don't pay her much attention. Not only do the local
papers have little interest in Frances Slocum, but people seem to
have picked the wrong stories to remember in their historic festivals.
"The white man in Wabash," she says with a look of cast iron, "will
not give an inch."

Every year Wabash reenacts the Paradise Springs Treaty of 1826,
celebrating the Indian cession of part of northern Indiana and southern Michigan. "It's a white man's enactment," Miley says, complain-
ing that a Miami medicine man was denied participation because his
beads and tepee weren't considered authentic. Miller, too, laments
the absence of native people at the event. "The heritage is there, and
we should see it," he says. "[The Miami] were the ones who made the

sacrifice, not us." He adds, a little embarrassed, that the local battle of 1812, also reenacted, has better Indian participation, though the Miami are only expected to stand around and get shot by the British.

The treaty was more than a decade old when Frances finally met her brothers, Miller resumes. But even a two-day family reunion at the Bearrs Hotel in Peru couldn't bring her back to Pennsylvania. However much the family tried to coax her, Frances wouldn't budge. By the 1840s, the Miami had been officially moved west of the Mississippi—except for a few sections of land, one of which was allotted to Slocum and her daughters. White encroachment had all but surrounded them; she had grown embittered toward the culture of her birth. After her second husband died, a nephew from back east came to purchase a section of land near Peru where he could live during her last days and hear out her full story. Miller looks at me square on for the first time since he started, a thin, gray chin beard framing his face. "There's something about living with nature that got into them," he says of the captives who didn't come back. Living at the edge of white society, unable to completely escape the culture she'd once been torn from, Slocum died in 1847. Her captivity, seventy years long, had sooner or later become her life.

However indignant she is at "the white man," Miley owes her celebrity to the fact that Slocum was born white. She's thankful the postmaster sent the letter on ("It was an act of the spirits," Miller adds), but if he hadn't, maybe Frances would have been spared the pain of having to choose between families. In that case, her descendants would probably never have known their link with the Slocum family. Miley says she was reunited with the other branch of the Slocums in 1992, the first time, to her knowledge, the two sides had met in 125 years. The reunion was held at the 1812 battle festivities, a likely place for the descendants of a war captive to catch up on everyone.

"That's more or less the story of Frances," Miller says wistfully, as though regretting it had to come to an end. At the insistence of her nephew, he says, Slocum was given a Christian burial. But as we leave the museum, Miller adds how mourners, in an Indian gesture, planted a pole with a white flag at the grave to show the Great Spirit where she rested. When it finally rotted away, it didn't bother local Indian people much—their sense of memory was different. In 1900, the new memorial was unveiled, the contribution of Slocums from across the country. The federal government ordered the cemetery relocated in the 1960s when a dam went in on the adjacent Mississinewa River. Miley was there from dawn to dusk the day Slocum's body was exhumed—the graves redug at the new site in precisely the same positions as before. "The Bible's right," she says, "when it talks about ashes to ashes." The cemetery where Slocum is buried with her husband and daughters was deeded to the Miamis by the county historical society in 1993. The land she lived on is under water in the Mississinewa Reservoir.

The chimes outside play a somber rendition of "John Brown's Body." Next door, a thirty-five-ton bronze of Abraham Lincoln on the courthouse lawn is inscribed "With Malice Toward None." In the other direction is the old city high school, boarded up and condemned, a swath of black graffiti painted on one wall: "Wabash Murders History." I pass the Frances Slocum Bank on my way out of town, its logo an Indian profile with feather headdress. The last thing I asked Miley was what she would ask Frances if she could meet her today.

"I would say, 'Grandmother, I need to know the language.'" Nobody on the tribal council speaks Miami today, she explains. For that matter, Frances never completely relearned English. A hundred and fifty years later, Phyllis Miley, like her ancestor, is something of a stranger to her mother tongue.

A WAMPANOAG AT PLIMOTH

On October 17, 1993, the citizens of Cherry Valley, New York, celebrated the most infamous event in their history: the Revolutionary War Massacre of 1778. That year, British loyalists and Iroquois allies attacked the town, killing close to ninety of its residents and carrying off a dozen others. The 215th anniversary merited a celebration sponsored by the Greater Cherry Valley Chamber of Commerce. The weekend schedule was busy: a craft show, a march to the massacre monument in the cemetery, a musket demonstration, a pancake breakfast. The night before was a colonial ball at the Tryon Inn, where, event chairwoman Nancy Erway said, "the Indians took most of the [costume] prizes," even if most of them weren't real Indians, she concedes. Publicity flyers for the massacre showed a tricornered hat with an arrow shot through it.

The next day the weather sulked. At two P.M. the sun broke through and the Tories and Indians made their charge across a field of corn stubble near the old high school, part of the original battlefield. They attacked houses, carried off captives, and tomahawked Colonel Ichabod Alden. (The rescue of the Campbell children by local slaves wasn't a part of the scenario, Erway says.) About 180 reenactors participated, many furnished by the Burning of the Valley Committee, a group that plans historical reenactments for the Schoharie and Mohawk Valleys. Cherry Valley seems enthralled with the story of its near destruction.

The reenactment is hardly unique. Every August, nearly a hundred people reenact the massacre at Fort Mims, where children have taken the roles of attacking Indians. On July 4 the people of Meeker, Colorado, celebrate the Massacre of 1879 with fireworks and full battle regalia—although one year they had so much rain they couldn't get the buildings to catch fire. In Medicine Lodge, Kansas, the signing of the 1867 Medicine Lodge treaty is reenacted every third year—Indians participating—and draws about twenty-five thousand people, who book motel rooms as far as a year in advance. To add a little color before the ceremony, they include a wagon train being attacked by renegade natives. Even President Lincoln shows up for the festivities, though by 1867 he had been in his grave for two years.

Thriving as they do on melodrama, reenactments are likely to recall native history with a bloody hand. Not so at Plimoth Plantation in Massachusetts, a historic reconstruction open at its current site since the 1950s, just a few miles from legendary Plymouth Rock. Interpreters portray people at the palisaded village of Plimoth as it appeared in 1627, lined with thatch, wattle, and daub cottages. Down the Eel River Nature Walk is Hobbamock's Homesite, the recreated dwelling of a Wampanoag family that lived near the colony in its early years. Through the modest rhythm of daily labors, interpreters at both sites offer a reenactment of cultural contact without the smoke and fuss of pitched battle.

Perched at the edge of Cape Cod Bay, Plimoth commands a grand view of the coast. But in the village proper is a less breathtaking vision of early New England, the more compelling for its dirt streets and cow dung. The tourist willing to part with $18.50 is free to amble at will and visit with pigs, cows, goats, sheep, horses, and, if not a pack of mad dogs, a rather motley crew of Englishmen. A carpenter tells of his journeyman years in the Old Country. The men perform a muster drill like a parody of the changing-of-the-guard. Women complain about how the men can be shiftless. A wife allows that, illiterate, she's content to have learned the Bible by having her husband read it aloud. The admission emerges that hardly any of the colonists can speak the language of the local Wampanoag—and frankly, why should they even bother?

It's taken years for Plimoth interpretation to evolve, shifting from life-size mannequins to costumed guides and candle-making demonstrations and then to the "first-person interpretation" that began in the late 1970s and continues today. The village "museum," as they call it, is based on painstaking research. A training period for interpreters includes sessions on Table Manners, Tool Identification, Elements of Theology, and Pilgrim Myths. In their apprenticeship, actors refine a role that ranges from imitating English regional accents to aping seventeenth-century posture as they stride down the street. Even in summer women wear full shifts and corsets.

Wearing the right undergarments is one thing; donning the uglier prejudices of the Pilgrims quite another. Assistant village supervisor Kathleen Wall remembers receiving a letter from a Native American who alleged that Plimoth was "encouraging the promotion of racial stereotypes." She remembered the incident that inspired the complaint, having been the cause of it while playing a Pilgrim woman in the village. Asked one day about her Indian neighbor Hobbamock, she displayed the English attitude typical of the day, responding, "We've improved him somewhat." But something got lost in the translation. "I could see his eyes sort of flare up," she remembers. "He said, 'I understand what you're saying. I don't like it, but I understand.'" Wall adds a little guiltily, "It's not a conversation you really want to be a part of. . . . You want to let people know this is the way they felt, but you don't want to encourage bigotry."

Bigotry was what helped bind the Pilgrims—and the later Puritans—together in an unfamiliar land. "People come in thinking Plimoth is the story of American democracy and that these are the founding fathers," observes John Kemp, director of interpretation. "Thomas Jefferson," he chuckles, "would have been ridden out of town on a rail." Kemp knows something about the intolerance of the early New England church, playing as he does the pious Deacon Fuller in the Pilgrim village. A thin man with graying beard, he's clad on this day in red breeches, a doublet with pewter buttons and lace collar, and custom-made "seventeenth-century" shoes that run two hundred dollars a pair. Bearing no resemblance to a former high-school teacher who once wrote a book on Robert Frost, Kemp concedes what it is that fascinates him about the place where he's spent over a decade: "There's a lot in the story about people finding their own way."

Find their way the Pilgrims did—with a lot of help from their friends. The most casual visitor to Plimoth sees that the plantation doesn't strike a balance between English and Wampanoag, if such a thing were even possible. The Indian homesite is much smaller than the village and is relegated to the end, not the beginning, of the tour. Native interpreters make no attempt to maintain the first-person historic pose of the villagers—though there was a time they did. To their disappointment, they learned the general public wasn't ready for anything much deeper than Fort Apache. "Have you scalped anyone lately?" was a common question. Other people wanted to see their horses (in 1627, the Wampanoag had never seen a horse) or tepees (shelters used by Plains Indian tribes, not eastern ones). Kids would come down the path doing their imitation of an Indian war cry.

In the early 1980s, Plimoth settled on a compromise. Indian staff would wear historical clothing but speak from a contemporary point of view—"third-person interpretation," as they call it. The New England accent of a Wampanoag dressed in deerskin leggings may be a little jarring, but it tempers those who come in expecting to find Tonto grunting in pidgin English. Even this doesn't preclude people from holding to the old myths. A young Blackfoot woman (nearly all interpreters at the homesite are Native American), told of a teacher who got up and walked out on her when she dared suggest that Squanto was a political opportunist, not the naive friend our folklore has made him out to be. While most comments are positive in the visitor response book at the village, one can still read remarks like "Make your Indians better," or "It was a great pity that the Indians were not expected to be 'authentic.'" Visitors tend to come to Plimoth with about as much baggage as the Pilgrim fathers did.

The subject of authenticity rankles Nanepashemet, a Wampanoag who's worked at Plimoth for two decades and is director of the Indian program. "Our homesite is probably—in scale—more authentic than the Pilgrim village," he insists. "The village had 180 people [in 1627], but there aren't that many there now." A stickler for historic detail,

Nanepashemet, at first glance, looks more like one of the harpooners from *Moby Dick* than a member of the preservation establishment. With the sides of his head shaved and his hair tied in a braid, he sports several earrings and pulls on a small, straight-stemmed pipe between questions.

The problem with the public, he complains, is that "they perceive size is quality." So concerned is he with misconceptions of Indian life that he oversees the Wampanoag site at Plimoth as a place where people build dugout canoes, cultivate corn, and fire clay pots with exacting historical precision. His staff, many staying during the winter months when Plimoth is closed, make their own crafts. In a world of theme parks and ersatz historic villages, Nanepashemet's motto is refreshingly out of step: "I'd rather have no pots than bad pots," he puts it bluntly. But he also seems to have made a virtue of circumstance. Taking a long draw on his pipe, he finally admits that it all comes down to more or less the same thing. "You can't build a [whole] village because it's too expensive to do and furnish and staff. . . . Sometimes it's just a matter of hanging on to what we have and improving that." The homesite, in other words, is not a Plimoth priority.

It's no surprise that the Wampanoag are not what draw some four hundred thousand people to Plimoth Plantation every year. Visions of stout-hearted nonconformists celebrating the first Thanksgiving in the "wilderness" are compelling still. And, as gate admissions and museum sales pay for 90 percent of operating expenses at this non-profit site, public expectations are paramount. Of total annual revenue and support—over $6 million—less than $300,000 goes to the Indian program.

As Kemp put it, the charm of Plimoth has to do with people "finding their own way"—a trait that most Americans still find attractive. It doesn't occur to many visitors that the success of Plimoth hinged on other factors too—such as the consequences of infectious disease. The visitors' film notes in passing that Plimoth was built on the site of an Indian village abandoned because of plague. But at a site such as Plimoth that relies on visceral impressions, how can one convey the real disaster of European-borne disease—by constructing a ghost village with abandoned homes and pots? The real debt Plimoth owed local tribes for its survival (half the colonists died during the first winter) is revealed only to visitors who know how to ask the right questions—"How did you get your food the first winter?"—and gauge the prejudices of their informants to boot. God-fearing Pilgrims were not given to crediting pagans with having saved them from almost certain extermination.

Muskets, disease, and demography enforced a political balance of power at Plimoth that is, in many ways, still in effect. "We have a folder with two hundred applications," says Kemp of the interpreters' program, "and Nanepashemet has to go out and knock on doors. For an Indian to work at a place called Plimoth Plantation, there's got to be a lot of negative feelings about that." Though Nanepashemet stresses the continuity of his staff, he admits that the program faces limitations.

In reconstructing Hobbamock's summer home, he says, they haven't even been able to find the names of the people who lived there, a problem that doesn't trouble the villagers up the path, given the wealth of materials on Plimoth specifically and English life in general. The record that both sides must consult is notoriously uneven. "Yea, he made [the Indians] believe [the English] kept the plague buried in the ground, and could send it amongst whom they would, which did much terrify the Indians and made them depend more on him, and seek more to him, than to Massasoit." Such is an account of Squanto playing for political position—but they have to scour a history written by William Bradford even to get a glimpse of him.

An intricate piece of "living history," Plimoth serves up a salty but familiar slice of life. Its effect is to enhance the experience of a favorite chapter, to correct the details of a story without questioning its point of view. The village is the big attraction, the homesite an illuminating sideshow. While Plimoth challenges our misconceptions of the Pilgrims, it reenforces their context by its very orientation. "In their story," says Kemp of the Wampanoag, "the Pilgrims aren't much more than a footnote." For most Americans, the Wampanoag don't even amount to that, a fact that Plimoth takes moderate steps to correct. "All of us would like to see a really top-notch Native American living history site," concludes Kemp, who is proud of what the smaller homesite has done, ". . . [but] there are reasons to wonder whether that top-notch site might not be better somewhere else."

Authenticity runs deeper than costume at Plimoth; conflict isn't resolved by the easy roar of gunfire. The depiction of two cultures living in a tenuous state of coexistence (even today at the Plantation the two sides seem to have minimal contact) is bound to be harder than staging a climactic event. The approach seems right—the two sides kept the peace locally for several decades after 1627. In fact, it may be more representative of Indian–white relations over the centuries than the common reflex of our public history, which has been to mark the occasion of great battles rather than the intervals between them. For living-history preservationists, peace is a more demanding state of affairs than war.

Travelers who venture from Plimoth up Cape Cod along the Grand Army of the Republic Highway, taking a detour on Samoset Road near Eastham, will find First Encounter Beach, where in midsummer the sand is strewn with towels, deck chairs, and sunbathers. A 1920 marker on a dune above the beach notes that "on this spot hostile Indians had their first encounter" with the Pilgrim fathers— many of whom, I realize as I read their names on the plaque, I just met in historical drag at Plimoth. What the sign fails to mention is that the hostile reception was probably occasioned by a previous encounter with an English privateer who had earlier taken some of the tribe captive.

Three weeks before, the Pilgrim fathers had unearthed a cache of Indian corn up the coast near Truro, another act that could not have endeared them to the natives, try as the English did to recompense them for it later. Near the bay, I find a small rock corralled by a fence with a flagpole next to it flying Old Glory. "'And sure it was God's good providence that we found this corn,'" the rock's script quotes a Pilgrim account, "'for else we know not how we should have done.'" It was the first step of the Pilgrim fathers in claiming the land, seven years before we find them in their palisaded village down the coast.

The locals, I suppose, must have been suspicious about these strangers poking about—but no more so than today. A few hundred yards away, Corn Hill—named for the cache the Puritans dug up—is the site of a housing development with posted signs on the road that warn "residents only" and "no trespassing." I get a few strange looks from people as I drive around the development. There doesn't seem to be any place fit for a picnic. I make ready for a return down the Cape as it occurs to me that the current residents of Corn Hill, if their public signs are any indication, remember the story of the Pilgrim fathers only too well.

Monuments are supposed to get the facts straight, but Melissa Fawcett Sayet doesn't think the one honoring her ancestor in Norwich, Connecticut, comes even close. President Andrew Jackson went to Norwich in 1833 to dedicate the resting place of the man who inspired Fenimore Cooper's *The Last of the Mohicans*—Uncas, sachem of the Mohegan tribe. Next to the Uncas monument on Sachem Street (inscribed with only his name), his grandchildren are also buried—so much for Uncas being the last of his line. A twelfth-generation descendant of the chief, Sayet rivets me with her pale blue eyes in the Uncasville office where she serves as Mohegan tribal historian. "They wanted to put a monument to Uncas somewhere," she shrugs, "but he's buried here on Mohegan Hill [near Uncasville] . . . and there's no marker." A new sign at the Norwich monument (1994), while giving a detailed resume of his life, doesn't admit that his burial place is disputed at all.

Sayet has worked to do something about recognition of the Mohegan, saying that Indian monuments too often recall a violent past. Part of a committee reporting to the city council, she helped design a statue for Norwich's Mohegan Park that would be a fitting memory to the tribe, today nearly a thousand strong. Unveiled in 1994, it includes a beckoning elder, a wolf, and a boy and girl—neither of whom appear to be full-blooded Indian—pounding and carrying corn. "It's a monument that doesn't mark conquest or the subjugation of one group to another," says Sayet, "but [one] that marks continuity, traditions, and peace between two groups—and that's not that common around here."

If anything, Sayet's ancestor was better known for making war than peace, a fact that has bearing on a controversial statue just fifteen miles from Norwich. In West Mystic, Connecticut, a large bronze commemorates the achievement of Major John Mason, who smashed the Pequot tribe in 1637 and so, history has it, made the area safe for English settlement. Set on a shady residential street on Pequot Hill, the oxidized image of Mason (or an idealized soldier)—striding as his hand draws a sword from a short scabbard—probably sees more joggers than automobiles in a typical afternoon. At the post office I have trouble getting directions to the statue, dedicated in 1889 in the pres-

"Preserving the settlements from destruction":
the John Mason Monument,
West Mystic, Connecticut

ence of the Connecticut national guard. In truth, Pequot isn't much of a hill anymore; nor, accounts suggest, was it much of a battle either.

Accompanied by Indian allies, the English cornered the Pequot in a wooden palisade called Mystic Fort—which has long ago disappeared—in the immediate vicinity of where the statue now stands. Anxious to end the struggle, Mason put it to the torch—filled, it seems, with men, women, and children who came pouring out to the fire of their enemies. "Great and dolefull was the bloudy fight to the view of young souldiers that never had been in Warre," wrote Captain

John Underhill, "to see so many soules lie gasping on the ground so thicke in some places, that you could hardly passe along." Another eyewitness related "no less then five or six hundred Pequot souls were brought down to Hell that day," an estimate that has never been significantly revised. With only a few dead on the English side, Mystic ranks, except for the most determined apologists, as an acknowledged Indian massacre.

The Mason statue—not to mention the high-minded motives that raised it—strikes a somewhat quaint pose at the end of the twentieth century. Had several hundred English settlers been killed, one supposes the site would have been consecrated as holy ground long ago. Permitting as it did the first English foothold in southern New England, the "battle" had greater impact than many a future engagement, though few Americans have ever heard of Mystic Fort. Since 1992, on the other hand, the people of West Mystic haven't heard much of anything else. That was when a Native American memorial service for the Pequot dead—on a site considered sacred by the tribe—initiated a controversy that, more than two years later in this small community, is still unresolved.

Complaints were lodged as far back as the 1950s about the Mason statue's failure to remember the fallen Pequots. In fact, the Victorian inscription hails the "heroic" Mason who "overthrew the Pequot Indians and preserved the settlements from destruction." In 1992 an effort supported by the Southeastern Connecticut Coalition for Peace and Justice, based in Mystic, organized opposition to the statue by gathering hundreds of signatures. Feeling public pressure, the Groton Town Council, with jurisdiction over the village of West Mystic, appointed a committee to study what might be done about the offending forty-five-ton bronze.

Composed of Indians and non-Indians, the committee struggled for a year, unable to resolve even the most basic issues: Were women and children killed, as an eyewitness account alleged, or was the narrative "exaggerated"? Were the Pequots aggressors—or were they defenders of their native soil? Was "genocide" applicable to the English tactics of slash-and-burn? Were there differences in the ways the two sides practiced war—or would the Pequot have done the same to the English in similar circumstances? It turned out to be a lot harder to resolve these issues than it seemed to be for those television images of happy crowds toppling statues of Vladimir Lenin in the closing months of the Soviet Union.

Some community members went so far as to advocate that the statue be melted down. Opponents countered that it might well be time to move the bronze—in front of the public library, a more prominent way to honor Mason. After extended wrangling, the committee finally reached a compromise: the statue should be moved from its current site. In March of 1994, the town council resolved to accept that recommendation. After several institutions respectfully refused the statue, Groton approved a most unusual invitation: they agreed to "loan" it to the Mashantucket Pequots in nearby Ledyard for their new tribal museum, not due to open until 1997. A more ironic setting for the statue of a Puritan warrior cannot be imagined.

"If somebody killed your parents, how would you feel if someone put a picture of [the killers] over their grave?" asks Joey Carter, assistant director of public relations for the Mashantucket tribe. The tribe, says Carter, wasn't opposed to the Mason statue, but to the fact that it stood on sacred ground where many of their ancestors had died. He believes the site was originally marked by the Pequot, but, like so many Indian cemeteries, was built over by the culture that displaced his people. Carter has been assured by the tribal council that the statue—when and if it arrives—will not be exploited for political purposes. He concedes that the Pequots fought their own wars of expansion, and that Mason (considered by many to be the founder of Norwich) was probably only following orders. "He did his job," Carter says with studied grimness, "and he did it very well."

"I don't trust them to interpret [the statue] in an even-handed way," counters Christopher Collier, Connecticut state historian, of the Mashantucket offer. "We can't undo the past," he insists, adding that "war was important in establishing security for Englishmen to settle." A professor of history at the University of Connecticut, Collier admits that history—and historians—haven't always been fair to the Pequots. But the problem of interpreting Mason should be left to professional historians, he says, not amateur "antiquarians," although he concedes that the monument wasn't put up by historians in the first place. Officials say that although the state-owned statue will probably be moved, the Mashantucket offer, because of the variety of interests involved, may well be ignored. As Collier puts it, John Mason is an "authentic hero" to many people in the state.

Standing at Mason's side during the Mystic inferno—a staunch ally of the English, as he would be forty years later during King Philip's War—was none other than Melissa Sayet's ancestor. Uncas was no more the last Indian to take sides with white newcomers than he was the last of his tribe, even if, as evidence suggests, he was shocked by the strategy of total war that Mason waged against the Pequots. The monument erected by the state of Connecticut long ago should have shown an Englishman striding, arm in arm, with the faithful sachem of the Mohegans. "Indeed he was a great Friend," wrote Mason of Uncas, "and did great Service" in a battle in which only a handful of Pequots were said to have escaped. Most of the rest of the Pequot tribe was rounded up in the months to come and sold into slavery to the English and the Mohegans.

Mystic Fort is another indication that the Indian battle wasn't only a contest over "race." I think of the Crow scouts killed with Custer; the Cherokees who fought on the winning side at Horseshoe Bend; the Deerfield attackers, a mixture of Abenaki, Mohawk, and French, many of whom were at least nominally Catholic; Squanto, the Patuxet, cutting deals with Wampanoag and English both; or the story of Frances Slocum, made popular by the culture she ultimately shunned. Not only a misnomer, the term *Indian* is unwieldy in categorizing peoples whose motives and loyalties were complex. Tom Quick, Davy Crockett, and Andy Jackson aside, some of the best Indian fighters in American history were Indian.

"What the gift of the Mason statue was," admits Sayet, conscious of the friendship between Mohegan and English, is a sign that "we're all reforming our relationships with each other." She calls the Pequot War a struggle of brother versus brother, acknowledging that Uncas had earlier broken from the Pequots—and that a time of "healing" has come. But she admits the Mohegans long profited from their relations with whites in educational level and socioeconomic success, even if profits from the Mashantucket gambling casino have made the Pequots newly powerful in the 1990s. Though the Mohegans remained silent during the controversy—no doubt feeling some embarrassment—she says that their stated support of whatever the Pequots decided was a show of solidarity. "If the Mohegans can stand up and say 'We did the wrong thing,'" she wonders out loud, "why can't other people?"

West Mystic reminds us of the stolid nature of monuments. In fact, it usually takes an act of nature to remove one. Unlike first press runs, cast metal or sculpted marble don't go out of print. By marking the past, memorials become historic events in themselves. Erected over a century ago, the Mason statue has importance as a Victorian antiquity, not just as a memorial to those who value their English heritage. But for tribes that would have once marked battles or cemeteries with a simple cairn of stones, an inscribed statue seems a perversion of the record—not to mention that the sacred site would have been casually erased by commercial development had the statue never been erected. Though hard to believe now, when the statue was unveiled in 1889, the charred remains of the stockade—already 250 years old—could still be seen.

There have been changes in how we tell the Indian battle. But after visiting battlegrounds, admiring statues, and reading cemetery stones and steel markers, almost anyone would conclude that it was not the native population that virtually disappeared by the turn of the twentieth century, but the white one instead. The image of *The Last of the Mohicans* may be a venerable one in our literature, but it is the last of the Custers, the Masons, the Wadsworths, the Bradleys, and the Sheldons that dominate our public spaces. From Plimoth to Frontierland, from Boonesborough to Fort Davis, evidence of the siege mentality that characterizes the public image of Indians is underscored. When the fort was one such as Mystic, however, the embarrassed consensus has been clear—better *that* stockade not be rebuilt at all.

2

The Plantation

THREE HUNDRED and seventy-five years later, the first Africans brought to America's English colonies in 1619 are about to step off the ship all over again. Hundreds of onlookers descend the slope from Jamestown settlement, packing telephoto lenses and minicams in expectation of the approaching ship. It's a boiling hot August morning on the Virginia tidewater. The crowd, mostly black, has come to remember a day as important for them as the docking at Jamestown in 1607 or Plymouth in 1620. The names of enslaved tribes are recited to the throng. People on shore link hands for a benediction. When the replica ship pulls into the pier, the crew hauls in the sails and the gangplank is lowered. "Ain't nothing to be ashamed of," a man behind me says.

The first black faces emerge from the hold—proud, buoyant. Twenty local dignitaries come forth, dressed in African and Western attire, stepping to a Liberian welcome song before being seated for a morning of speeches and spirituals. A choir is on hand to sing "God Is a Wonder to My Soul" and the first black Miss Williamsburg renders "America the Beautiful." Descendants of Nat Turner, Patrick Henry, and Pocahontas are said to be in attendance. Though a woman next to me complains that she came to see slaves in shackles, few people seem to be disappointed. There's barbecued chicken, plenty of crafts, and T-shirts commemorating "The Arrival" for $15.95. "We saw Mount Kilimanjaro," exudes a Baltimore pastor before the hushed crowd, "before McMillan ever put it on the map!"

There were few white faces at Jamestown that day, a fact that somehow seemed fitting. From the European "discovery" of America until the end of the eighteenth century, six out of every seven immigrants to the New World came from Africa, not Europe. Although only a small percentage found their way to North America, their numbers were still impressive. By 1720, blacks were a majority in South Carolina; by 1840, in Mississippi. The very word *plantation* grew up with America, denoting a "colonial settlement" in the late sixteenth century; by 1706, it had come to designate a tropical estate worked with forced labor. The indentured servants of Plimoth Plantation were a world removed from the chattel labor that would cultivate the corn and tobacco of Mount Vernon.

Most of today's Tidewater tourists aren't black, however, and are more likely to trace their ancestors to John Smith than the African indentured servants of Jamestown. The plantation has long catered to an audience that is basically white and well-heeled—and they do so successfully. Washington's Mount Vernon admits almost a million visitors a year; half a million make the trip to Jefferson's Monticello; a quarter million go to Andrew Jackson's "Hermitage" in Nashville, Tennessee. Curators will admit reluctantly that they don't draw many minority visitors, try what they will to encourage them to come. Pilgrimages, housewalks, even candlelight tours ply magnificent estates across the South for a simple reason: the Plantation is the symbol of the Good Life.

The planter homes are the closest we come to the manorial estates of Europe, built on a sweeping scale more in keeping with America's own ethos of expansion. The plantation promises to edify its visitors: architectural grandeur, riverine panoramas, sideboards full of family china. After all, the Indian battle is over. Ownership is secure. The land has been cleared, a veranda added to the cabin, political broadsides traded for estate inventories. But a bothersome question remains back of the Big House: just who's going to do all the work?

The market for slave labor touched masters north and south, wealthy and hardscrabble, urban and rural. It's no surprise that the famous made it a particular habit. Over half the presidents before Lincoln owned slaves. In 1799, George and Martha Washington together owned 314 slaves at their 8,000 acre estate in Virginia. By 1796, Thomas Jefferson owned about 170 slaves to work his properties in Albemarle and Bedford counties. Many of the gentry lived on estates

where the population was, in fact, overwhelmingly black. They inhabited a world that was profoundly—if arbitrarily—integrated, something that most plantations today would just as soon have us forget.

GEORGE WASHINGTON SLEPT HERE—A LOT

For an April day, it couldn't have been more perfect. The redbud and
forsythia were in full bloom. Gordon McCrae was on the radio croon-
ing "Oh What a Beautiful Morning" as I cruised down the George
Washington Parkway, leaving behind the urban blight of the capital
for a pleasant day in the Virginia countryside. Tired of signs up and
down the east coast that brag "George Washington Slept Here," I decided, like more than fifty million people before me, to see where it
was he came back to after all those arduous journeys. On a belated
pilgrimage, I had finally come to Mount Vernon.

I paid my money and walked up a lane lined with red brick, steering a course between a white four-rail fence that pointed the way
back through time. I crossed the broad bowling green and got in line
for the house tour. The plastered Palladian window was there; the key
to the Bastille that Washington was given by the Marquis de
Lafayette; and the bed on which the general, in 1799, as the guidebook puts it, "answered the final summons." I marveled at the library,
saw the copy of the Houdon bust in the museum, and had to fight off
the temptation in the gift shop to buy some nice-looking Chardonnay
bottled especially for the estate.

But something was missing. The day had been a little too glorious.
Sailboats glided up the Potomac. I overheard a guide reassure a
school group that slavery had been practiced for thousands of years,
not just in America, and that it hadn't been invented expressly for
black people, either. I decided to plan another trip—out of season,
this time. When I found my "guide" one morning in late November,
he was excavating a trash pit on the south side of General Washington's mansion. Head archaeologist at Mount Vernon since 1987,
Dennis Pogue is a little more skeptical of legend than most. After all,
he spent four summers digging up and cataloging garbage left by the
family of the Father of Our Country. "You're not going to get me to say
that George Washington was a good slaveowner," Pogue says a little
testily when I broach the subject. "That's an oxymoron."

Apologies for slavery, he explains, are common at plantations preserved for the public. Pogue calls it a "bunker mentality" on the part of administrators, a defensive reaction that tries to keep embarrassing questions at bay. A perusal of the Mount Vernon guidebook bears him out. One can read that Washington was a compassionate master, that the field hands were warmly lodged, that he emancipated his slaves in his will, that many stayed on as pensioners after gaining their freedom. While that may be true as far as it goes, it also smacks a bit of gift wrapping a lump of coal. "[Slavery] is a big part of our story here," Pogue says between trowelfuls, then pauses to reconsider. "Or should be."

As the vast majority of slaves were kept illiterate, the record of plantation life is sketchy and one-sided. In recent decades, however, a raft of testimony has come to light—letters, narratives, oral histories, and interviews—enriching our understanding of slave communities. Whether or not slaves could write, they left evidence of their material lives in the form of bones, bottles, tools, and pottery shards—in short, garbage. Although house tours may still be the mainstay of historic preservation, archaeologists have lately argued that a big part of our history is to be told by digging root cellars, not repapering the entrance hallway of the Big House. Thus a public history version of *Upstairs Downstairs* was born.

"What we find is that people are extremely interested in the process of archeology," Pogue says brightly, brushing dirt from part of the exposed brick pipe that leads to the house midden. He looks up at the mansion with a mixture of awe and misgiving. "This is such a static site. . . . We get a million visitors a year. For 90 percent of them, the only time they actually even talk to somebody is when they go to the mansion. . . . All you get are answers when you go through the house. The answer is 'yes,' the answer is 'no.' It's very stultifying. . . . Something like this is exactly the opposite."

"This" happens to be the first family's trash pit—twenty-five feet in diameter, one and a half feet deep—where Pogue and assistants were engaged in retrieving some high-class detritus, including broken ceramics, glassware, and a copper plate with Washington's name engraved on it. Curious visitors stop by to inquire just what they're doing. Unfailingly polite, Pogue's answers range from the ridiculous ("That's the Potomac River, ma'am") to the faintly sublime ("You see, in the eighteenth century, they didn't have any garbage trucks"). In the months to come, he adds, they'll be digging up the animal dung repository nearby, yet another example of doing history from the bottom up.

Some of the digging has explored the lives of other people at Mount Vernon. In 1990, Pogue and his team excavated, a few hundred yards away, the cellar of the House for Families, a slave quarter demolished by Washington in 1793. What they found on site was a rather surprising assortment of remains: duck, turkey, deer, and quail bones; wine bottles; clay tobacco pipes; Chinese export porcelain; Staffordshire slipware plates and pewter spoons. It may not have been a kingly take, but it wasn't the kind of inventory you'd expect from the poor and downtrodden.

"One of the findings that we made at the House for Families was that [the slaves] were eating better than we thought," says Pogue. "There are people who would like to draw from that conclusion that the slaves were better off." But the quality of life, he cautions, is hard to infer from plateware and bones. The ceramics, after all, were probably hand-me-downs from the Big House. And "just because they had some porcelain," he asks, "does that really mean things were better? Just because they had a greater diversity of diet, does that mean the quality of life was very good? . . . Maybe what that means is they weren't getting enough to eat so they had to go out and get it themselves. . . . How benevolent is that?" Finally, Dennis Pogue is starting to talk some trash.

"I'd like to see an Afrocentric tour of Mount Vernon," he says, "where people come in the front gate and it's flipped—instead of being a tour of George Washington's house, it's a tour of African Americans who lived on this plantation." It would be only an occasional event, he's quick to point out, but the tour would ignore the Big House, since most slaves didn't have any business there in the first place. In fact, they wouldn't even mention the general on such a tour, he speculates, just call it the "planter's house." "We don't name slaves," argues Pogue. "Why should he be named?"

Although some of the remains from the House for Families are displayed in the museum annex, elsewhere at Mount Vernon slave life is given barely a nod. The labor that raised the mansion is barely mentioned in the guidebook. The horse stables take up more space than the Greenhouse Quarters (the reconstructed lodgings of domestic slaves), and the flimsy shacks of field hands aren't represented at all.

Near the Big House, the closest one gets to someone breaking sweat is the gardener in the cabbage patch or the occasional craft demonstration during Colonial Days. The guidebook points out that General Washington, after all, was not a wealthy man: "Poor soil, indifferent labor, and dilatory overseers were limiting factors every year." Life could be pretty hard for the Tidewater gentry.

To its credit, Mount Vernon dedicated a memorial to the slaves in 1983: a granite column standing in a grove of trees near the original slave burial ground. Dedicated to the "Afro Americans Who Served as Slaves at Mount Vernon," it suggests a rather ennobled sense of their position—no doubt a reaction to a marker that earlier noted where the "colored servants" of Mount Vernon are buried. An annual service celebrates the memorial with songs, prayer, and the reading of a list of slaves from an estate inventory. Not far from Washington's tomb, it offers a poignant, if hidden, reminder of just who made it possible for George Washington to become a successful gentleman farmer.

For adults who spend the seven dollars to visit Mount Vernon today, it's hard to imagine why anyone would have ever wanted to run away from it. But perfectly sane people did. Washington wrote of an absconding charge in 1796: "The ingratitude of the girl," he fumed, "who was brought up and treated more like a child than a Servant . . . [she] ought not to escape with impunity if it can be avoided." Although black slaves provided the bulk of his labor force, Washington could hardly afford to limit his surveillance to people of color. In 1775 he advertised a forty-dollar reward in the *Virginia Gazette* for the return of two indentured servants—a pock-marked English carpenter and a Scottish brickmaker who "talks pretty broad"—the fellows having escaped down the Potomac in a small boat.

A prominent historic site, Mount Vernon is also a refuge for the imagination. "You see these people here," Pogue gestures at a group lined up to enter the mansion. "They're all thinking, 'In the eighteenth century, I could be living in this house.'" He shakes his head dubiously. Most white people lived in shelters more like those of slaves, he says. Besides, "it didn't look anything like this." The midden was full of trash. The trees that stand nearby weren't even there. "Most people . . . [who] come here don't want to see slavery," Pogue concludes. "They come here to walk through that house and see where the great man lived and where the great man slept. . . . There's no secret about [these sites]—they're a way of making some linkage with a past that we somehow see as good."

Of course, Mount Vernon's pedigree is better than good. In 1858, two hundred acres of the original estate were purchased by the Mount Vernon Ladies' Association—America's first national historic preservation society—from a great-grandnephew of Washington himself. The Ladies, who still own and administer the site, call themselves "the oldest women's patriotic society in the United States," their mission to preserve the estate as a national "shrine." With an operating budget of $8 million, Mount Vernon receives no federal or state funds, though part of the estate was first purchased by public subscription. A private site with the most public of profiles, Mount Vernon is a slice of history for the whole family. At least, some families.

"We are trying to avoid the sort of bleeding-heart approach to interpretation," says head curator Christine Meadows during one of my visits to the estate. "One of our problems is helping our interpretive staff deal with the black visitor who is very critical and angry." Admitting they haven't reached out sufficiently to African Americans, Meadows is still worried that the momentum of the New History may swing too far the other way. After all, she says, not everything that happened at Mount Vernon was all that terrible.

Over thirty years at the site have given her a practiced hand at deflating stereotypes. The estate had a mixture of laborers, she explains, including white servants, hired blacks, and black overseers; some of the whites had sleeping accommodations little better than those provided to blacks. Virginia had laws prohibiting masters from manumitting slaves, she goes on. Such laws, however, weren't an obstacle until long after Washington had died. Some slaves freed in 1799 were still living on the estate in the 1830s—"that's a pretty long time," Meadows notes, capping her claim that the Washingtons looked after their own.

"There's no question but [the Washingtons] were outnumbered," she says, affirming that Mount Vernon was a black community. But her way of putting it more recalls the conditions that would have faced General Custer than a respected member of the Tidewater gentry. It seems ironic to think of the masters surrounded or even threatened by their chattel—especially now, when signs of the slaves are virtually invisible. Though the Washingtons were outnumbered, visitors would hardly guess it today. "You really wonder that there was as much stability as there was on these plantations."

Acknowledging that Washington's farm records are an excellent documentary source, she's afraid that some subjects he wrote about will need to be handled with care. "One thing I think we're going to find it difficult to deal with is the theft by slaves," she says hesitantly. Noting that some objects retrieved in archaeological digs were hand-me-downs from the Big House, she adds that others would have found their way to the quarters by different means. Theft was "a natural and normal part of the economy," she concedes, quickly adding that "all of us have gone home with a pencil or a pen from the office," striking the conciliatory pose that seems like a reflex at Mount Vernon.

"Washington is criticized by the black community for not freeing his slaves before he died," she says dejectedly. "We hear that a lot. It was not as easy as it might seem to us. First of all they had to be educated—they had to be able to read and write. . . . In order to make their way as freemen they certainly needed more education than they had. . . . In some ways it would have been a harsh thing to do. I know that's not palatable to people whose ancestors were slaves—but you couldn't just open the gates and say 'go.'" No doubt some of the slaves regretted that they hadn't been provided with an education in the first place. In 1846, one of Mrs. Washington's former chamber-maids complained to an interviewer that "she never received the least mental or moral instruction, of any kind, while she remained in Washington's family." She had escaped to the north and resisted family efforts to return her by force.

Meadows admits there have been interpretive mistakes at Mount Vernon. After consulting the farm inventory a few years ago, they realized the domestic slave quarters were "overstocked"—they thinned out the furnishings, replaced the quilted coverlets with blankets, and roughed up the woodwork a bit. Reconstructed in 1950, the quarters, of course, are far from representative. In the surrounding fields, Washington would have directed the more numerous field hands where to "take their cabins," she says, which they picked up and moved as ordered. These were wooden shacks, hardly the stuff of a restoration intended to preserve relics for a national shrine. Most of the original eight thousand acres have been bought by private developers, and it's hard to imagine that part of Mount Vernon today. Washington wrote that the hands worked better when he was on site,

Looking into slavery: reconstructed slave quarters,
Mount Vernon, Virginia

Meadows adds, reflecting that "they did pretty much as they pleased probably most of the time."

As newly appointed director of restoration, Pogue tells me the attitude toward slavery is changing at Mount Vernon—slowly. He's proud of the Pioneer Farmer exhibit that's producing bricks, nails, and lumber to rebuild a sixteen-sided grain-treading barn—a way of using outbuildings to tell the story of Mount Vernon labor. Although the site is planted with tobacco and corn and harvested by workers, Pogue admits that fewer than half of estate visitors even find their way down to the riverside exhibit. This is all the more reason he's anxious to unveil a new "slavery tour," though maybe not as radical as the Afrocentric one.

April or November, Mount Vernon makes for a tidy outing. But the hemming and hawing employed by the Ladies is nothing new. A few years before his death, Washington wrote of a runaway, "It is highly probable Paul has left these parts (by water or land). If Mr. Dulany is disposed to pursue any measure for the purpose of recovering his man, I will join him in the expence so far as it may respect Paul; but I would not have my name appear in any advertisement, or other measure, leading to it." Without taking a breath, he passes on to a discussion of dressing artichokes—still grown, by the way, in the lush Lower Garden. Protecting a reputation, the Ladies don't do anything the General didn't once do on his own behalf. Two hundred years later, slavery at Mount Vernon is still all in the family.

A PLANTATION SAMPLER

"Old Nurse," the Mount Vernon gatekeeper said to be in the general's room the day he died in 1799, was among those slaves accompanying George Washington Parke Custis—Martha Washington's grandson by her first marriage—when he moved in 1802 to Arlington, Virginia. Across the Potomac River from the nation's capital, the view from Arlington House was described by the Marquis de Lafayette as "the finest in the world," perhaps the reason the privileged slaves were given cabins along the ridge to enjoy its panorama. From the Greek Revival pillars facing the river, today's skyline—the Capitol, the Washington monument, the Jefferson and Lincoln Memorials—looks something like a cluster of grand paperweights, the tools of a busy Enlightenment geometer at work. This is no kind of place for Uncle Tom's Cabin.

Behind the Custis/Lee mansion—owned by the National Park Service—stand two stuccoed brick houses that, at a glance, could probably pass muster at Virginia's better-known and more elegant Colonial Williamsburg. They would have housed the domestic slaves of the Custis family that Robert E. Lee married into on these very grounds in 1831. One house has been partly converted to a bookstore, a variation of the slave-quarter-as-rest-room found at Jefferson's popular estate at Monticello; the other is furnished with a high-backed chair, cradle, brass candlesticks, and peeling interior paint that has more neglect in it than historical authenticity. Garbed in sunbonnet and colonial dress, an interpretive ranger tells a group of schoolchildren peeping into the furnished room, "Everything's relative, but if you lived here, you were well taken care of."

In fact, some of the "Arlington People," as the Custis slaves are known, were educated—learning enough to read the Bible for their own self-improvement. Their descendants live in the Washington area today, some tracing their lineage to Mr. Custis himself. Park historian

Agnes Mullins isn't sure whether such a claim is accurate, saying only that "there's more smoke at Monticello," alluding not to Jefferson himself, but the less-disputed affair said to have taken place between slave Sally Hemings and his nephews. The Park Service is anxious to acquire a hunting piece that Custis gave one of "his people," currently owned by descendants of an Arlington slave family. The gun, says Mullins, would put to rest the stereotype that slaves were never allowed to bear arms. "[Arlington's] a farm," she wants to make sure I understand of the former 1,100-acre spread, "not a plantation."

Whatever their ennobled status, evidence of the Arlington people isn't easy to find today. A small exhibit on the slaves is hidden in the winter kitchen of the Big House. The nearby museum includes a lock of General Lee's hair and another from his favorite horse. But little is said of the slaves except to note that the Lees inventoried sixty-three of them in 1858. Freed by the Custis will four years later, many decided to remain on the land until the end of the war. "Uncle Charles" Syphax saw that his children were freed, Mullins tells me, but refused to follow course, such was his loyalty to the family. Even those slaves who ventured far from home carried with them something of the Custis manner. "I have some native children in my family which I am trying to Civilize and Christianize," wrote William Burke in 1858, who had emigrated to live in the free colony of Liberia and advance the cause of Christianity, "so if possible to do something for the heathen around us."

Today Arlington House resembles nothing so much as a polished headstone, the body of the estate now hidden from public view. It wasn't just the memory of the white South that was being blinkered when General Lee's "farm" was confiscated in 1864, part of it set aside for the new Arlington national cemetery. Many slave cabins were torn down. Nothing remains of the slave burial ground near the cemetery's northern border, nor of the Freedman's Village, established during the war to educate escaped slaves. "Several thousands are now in the settlement," wrote a visitor in 1865, "which is composed of a number of streets of log huts, all clean and neat as model lodging houses." Some Arlington people—given life tenancy on the land—were moved off, though a few returned to work at the cemetery later.

If the Custis estate seems a bit moribund in its surroundings, elsewhere in the South the business of historic tourism is booming. In Natchez, Mississippi, the brick slave quarters at Monmouth planta-

tion, my guide says, "were built by slaves by moonlight," a pretty notion, though she doesn't explain why they didn't have time to do it
while the sun was up. Monmouth boasts that it's "a glorious return to
the antebellum South"—compliments of southern California. Bought
in 1978 by Los Angeles developer Ron Riches, the estate has been lav-
ishly restored to a time when, as the guidebook says, fireflies danced
in the yard, the lady of the house made macaroons, and the bells of an
ice-cream wagon could be heard on a hot summer's day.

Monmouth, a national historic landmark, isn't just there to walk
through—people come from all over America to spend the night.
Glamour magazine and *USA Today* have called it one of the ten most
romantic places in the country. On twenty-six acres landscaped with
terraces, gardens, and a small pond, visitors find two cottages built on
the foundations of slave cabins where one can spend the night after
taking a thirty-five-dollar set dinner menu in the mansion, compli-
mentary house tour included. Those seeking a more authentic experience lodge on the second floor of the restored "servants' quarters"—ninety-five dollars a night, including color television and full
southern breakfast. "Monmouth was usually a very happy, pleasant
place to be," the guidebook chirps, stopping to note that on Christ-
mas Eve "the servants would party at the gardener's house."

"I doubt they have blacks in who have to wear handkerchiefs [on
their head]," sighs Mary Lee Toles when I tell her of my visit to Monmouth. Although admitting the importance of tourism, the president
and co-founder of the Natchez Museum of Afro-American History and
Culture says there's another story "we believe is not told when many
visitors come to Natchez." Thousands flock to the city for the Spring
Pilgrimage, she says, where ladies in hoop skirts usher the public
through antebellum estates lined with azaleas and boxwood, where
slaves might be mentioned as "servants" among the magnolias.
Blacks—and many whites—are excluded from the planning process,
says Toles, making the pilgrimage the preserve of the city's old money
and migrant professionals. "Natchez," she rues, "is still a tale of two
cities."

Toles explains how the city, dependent on tourist dollars as industry has relocated, is vulnerable to nostalgia. "They sell what they
think people want to buy," she says of the tourist establishment, "a
'happy experience.' We can't totally blame them." Still, she's cautious
about catering too much to expectations. Her own museum stresses

the enduring role of the black family, contrary to negative images that fill the press. Some people come to town to find out how the houses were built, Toles exclaims, not just to view their elegant exteriors or gaze at the china. But "Natchez is still not ready to tell that story," she admits.

Across the South, it's hard to find a plantation that demurs at the vision of cultured folks leading the good life. I pay my respects to the Andrew Jackson estate near Nashville, owned since 1889 by the Ladies' Hermitage Association, and a purveyor today of high-tech antebellum. Visitors are equipped with tape recorders and headsets for their stroll through the Hermitage mansion and its six hundred acres—the house and most of the land donated by the state of Tennessee. The recording begins with an overseer's voice acknowledging that the estate was worked by slaves; many of them gathered on the porch outside when General Jackson died, we're told. Hannah, slave wife of the blacksmith, recounts the demands of rearing her children, only to conclude with an invitation that we come back to the Hermitage the next time we're in the neighborhood.

Whether the quarter of a million people who annually visit the Hermitage enjoy themselves is hardly in question; the remarkable thing is that Hannah, her voice upbeat if not uppity, appears to have had such a good time, too. The Ladies, sure enough, have done their homework. Hannah (born around 1792)—commonly known as "House Hannah"—was a personal servant to Mrs. Jackson. In 1814, the future father of her ten children, Aaron the blacksmith, dared an altercation with a white man near Nashville who "shot a large load of Small Shot into his back which is still in him," a Jackson in-law reported, a fact that goes unstated during Hannah's few moments in the limelight.

"Jackson had genuine compassion for the weak and less privileged," the guidebook declares, a fact demonstrated by his adoption of a Creek boy, Lyncoya, whom he raised at the Hermitage until his untimely death at age sixteen. Old Hickory was a kindly master who appreciated loyalty in his dependents. Why else would Uncle Alfred, slave husband of Mrs. Jackson's seamstress, decide to live on at the estate until his death in 1901? His funeral was held in the hall of the Big House, his grave dug near Jackson's tomb in the family cemetery, proof that master and servant can walk (in the next world, at least) hand in hand. Andrew Jackson was more than just the ruthless victor of Horseshoe Bend.

Of course, the general's compassion had its limits. On 3 October 1804 the *Tennessee Gazette* advertised a fifty-dollar reward for a mulatto runaway ("stout made and active, talks sensible, stoops in his walk,") with the added incentive of "ten dollars extra, for every hundred lashes any person will give him, to the amount of three hundred," the ad signed by Andrew Jackson of Nashville. The Ladies have removed evidence of Old Hickory's temper, making him sound downright accommodating on the tape tour, which he no doubt was if you came from the right kind of family.

Today, the harsh hand of King Cotton is barely remembered at the Hermitage. The estate projects a contented human community instead, a virtue it hardly possessed in Jackson's day. "I have been obliged to tell [the overseer] he should not keep his hands a doying nothing," wrote Mrs. Jackson's brother-in-law in 1814, "as [the slaves] did not Tread out thirty bushells or more of oats in three days he cannot command the negro women I wish he would answer I pity him." The next year the protesting "wenches" were handed out a stiff dose of hickory oil in punishment. The museum film comments that the site answers "our need for a place to call home," but the only interpreted slave cabin on site is Uncle Alfred's. Most of the homes at the Hermitage are no longer there.

How best to restore the vestiges of the plantation is a common problem. Near Charleston, South Carolina, the National Trust for Historic Preservation—a nonprofit organization established by Congress—has preserved a Georgian mansion with spartan reserve, eschewing the idea of filling space with period furniture. Even so, the story of those who built the wonder known as Drayton Hall is hardly mentioned when I take the house tour. Aside from a privy, other outbuildings have disappeared. Hung with strands of Spanish moss, the gnarled live oaks give it a photogenic feel. The twentieth-century caretaker's cottage was moved off to the side, our guide says, to "get it out of the picture." That decision was made in the same spirit as that of the architect who had sham interior doors installed to complement real ones and thus maintain symmetry. Drayton Hall, then and now, is meant to be pretty.

For many years, informal tours were led by gatekeeper Richmond Bowens, the grandson of a Drayton slave, who was born and grew up

Field of dreams: Drayton Hall, Charleston, South Carolina

on the site—an original way of bringing a black perspective to the estate. Though Bowens retired in 1993, a videotape of him recounting life in the early twentieth century lends valuable insight about life at Drayton. But other reminders of the more than 180 slaves who lived at Drayton in 1810 are more fragile. The slave cabins were long ago removed in order to do lucrative phosphate mining. The slave cemetery, marked by families with shards of glass and pottery, was accidentally raked over in the 1970s by a volunteer group on a clean-up campaign—the volunteers just didn't recognize the sites as graves.

Drayton director George McDaniel is trying to tie material culture—the mansion itself—to the people who inhabited the grounds. As he puts it, "everything we see is the product of human hands." Still, some of his own guides don't feel they have time to discuss slavery in house tours that are barely an hour in length. Instead, he admits, they may focus on things such as mahogany brackets and sham doors—not the workforce that would have put up, as their publicity puts it, the South's "finest surviving example of Georgian Palladian architecture." Sometimes, he says, there are more basic battles to be fought. McDaniel tells how, aligned with local citizens, the trust fought a proposed boat ramp on the adjacent Ashley River, a development that would have ruined the mood of the place. "We want you to come to a

site and be able to imagine," he says of Drayton and its serene environment, citing the movie *Field of Dreams* as an example. It's a fitting
image—and one of a lost, pastoral America that belies the conditions
under which the bricks of Drayton Hall would have been fired.

The plantation seems typically southern—in South Carolina,
slaves comprised almost 60 percent of the population by the Civil
War. But my trip to Deerfield taught me that slavery was sometimes to
be found in surprising places. At the Royall House in Medford, Massachusetts, stands a brick slave quarter and summer kitchen from the
1730s, near the mansion built for merchant Isaac Royall Sr. on six
hundred acres of land first deeded to John Winthrop in 1631. Only a
few acres of the estate remain intact today, a small island in downtown Medford. When the federal government put the house on a commemorative stamp in 1990, the Royall House Association, owners of
the estate, drew fire from opposite sides. Although some people objected that the stamp failed to include the slave quarters at all, others
regarded it as an unnecessary reminder of a painful chapter in American history.

The outcry called into question the efforts that had restored the
Royall House and slave quarters from the beginning. "It celebrates
slavery, not freedom," says the Reverend Eugene Adams of the Royall
estate, himself a former member of the Association. Minister emeri-
tus of the Unitarian Universalist church of Medford, Adams explains,
"Slavery's the furthest thing from our mind now," noting that more
pressing political issues are at hand and that the fixation on bondage
only perpetuates a backward perspective.

Resistance developed in the black community, too. Local historian
Mabray Kountze long criticized the major role Royall had taken in
Medford public history. "Medford never had hundreds of slaves," he
wrote in a 1969 account of the city, emphasizing that "[its] current
colored population came from the settlement of free men." Noting
that the forty-nine slaves inventoried in Medford had been freed by
1764—a century before emancipation—he argued that the city's slave
history had been exaggerated at the expense of the more uplifting tale
of early free blacks who became artisans, participated in the Underground Railroad, and, though the record is scanty, probably fought in
the Revolutionary War.

"We don't look at this as a monument to slavery," counters Jay
Griffin, Royall House curator. "We look at it like the death camps, as

a memorial to the people who suffered an injustice." Saying he received bomb threats during the stamp controversy, Griffin proudly shows me a pair of Medford slave handcuffs now displayed in the quarters, rooms long used as a meeting place by the Daughters of the American Revolution before the Association bought the buildings in 1908 and restored them. The second floor of the slave quarters house Griffin and his family, while the downstairs is full of folding tables, bric-a-brac, and a nine-foot-long fireplace. Only in the last year, he admits, has the social history of Royall slaves been interpreted in any detail. And if the controversial stamp didn't show the slave quarters, I notice, neither does the site brochure.

Public reminders of slavery are taken seriously in Medford, says Griffin. A plaque put up on "Pompey's Wall," built of bricks by a local slave on a street elsewhere in Medford, hasn't stayed put. "We've marked it, but they've ripped off the plaque every time," he complains, not elaborating on exactly who "they" are. A mural depicting the triangular slave trade in a Medford post office also came under fire from part of the black community, who argued that the images of slavery gave an incomplete impression of the past. Griffin adds that no one has torn down the local marker acknowledging a stop on the Underground Railroad—evidence, he notes, that good memories are easier for people to accept.

After a tour of the plantations, Medford's history bears out a valuable reminder. There were slaves in the North. There were slaves who lived in cities. Just as important, there were many free blacks before emancipation—almost half a million in 1860, most of them in the South. However restricted the freedoms of free blacks, their story is unknown to most Americans. Griffin remains aghast that the motives of the Association could be so grievously misunderstood. "I went to Dachau," he says, urging on me the need for poignant memorials, "I know."

But not everyone agrees on the purpose of remembering the plantation. As some whites have neglected the story of slavery out of embarrassment or condescension, some blacks have doubts about remembering their early roots in the Americas too. The problem is how we have come to see slavery as a degraded existence, forgetting the humanity of the people who endured it. To see them only as "slaves" is one of the most difficult legacies of the plantation—for black and white alike—to overcome. As I saw in my excursion to Jamestown,

thousands of African Americans, given the chance, came out to celebrate the memory of ancestors who arrived in the most tragic of circumstances—in bondage—but still with a hope of leading lives beyond the shackle and the lash.

THE IMAGINARY PLANTATION

America's plantations have suffered the effects of time: some were destroyed outright during the Civil War, many more have crumbled
from sheer neglect. Most of those open to the public are fortunate to
have anything to preserve at all. But in our zeal to recreate the past,
says John Michael Vlach, professor of American Studies at George
Washington University in Washington, D.C., sometimes dubious
methods have been employed. Some estates simply "don't have
enough to make up a site," says Vlach, "so they get a barn from one
place and a house from another place, and a watering trough from another, and then just bring them together generically in a way that
matches a Currier and Ives print." The result ends up being, to his
mind, an antiseptic and distorted view of the past.

Vlach has written widely on plantation architecture, but is less
taken with the Big House than the myriad outbuildings that supported it. Built of wood, average slave quarters might last for thirty
years under ordinary conditions, he says. Many were converted to
storage sheds or barns after the Civil War and eventually decayed, unless someone happened to be living in them. In 1860, there were
twenty-three hundred plantations in America that had a hundred or
more slaves. Although scores of these sites still have standing slave
quarters, Vlach says, only a tiny number of them have more than one
or two—further minimizing the memory of slavery on the plantation.
The others won't last, he predicts, "without particular care and refur-
bishment," for another twenty-five years. If some people want to forget about slavery, the passage of time is doing them a big favor.

"This is vernacular architecture," Vlach emphasizes, "and most
states are oriented toward monumental buildings. If somebody important slept there, they'll save the building. If it's just a very good example of its type, [they'll say] 'we still have a lot of great men and
women to look after.'" He adds disapprovingly, "It's not glamorous
enough," even if some structures would prove to be, as he puts it, the

The common fate of slave quarters:
Kingsley Plantation, Fort George Island, Florida

Rosetta Stone for understanding life in slave quarters. "It does throw some ink on the heroic moment of the founding fathers," he says of bringing slavery out of the closet, "but it's not a secret—the history profession's been writing that for thirty or forty years."

For all the plantations that have fallen into disrepair, tourists are invited to sample a unique one in upstate Mississippi—the antebellum estate "that never was." In 1976, the state-run Florewood River Plantation, where twenty-five thousand people a year come to sample life at a "typical" cotton plantation of the 1850s, was opened to the public near Greenwood. The crepe myrtles and cotton fields are bare, and the tram isn't running for out-of-season tourists the day I visit. No doubt splendid in the spring, the estate seems, in mid-January, a bit like the lady of the house caught in an embarrassing state of undress by an unannounced caller.

Florewood recalls the name of Greenwood LeFlore, a Choctaw chief who owned over four hundred slaves in 1860 and was a leading member of the local planter community. Though LeFlore owned a nearby estate, the Florewood mansion is modeled after nearby Roebuck Plantation, a private site. Since the city of Greenwood and Leflore County are both named for the Choctaw chief, however, a state park along the same line seemed only fitting. "It is a romantic name," reads the plantation guide, "rhythmical and fluid, that trips lightly on the tongue and evokes images of dashing gentlemen and demure ladies." In season, guides don period dress for candlelight tours of the Big House. In the outbuildings are craft demonstrations, some by African Americans, that include pottery making, candle making, and cooking. Home-baked biscuits and molasses, I'm told, are a favorite with school kids on the tour.

Situated on one hundred acres of land, Florewood is meant to represent a plantation ten times its actual size. The grander estate of one thousand acres would have typically included some eighty slaves, though there are only a couple of cabins for them at Florewood—intended to be "representative." Then, too, Florewood's buildings are closer together than they would have been on a large estate, yet another concession to scale. As I walk the grounds, I'm bothered by a question: Why not recreate a site that would have fit the available acreage in the first place? "[Because] you wouldn't have had such elaborate stuff," manager Scott Dean replies matter of factly, saying that a one-hundred-acre site wouldn't have been much more than a "sharecropper's farm [with] a couple slaves." The moral is simple: who would pay even two dollars a vehicle to visit a poor dirt farmer? Florewood is built to accommodate an epic memory of the Old South.

Distinguishing the real from the surreal at Florewood isn't always easy. A weatherbeaten book in the slave hospital lists ailments—cholera, cold, strained backs—but my tour guide doesn't know if it's a real document or a facsimile. The field hands' cabin is as solid as if it were built last week. But Marion Johnson, from Louisiana, recalled what would have been just as close to the typical experience: "The log cabin where my mammy lived had so many cracks in it that when I would sleep down there I could lie in bed and count the stars through the cracks." Managed by the Department of Natural Resources, Florewood doesn't have any cracks. Little may go to seed except the seasonal half acre planted in cotton that gets picked by visiting schoolchildren in the fall.

What, after all, is "typical" of Mississippi slave life? "We sho had plenty t'eat"; remembered Polly Turner Cancer of Lafayette County, a former slave, in the 1930s, "dey wud kill hogs an' make sausage, an' dey wud tak de guts an' turn dem an' stuff dem wid sausage; we wud hav' more meat dan you cud put in two rooms lak dis." Or would "typical" be what Aron Carter of Lincoln County remembered during the same period: "Us chillun use get fed in a long trough. Yassum you knows, a trough. Long, wooden contraption thing jest like de pigs are fed outten of. It wuz a fine thing an' dey keep it spic an' span an' feed us good." The Florewood grounds don't have any troughs for slave children that I could find. In fact, Mississippi hasn't so much recreated "the plantation that was" as done a passing good imitation of the one "that could have been," a clean, well-stocked, orderly improvement on the past.

That Florewood is set Before the Fall is no coincidence either. *Antebellum* has all the magic pull in Mississippi that *pioneer* has in Montana or *minuteman* in Massachusetts. What's rebuilt at Florewood is a time when, as tradition would have it, the South was at its zenith. The land is "pristine," we read, the soil as rich as "the famed Nile Valley." A gazebo near the mansion "hints of the pleasure of solitary contemplation and the intrigue of romantic interludes." Whoever is speaking here, it's not Cato the blacksmith. The point of view assumes that the 1850s were a pleasant time for just about everyone living on the Delta, a rather risky assumption when we remember that over half the people living in Mississippi in 1860 were slaves.

The fact is that Florewood might just as well have educated visitors about the 1870s as the 1850s. (The adjoining museum includes the post-war era, but only as a showpiece for cotton technology.) Such a setting, alas, would ruin the romance that engulfs the pre-war plantation. While slavery has more or less been digested by the public as a fact, the murky years of post-emancipation are buried in the very places most capable of resurrecting them. Sharecropping, Jim Crow laws, land reform failure, temporary black political gains during Reconstruction—these are rarely discussed, so discomfiting is their legacy. If slavery is talked about little, Reconstruction, at such sites, gets still less attention. While emancipation can be pointed to in the text of the Thirteenth Amendment, it's harder to explain what happened to the proverbial forty acres and a mule.

But these are questions of strategy. Abundantly furnished with period antiques, Florewood is also an object lesson in the limitations of material culture—the physical objects of the built environment. To be sure, plantation life for slaves can be evoked through the display of rope beds, wash pots, cornshuck mattresses, flatware, smithy's tools, and a functioning gristmill—as Florewood most competently does. But material culture, as has often been noted, poorly suggests the realities of social status, especially on an antebellum plantation that has been made out of, if not whole cloth, 100 percent Mississippi homespun.

Much is invisible at Florewood, a fact some visitors will no doubt be thankful for. How, for example, does a curator acknowledge corporal punishment in "good taste"—by hanging a bullwhip in the overseer's house? How, using an object, does one evoke slave resistance—a mock advertisement for runaways? How does one suggest the presence of "paddyrollers" (police who roamed the South looking for runaways)—will tacking up a typical pass from the master suffice? Possessions, in short, are hard put to show dispossession. Aside from displaying weapons, the drama of conflict is hard to convey. Things have to work overtime to prove a "negative," especially in a culture that, due to its own view of history, prizes period antiques as collectibles of considerable value.

Nor are all the Florewood antiques quite typical. Its best-known piece is the bed that belonged to Confederate General Nathan Bedford Forrest, grand wizard of the Ku Klux Klan following the Civil War. The informed visitor may have difficulty admiring the big four-poster while remembering Forrest's summary execution of black Union soldiers at Fort Pillow in 1864. Our experience is not quite imaginary after all. From one point of view, Florewood is a well-meaning reconstruction of a bygone era. From another, it's the shell of a bad dream, rebuilt so that people can savor an illusion that, aside from its furnishings, doesn't contain much more history than an elaborate recounting of "once upon a time."

Florewood is a feel-good tableau, a regional act of historic engineering in the style of Disney. It may be better stocked than Frontierland, but comes close to being a Delta cousin of *Song of the South*. It exploits the cliché of the plantation as a noble, manorial farm. It recreates the buildings and crafts of a period (including gift-shop slave dolls dressed in headwrap and homespun) without calling much attention to those who would have produced them—or under what circumstances. "It's offensive to some black people," admits Dean, referring to a small minority, he says, who are sensitive about how life at Florewood has been portrayed. The slave cabins are referred to as Servants' Quarters and Double House on the map, a sign, he says, of not wanting to offend. "We're careful," he adds, "about what we say."

Yet, for all its flaws, Florewood doesn't do worse than many of its genuine counterparts. An attempt has been made to rebuild the plantation beyond the Big House, even if it is misty eyed and incomplete. It's more honest than estates such as Monmouth that would dismiss slavery with a word about the butler before passing on to reservations for bed and breakfast. Counterfeit by design, Florewood at least has the excuse of having copied inadequate models. That's probably why Dean, without a hint of irony, finally told me, "We pretty well tell it like it was."

TOUR DE FORCE

Visitors to the plantation will be expected to submit to the cleansing ritual of "the Tour." While painless for most of those who have attained their majority, it may be excruciating for toddlers, misfits, and general malcontents. Offering a catalog of material culture in the Big House—Hepplewhite chairs, broken pediments, baseboard moulding, ornamental quoins—the Tour will say hardly a word of the people who managed the estate. There will be little mention of the conjurer born on the Guinea Coast, the blind slave inventoried as "useless," the woman whose brother was sold in Nashville, the boy whose closest brush with education was propping up his master with a dictionary at the dinner table, the woman who agreed to become her master's mistress and bear his children in return for their freedom, or the free Creole girl kidnapped in New Orleans and taken to Kentucky so she could teach massa's children to speak French. Repeated from manor to manor, the Tour will come to seem as much the work of a divine mandate as that of any mere human effort.

The Tour begins in the Big House. The mansion will be said to have been "built" by its owner—a way of making invisible the gang labor that raised it. The front hall is filled with portraits of the ancestors, furthering a family claim on the land and its fruits. Dinner is set for eight in the dining room, the servants, of course, having retired for the evening. Curiosities include a trundle bed in the master bedroom, an Empire couch in the salon, a spotless Staffordshire service. The servant bells in the corridor, each pitched to a different room, may be of interest to antiques enthusiasts. If shown at all, the semi-attached kitchen may have hot biscuits for the children, a reward for enduring what, it turns out, is only the first leg of the ordeal.

The Tour takes an exterior turn to capture the full grandeur of the estate. A French ornamental flower garden—a statue of Hermes at the center—will awe the botanical set. A swan gently treads the surface of a large pond. The outbuildings shelter exhibits on blacksmithing, spinning, or horse-drawn carriages. At the border of the tourist map (if not off the edge) stands a restored slave quarters building; if not that, the foundation of one; if not that, a sign that notes where something like it might once have stood. Local arboreal varieties are likely to be better distinguished on the grounds than the people who once lived there. Other than the uniformed gardener trimming a hedge of boxwood, the restored plantation is a landscape without hands.

The larger community is recognized by trotting out the story of a trusted servant. Call them "affirmative action slaves"—avuncular figures who reassure us that life on a plantation didn't have to be all that bad. At Monticello we meet Isaac, the literate blacksmith who was a personal favorite of Mr. Jefferson. At Middleton Place, South Carolina, they tell of Ned and Chloe, two slaves who stayed on to help the family "reorganize their lives in the difficult post-war years." At Hampton, Maryland, it's the loyalty of a slave nurse, Ann, that merits her a funeral in the main hall—just like Uncle Alfred at the Hermitage. Recalling real human bonds that were certainly a part of the peculiar institution, their stories become pat symbols of a community that was much more vibrant and complex.

We hear about those whose conduct reflects well on their owners. Activities such as theft or miscegenation are scrubbed as clean as the Big House entryway. Tour guides will wax about a portico of Corinthian columns, but it's the rare one who mentions the black overseer—a compelling study in human dilemmas if there ever was one. How were slaves or indentured servants purchased? Did many abscond? What happened if they were caught? What characteristics did the master encourage in "his people"? Did they have a varied diet? Were their houses more African than American? At what age did children begin to work in the fields? Were slaves allowed to marry? What did they do with their free time? "The plantation supported eight hundred slaves," my guide at Middleton Place tells me, a strange way of remembering the people who built the terraces and lakes that tourists today spend fifteen dollars to admire in the old rice country of South Carolina. Just who, the visitor has to wonder, was doing the supporting?

When "the help" are mentioned at all, issues of local pride are at stake. At Middleton they tell me slaves might well have run away from the plantation—only to be forced by invading Yankees to help them build army latrines. At Kingsley plantation, Florida, the task system of defined chores is cautiously put forward as an improvement on the sunup-to-sundown labors of slave gangs in other areas. At the Stephen Foster Folk Center in northern Florida, I'm reminded that Yankees, once upon a time, had slaves too. At Monmouth, in Natchez, the guidebook claims that John Quitman was a "kindly master," echoes of General Washington. For those inclined to feel uncomfortable, the Tour ministers a painless remedy: if not "holier than thou," the common retort amounts to "no worse than them," "better than average," or "what would you have done in their place?"

There are, in fact, as many good reasons to minimize public discussion of slavery as there once were to defend the institution itself. It's not that "slaves are ignorant" anymore, it's that "we're ignorant about the facts of slave life." It's not that "they lived better than northern factory workers did"—a common defense of slavery in the antebellum period—it's that slaves could earn money "equal to the daily wage of a skilled bricklayer" in their free time, as I learned at the Thomas Jefferson Visitors' Center near Charlottesville, Virginia. It's not that slavery was ordained in the Bible (as slaveholders took pains to point out), but that "people of all colors have been enslaved all over the world," as I heard it tenderly explained to a group of schoolchildren at Mount Vernon.

If you take the Tour enough times, there seems to be no alternative. So it's with something close to shock that I watch one July afternoon as slave-quarters interpreter Sylvia Tabb-Lee, surrounded by two dozen children and adults, points out a rebuilt slave house at Carter's Grove, Virginia, near the banks of the James River. With an eighteenth-century Big House and a state-of-the-art archeology museum, Carter's Grove—unlike its counterparts—takes a multifaceted look at the plantation that includes early Native American occupants, African American slaves, and white indentured servants. "That's where most people—white and black—would have lived in the eighteenth century," she says of the plain-looking cabin and garden. Dressed in a cotton skirt, a drawstring blouse, and a straw hat with the top cut out,

Tabb-Lee, an African American, talks about a subject that most sites wouldn't dare touch: the life of those not to the manor born.

She tells the crowd of the average life expectancy for eighteenth-century Virginians—in the low forties, even for white males. Using a group of school-age girls, she demonstrates the difference between lying slaves in a ship shoulder-to-shoulder on their backs ("loose packing") and on their sides, stomach-to-back ("tight packing"), the latter more economical—and cruel. She stresses that cabins such as the one they're near would have housed "privileged" slaves—workers on a subsistence farm rather than a big rice plantation in the Carolinas. She tells of the black foreman who would have bossed fellow bondsmen for a few privileges—and been despised in return. Women, she adds, would have probably had several children by the time they were eighteen. It's a sobering picture for people in bermuda shorts pushing strollers.

"I think a lot of African Americans are afraid we're going to polish this up," she tells me later. " 'You're going to tell me a story,' they think." White people are worried they'll be made to feel guilty, so her philosophy is simple: "You cannot do this job with an attitude." Her objective is to steer clear of shame and resentment both, while never denying the pain of the people she gives voice to. What drives her to do a job that makes stand-up comedy look almost easy? "I'd rather see people walking through the slave quarters and talking about it," she confides, "than people walking through and saying, 'I hate white people.' "

I watch as she goes back out to work the crowd, something she'll do more than a dozen times on a busy day. A cross between a stump preacher (her father and brother are ministers) and a pickpocket who deprives people of pet delusions, Tabb-Lee gives something valuable to her audience they weren't expecting. People smile, grimace, ponder, look intently at the ground as she talks for a quarter of an hour, ending by inviting us all over to have a look at the cabins for ourselves. "This," she declaims, "is the world we made together."

Carter's Grove is owned by Colonial Williamsburg, Inc., whose nearby historic district has been a fixture in public history since the 1930s. When the slave quarters opened in 1989, they were used as craft shops for colonial trades, much as is done in Williamsburg proper. The eventual decision to use guides to interpret slavery left some people, including then Director Lawrence Henry, skeptical. Such an effort, he feared, would "undervalue the artifact"—decreasing the attention

"The world we made together":
reconstructed slave quarters, Carter's Grove, Virginia

paid to physical objects is a cardinal sin in most preservation circles. "I'm convinced that while all that reconstruction . . . has been useful and necessary," he says now, having seen what the personal tours can do, "what has made that a successful and powerful interpretation is the people." Now, says Henry, the artifact is the backdrop of the story, not the subject. Carter's Grove has brought slavery almost to the front lawn of the plantation. To get to the Big House on site, he reminds me, visitors have to walk by the slave quarters.

So why haven't more estates followed the lead of Carter's Grove? The reasons range from "an issue of racism," Henry says, to the more mundane question of " 'Will we be able to pay the electric bill?'," a concern of administrators if they offend too many sensibilities. He notes that visitation at Carter's Grove is a quarter of a million people a year. "The number of African American visitors has noticeably increased in the last five years," he says, even if a few complain that an "ugly story" like slavery has no reason being revived. "For every person who walks out in a huff," Henry adds, "there are ten or twenty more who are glad they came."

In one sense, at least, Carter's Grove is no different than its peers. The restored colonial and antebellum properties are usually the larger ones—not the one-hundred-acre Kentucky farm, but the five-thousand-acre estate with palatial mansion. On many slaveholding farms there would have been no overseers, no row of cabins, no pretty garden, no Big House worthy of the name. Master and slaves would have labored together in the fields, an incongruous and uncomfortable image for many who think they understand the realities of slavery. In 1850, 75 percent of American masters owned ten or fewer slaves, living a life far removed from the planter elite to which Henry Middleton, Thomas Jefferson, Robert Carter—and Scarlett O'Hara's father—belonged. The image of the slaveholder needs to be rehabilitated too.

After the President's Plantation, the Georgian Plantation, the Bed-and-Breakfast Plantation, the Model Plantation, the Hands-Off Plantation, and the All-American Plantation, Carter's Grove reveals the empty facade of the Tour. What might be useful at such sites is a disclaimer that the movie industry made obligatory long ago. In front of the Big House might stand a sign in view of all who enter: "This estate is loosely based on a true story," the words would read. "Most of the people who built and maintained it are not talked about because we're too embarrassed and confused about how to respond to your questions concerning them. We hope you enjoy your tour of the house and grounds. Have a nice day."

INTEGRATING HISTORY

People can talk about the past all they want—it's what they don't say that scares Dorothy Redford. Site manager at Somerset Place near Creswell, North Carolina, Redford has her own idea about why slavery is a taboo topic on the plantation. "I may be a little charitable," she begins cautiously, but "[people] have no idea how to integrate history. Part of it is ignorance, the other part of it is a genuine wish not to offend." She offers me a chair in an upstairs office stacked high with papers and files. "I don't think it's a deliberate attempt at omission," she reflects further. "I don't think it's any longer a need to protect one's own history. . . . I think people are just very uneasy."

Herself a descendant of Somerset slaves, Redford recalls the glory days of the Old South differently than some. She began a search for family roots in the 1970s that led to what became a life's mission—to uncover the story of the people who built and ran Somerset Place. In professional circles she's known as a nontraditional historian: her training is in social work rather than historic preservation. Having organized a family reunion in 1986 for the descendants—black and white—of Somerset's former inhabitants, Redford was hired by the state to develop site interpretation of the slave community. When she arrived at the site as program coordinator in 1987, the estate tour resembled something out of an antebellum edition of *Better Homes and Gardens*: they hardly mentioned the Somerset slaves at all.

"Five years ago nothing was going on here," Redford remembers. "They would have walked up to you and said, 'Welcome to the home of Josiah Collins.' And they would have walked you past every one of these outbuildings that is now open, through the main house, and then told you about Josiah Collins III and his family and every piece of furniture in the house." She smiles, on the verge of an admission that would make most preservationists choke. "I personally don't know the names and don't even encourage my staff to remember the names of the furniture." She had to rope off several pieces just to keep the guides from going on about them too long.

Redford wanted to undermine the image of white folks sipping mint juleps on the veranda, though she had no intention of abandoning the Big House. Adamant that Somerset would be interpreted as a whole community, she included the story of slavery inside the mansion—where the *S* word usually isn't spoken. "What we do when we go into a bedroom in this house is to say, 'This was a guest bedroom. It's also the size of a slave quarter,'" she explains, noting that the number of inhabitants in the two would have been far different. "When you get into the master bedroom and you're talking about what Mary Collins would have worn, you talk about what black women on the plantation would have worn. . . . You have to use existing space to integrate history."

The mansion tours are no longer the focus of the average visit. Few of the earliest Somerset residents, after all, would have ever set foot inside the front door. "No other slaves were allowed to go to the house," remembered Uriah Bennett in 1937, born a slave at Somerset. "If you wanted to see the master, you had to see the [house] servant, and the servant told the master." Bennett recalled a life where freedom of movement was severely circumscribed, a fact difficult for visitors to envision today. "For months and months at a time, we were never allowed off the farm, sometimes we would get as far as the gate and peep over."

Today, a child could hurdle the white picket fence, put up in the 1950s, that surrounds the estate. The quarters where Uriah Bennett lived are long gone. But even if it has no standing slave quarters, the estate has retained some of the original outbuildings that supported the mansion—kitchen, ice house, smokehouse, and dairy. Long ago converted to storage buildings, the "dependencies" have returned to being places of work. Although the working farm has become a popular historic attraction—Old Sturbridge Village, Amana Colonies—the working plantation is a long way from the traveled road of most tourists. Under Redford's direction, Somerset Place has once again become a hands-on plantation.

Over the years, Redford has been approached by people with different ideas of how to remember American slavery. Someone offered a plan for a "Tomb of the Unknown Slave." Another wanted to design a Vietnam Veterans–type memorial, inscribing it with the names of enslaved people. But the extended time span, the numbers involved, and the lack of extant records, says Redford, all make the latter project, at least, implausible. She admits to not having much use for "huge granite things," preferring a "living memorial" to those who built the Big House; dug the canal; raised the outbuildings; cultivated the rice, corn, and wheat; ground the meal; gathered the sugar pears, ginned the cotton; cooked the dinners; served the tureens; cleared the plates; cleaned the cisterns; and made way for the two-horse carriages with glass fronts and footmen that frequently brought friends and neighbors of the Collinses to attend services in the local chapel. "The roads were kept good by laborers," Bennett remembered. "All roots were kept off the road."

"Clothing is subject to wax and food spatters," warns the visitor's brochure—what turns out to be no idle boast. Adults take a guided tour and are encouraged to discuss what they find at Somerset. But groups of students from fourth grade to post-secondary school are greeted with the prospect of making gourd bowls, shingles, baskets, brooms, candles—even picking cotton. Greeted by costumed staff who assign them tasks, they're expected to don period slave dress and take part in the labor that would have maintained a plantation, even if it means playing an unfamiliar role.

"If a young man happens to get the lot of being a cook for the day, I also dress him in women's clothing," Redford beams, pulling from a filing cabinet a 100-percent cotton shirt spun by the staff. "[The kids]

"Africans cut canals before I remember":
a slave-built canal, Somerset Place, Creswell,
North Carolina

actually grind corn, they fry corn bread, they work over the open hearth. When they leave, they not only understand what it was to cook a meal over a hearth, they understand what it was to be a woman." And not everything, she brags, goes quite by the book. "They burn our clothes," she exclaims of the odd accident. "That's an important lesson. . . . They understand that plantations were places of work, not just mansion-type houses." Issued two sets of clothes and a pair of shoes every year, Somerset slaves, of course, wouldn't have had the luxury of changing out of work clothes at day's end.

A place of dreary and magnificent vistas, Somerset symbolizes the paradox of the plantation. The carriage drive to the Big House, lined with cypresses, is a pleasant stroll from the parking lot. The yellow clapboard buildings nestle under sycamores and cypresses that crowd the edge of Lake Phelps. Behind the lake, the setting sun recalls the grandeur that seems a cliché of the Old South. But the windbreak along the carriage path is a romantic canopy of foliage only so long as one ignores what lies beneath it. "Africans cut canals before I remember," Bennett recalled, and one can still see the transportation and irrigation canal—once twelve feet deep, twenty feet wide, and six miles long—dug over a period of two years by the Somerset slaves, many of whom came directly from Africa to give their lives digging a ditch through a malarial swamp in the Carolinas.

Meanwhile, the Big House slowly diminishes in Somerset's big picture. The state legislature awarded $300,000 in 1993 to begin research and design for the reconstruction of a long-absent row of buildings. Collectively called "the Street," the structures will include a slave hospital, chapel, field-hand kitchen, and two representative slave quarters—one much like the building where Redford's ancestors would have lived. The original quarters, made of hard cypress, had disappeared by 1920; many, Redford guesses, were disassembled and put up as storage buildings elsewhere. Preliminary digging has yielded buckshot, medicine bottles, beads, even the arm of a porcelain doll. For a community that was over 90 percent black (there were more than 320 slaves on the estate in 1860), it should become the Main Street of Somerset Place.

But funding didn't just fall from the sky, a fact Redford's ancestors would have no doubt appreciated. She landed money for the Street by stressing public/private partnerships with the legislature; founded the Somerset Place Foundation, creating a gift shop to funnel proceeds into research and acquisition; held a legislative caucus meeting on site, feeding the guests deer stew ladled with a gourd dipper out of a cast-iron pot; and now gets a discretionary grant of several thousand dollars a year from R. J. Reynolds. She buys corn for the educational program from the descendants of Somerset's former masters, the Collins family. "If I had to wait for the state of North Carolina to buy everything we needed for our programs," she says, "I would be crazy."

Somerset paints a different picture of antebellum than most plantations do. A one-fold brochure replaces the usual pricey guidebook. Few tomes are for sale in the old Colony House residence. There's no slide show or video, barely an interpretive sign on the place. Walking the grounds between tours or after hours, one could be fooled into thinking that Somerset didn't have anything to do with the story of a mass of people bringing to market a hard-won harvest for the lucky few. Unlike most plantations, Somerset sees many African American visitors. "Black people won't go where they're not represented," avows Redford, "or where their representation is not an ethical and honorable one."

In the last light of a winter afternoon, Somerset seems peaceful. Redford goes back to researching the case of seventeen slaves—one of them her great-great-grandmother, Elsy Littlejohn—who were sold down the river for trying to poison a white overseer. A published collection of letters from a neighboring family of the Collinses—a major source for her understanding of the region—didn't mention the plot at all. Only later did Redford find evidence of the revolt, as well as evidence of a rent strike by ex-slaves who stayed on after the Civil War. The insurrections had been edited out of the family's correspondence, much the way, Redford believes, the story of slavery has been distilled for the public. That's why she's not bashful about rebuilding the Street from the ground up next to the original structures, an act many purists wouldn't condone. "You make choices," she says evenly. "If we don't . . . we present a skewed view of history."

FREDERICK DOUGLASS GOES TO THE BIG HOUSE

On a terraced hill in Washington, D.C., is the estate of one of America's greatest success stories—a man born a slave, not a wealthy planter, in Talbot County, Maryland. Frederick Douglass, in fact, symbolizes the complexity of our racial past: a child born of a white father and slave mother; a slave boy who learned to write by having white children teach him his ABC's on the sly; a young man who escaped to freedom to become a leading abolitionist, only to be spurned later by many of his white colleagues; a husband twice—first married to an illiterate black woman, then to an educated white one. The latter time he bore up under complaints of those—white and black—who disapproved of mixed marriages. The classic self-made man, Douglass's humble roots make Lincoln's log-cabin origins seem genteel by comparison.

Although Lincoln's humble birth is celebrated at a number of public sites, one doesn't dwell for long on Douglass's roots at Cedar Hill, the home where he resided from 1877 until his death in 1895, and the only national site devoted to his life's story. A video in the visitors' center offers a rather mawkish overview of his career, but tourists, once they ascend the terraces to the mansion, will hear even less about the early Douglass. Entering the front door of a pillared and trellised facade, I'm asked by the ranger—the Park Service has administered the site since 1962—to imagine myself an "abolitionist" come to pay my respects to the eminent Mr. Douglass. Playing the role of the house butler, he leads a group of us through the mansion, which sports a magnificent view of the monuments across the Anacostia River, even if a large chain-link fence surrounding the property is a reminder of the sharp divide between past and present.

It's a jivey, vernacular tour that acquaints us with Douglass's library, a classical bust of abolitionist William Lloyd Garrison, the leather rocking chair given Douglass by the people of Haiti, where the owner of Cedar Hill was minister under President Benjamin Harrison. In spite of the banter, the visit takes the traditional path—through the parlors to admire the furniture, a peek at the upstairs bedrooms, a swoop through the kitchen to see the rugbeater and flatirons the hired help used. As at countless Tidewater homes, the visitor is awed by the trappings of a tasteful decor set out in precisely the way the Park Service believes it would have appeared at the end of Douglass's life. The furnished home, presented as a kind of living mausoleum, presents in typical fashion the surroundings of a man whose life— even among giants—was anything but typical.

The house Douglass bought in 1877 was built for real estate developer John Van Hook, who in developing the area of present-day Anacostia, zoned the suburb "for the use, benefit, and enjoyment of white persons only," a stricture that Douglass was to break as he did so many others in his life. Eventually purchasing up to fifteen acres, the new owner had seven outbuildings put up, including a carriage house, stable, barn, and servants' quarters. Our guide assures us, a little defensively, that the servants were well paid and that Douglass "gave them lots of holidays"—even if the building where they lived is no longer extant. The only rebuilt dependency is the "Growlery," a wooden cabin to which Douglass repaired on occasion to escape the workaday world. It's a symbolic reminder of where he came from, but the only substantial one on a tour dedicated to establishing, among other things, his extensive knowledge of English etiquette. The young slave hired out as a Baltimore ship-calker is no more in evidence in the Anacostia house than Hercules the cook is at Washington's estate on the Potomac. Cedar Hill, not surprisingly, has been called "the black Mount Vernon."

The man on official government business, the liberator in his dotage: this is the Douglass we see. The estate rightly prides itself that most of the furnishings are original—a rare thing at historic houses. Yet the house tour is unprepared to give us a sense of the radical spirit that infused Douglass. Cedar Hill is testament to the common reflex of the plantation: the past, preserved on a grand and uplifting scale, affords us a glimpse of a country gentleman. Just as some of his contemporaries could not believe Douglass was an escaped slave for all his eloquence and bearing, at Cedar Hill the impression would seem similarly fantastic that this was a man who had never seen his mother by the light of day, had suffered numerous beatings, and did not even know the date of his own birthday since slaves were customarily denied such knowledge. Going through his library on W Street, it is hard to remember these things.

Houses inhabited during adulthood may not say very much about one's youth—perhaps they shouldn't be expected to. But rarely in one life is there such a paradox between beginning and end as there is in the career of Frederick Douglass. The gentrified roots of Washington and Robert E. Lee, for example, are reinforced at their adult homes— Mount Vernon and Arlington—not contradicted by them. What's more, for all their substance, houses can be shadowy artifacts in the historic record. In his last, and longest, autobiography (*The Life and Times of Frederick Douglass*, 1892), Douglass does not even mention Cedar Hill, where he lived while writing the book, though several of his other homes are noted. Such is the difficulty of capturing a dynamic history in any mansion—as Dorothy Redford has discovered at Somerset Place—whether it happens to be a plantation or an urban estate intended as an emblematic antidote. On a hill in Anacostia, the Park Service has managed to cage the old abolitionist.

In ways only rarely acknowledged, Frederick Douglass is one of our founding fathers. Douglass—a child of racial enmity, likely sexual coercion, and mixed identity as a result—is a symbol of the plantation's bitter fruit. Even more, he is an example of the limitations of ancestor worship as we know it. His roots were confused, as he himself conceded, his father perhaps his own master. One half of the Douglass family tree is thus an unseemly mystery, the other a point of racial pride. His own genealogy is at once a celebration and a bitter lament. He was black and white. He was wealthy and poor. He was a slave runaway and a government minister. Everyone can claim a piece of Douglass; it's the whole man that's harder for us to embrace. Today, the neighborhood where he bought his house, once zoned for whites only, is almost all black. In a mirror image of Mount Vernon, the vast majority of visitors to Cedar Hill are African American. The most integrated of America's heroes, I think, would be surprised to see how little has changed.

The Mission

THE UNITED STATES shares a twenty-five-hundred-mile border with Mexico. In 1990, over seventeen million American residents reported speaking Spanish at home. The minority referred to as "Hispanic" on census forms is the fastest growing one in the country. Yet our public history of the Spanish borderlands has gaps about as wide as those in the official story of the plantation. Just what are "Hispanics," anyway? Puerto Ricans, Salvadorans, Spaniards, Peruvians, Cubans, and their various American descendants. The language is rich with distinctions: Latino, Chicano, Hispano. Even "Mexican" represents a mixture—*mestizaje*—of Spanish and native blood that doesn't easily fit North American definitions. "Hispanic" is a microcosm of the melting pot, a category that contains multitudes.

Yet for many Americans, "south of the border" is code for the gringo's Down Under, a tropical id bursting with illegal immigrants and drug traffickers who crowd the front page of the morning papers. Poor, Catholic, *mestizo,* the south seems the antithesis of the progressive, enlightened north. In school we learn to be repelled by Cortez but enamored of Francis Drake; to condemn the Spanish lust for gold while condoning the foibles of the forty-niners. Popular culture celebrates a figure such as Zorro, only to show his campaign for justice in a backward, feudal society. Latin America is the rude neighbor the north has sworn, at various times, it would tame, reconcile, exploit, or, lacking other alternatives, simply ignore.

Centuries ago began the Black Legend of Spanish cruelty, the image of the conquistador putting innocent natives to the sword. In recent years a White Legend, stressing a benign influence, has done its best to supplant it. Together they've melded into the dual romance of the Spanish and their descendants—conquistador, padre, border bandit, freedom fighter, veiled duenna—that feeds on equal doses of fear and pride. Several Spanish explorers have national monuments in their honor. The mission is represented by sites in New Mexico, Texas, Arizona, and California. In fact, the unsuspecting tourist would be tempted to think that every Spaniard who crossed the Rio Grande before the nineteenth century was either waving a crucifix or a blade of Toledo steel.

Built originally as a buffer against colonial powers such as France and England, the missions were part of a vast network constructed by Spain to protect territorial claims in the New World. When Mexico achieved independence from Spain in 1821, it inherited what remained of the missions, though most had either disappeared, been abandoned, or removed from control by the church. A mission such as the Alamo, in Texas, would eventually take on a strategic role completely at odds with its stated objective of "civilizing" the natives with the benefits of a Roman Catholic—and Spanish—heritage.

Heir to the Conquest, the Mexican differed from the Spaniard. A *mestizo* identity, combining Spanish-born and native populations, developed to a degree otherwise unknown in North America, a transformation that still clouds our understanding of terms such as *Hispanic*. Although the Spaniard, in spite of the Black Legend, is possessed of a certain cachet in our public history, the Mexican is a poorer relation. It's one thing for museums to celebrate the arrival of Hernando DeSoto in 1539, another to discuss frankly nineteenth-century border issues along the Rio Grande. Aside from Palo Alto battlefield in Texas (not yet open to the public), from the point of view of the National Park Service, one would hardly know that the Mexican War, for example, had even occurred. Inherent in the legacy of the Spanish mission— later the Mexican one—is an American family secret.

I DREAMED I SAW ST. AUGUSTINE

Once wary of intruders, St. Augustine, Florida, welcomes them today with open arms. Tourists spend an estimated $100 million a year to soak up the temperate climate and exotic colonial roots of St. John's County. It was late in the last century that city planners turned this backwater town into a boom of Spanish Revival architecture for a burgeoning tourist trade. Today, the former Ponce de Leon Hotel sprawls across King Street from Zorayda Castle, a reproduction of the Alhambra. Tourists find free parking on the plaza, more public restrooms than panhandlers, buskers who play fiddle tunes in the restored Spanish Quarter—and the waitresses can even speak English. A stroll along narrow residential streets reveals the main cottage industry of St. Augustine: keeping its cottages in good repair.

The city, in fact, was a piece of disputed property from the start. The Timucuan Indians were dislodged when the Spanish came in 1565 to begin a colony. After pirates sacked the town a century later, the English burned it in 1702. Surrendered by treaty to England in 1763 and returned to Spain twenty years later, the town was finally ceded to the Americans for good in 1821. It's arguable that St. Augustine has changed hands more times than Poland, an impression reenforced by the fact that there seem to be more antique cannon per square mile than in any other city in America. A reformed garrison town, St. Augustine finally learned how to make a dollar without having to fight a war to get it.

If all this seems exaggerated, it's only because the town is rather fond of superlatives. In addition to being the oldest permanent European settlement in the United States, it boasts of being home to the oldest masonry fort, the oldest wooden schoolhouse, the oldest mission, the oldest European house, the oldest store, and the oldest Christian parish north of Mexico. It comes as no surprise that a Ripley's Believe It or Not museum, three floors chock full of unlikely facts housed in Castle Warden, stands just outside the old city gates. No wonder the Chamber of Commerce has made it a foregone conclusion: St. Augustine (believe it or not) is really old.

It's as though the locals don't completely believe the hype themselves—and for good reason. In 1990, the population of St. John's County was 2 percent Hispanic. Even the Indian population, once considerable, is now tiny. Imagine Santa Fe, New Mexico, with no native people on the plaza; or the fact that Spanish is more likely to be spoken by foreign tourists than local residents, and you have the irony of St. Augustine—a largely Anglo town that makes its tourist dollar remembering the good old Spanish days. The ethnic diversity of the old city, long since disappeared, has given way to more noble roots in the tourist literature: baroque, Spanish, and Mediterranean. The complex *mestizo* history of St. Augustine isn't quite ready for prime time.

Centuries before the phrase gained currency, St. Augustine was a melting pot. It was, by local definition, the dregs of the pot who provided the city with its greatest public work and what is still the most famous attraction in town: Castillo de San Marcos, the stone fort erected in the seventeenth century and a national monument since 1924. It's a point of local pride that the garrison, many times besieged, was never taken by an attacking force, even if the nearby town was burnt to cinders and pillaged several times over.

"Spain built Castillo de San Marcos in 1672–95," reads a sign in front of the fort, "to defend St. Augustine from pirate raids and English invasions." Nothing could seem more straightforward than this fact—and nothing is so misleading. Spain, in fact, built the castillo in much the way the pharaohs built the pyramids: by pressing large gangs of forced laborers into doing the work for them. The job of clearing underbrush, quarrying and moving stone, firing limekilns, digging foundations, and setting the blocks for walls that were thirteen feet thick at the base and twenty feet high was done by a crew of Spanish unskilled workers, convicts, English prisoners, black slaves, and, most significantly, Apalache, Guale, and Timucua Indians from Georgia and Florida who would provide the bulk of San Marcos muscle.

The city guide published by the St. Augustine Historical Society emphasizes that Indian labor at San Marcos was "paid, not slave," anxious to quash any nagging doubts we might have about the affair. A Park Service publication, however, tells something closer to the truth. The native workers were paid one-fourth the daily wage of Spanish workers; many were conscripted by labor levies and held against their will for extended periods. Still more Indians—men and women—were brought in to grow maize and feed the hundreds of workers who labored on the fort. Never exactly a model of self-sufficiency, St. Augustine, even in its prime, needed a steady flow of guest laborers to thrive.

On a Saturday morning in the castillo's courtyard, a ranger in eighteenth-century costume gives a talk on "the birth of the nation," a lecture from a modern perspective. Dressed as a Spanish soldier, our guide reminds us that civilization in the old days extended about

Hard labors: Castillo de San Marcos, St. Augustine, Florida

as far as a cannonball could be fired from the fort ramparts. Beyond that was terra incognita: mosquitoes, dangerous animals, Indians "who would just as soon sever your head from your body as anything else," he says. We're suddenly a long way from the Indians who built the castillo, it occurs to me, but the Park Service hasn't provided a scorecard to tell them apart.

San Marcos, it turns out, has more to say about native boarders than builders. While laborers are given limited mention inside the fort, a larger exhibit tells of those Indians who lived at the castillo free of charge—nineteenth-century prisoners of war. Arapaho, Cheyenne, Comanche, and Apaches slept here, the latter of whom scouted for the government in large numbers and found themselves confined to the ramparts of San Marcos in return for services rendered. The exhibit briefly notes their suffering, with the caveat that those who went off later to Carlisle Indian School in Pennsylvania changed their appearances and attitudes for the better—a one-sided perspective for anyone familiar with the history of Indian boarding schools.

The arrival of the Apache prisoners of war—the Apaches were the last to arrive, in 1886—coincided with the time when St. Augustine first tested the waters of large-scale tourism. Henry Morrison Flagler, railroad magnate and associate of John D. Rockefeller, steered construction of the railroad south from Jacksonville and so secured the future of the town. It was Flagler who realized the immense architectural appeal of, if you will, Born-Again Castillian and funded construction of the Ponce de Leon Hotel, now named Flagler College in his honor. Tourists escaping harsh northern winters would find that the only colonial structure that had survived the sack of St. Augustine in 1702 was indeed the castillo. San Marcos was to offer them a unique treat, a twist on the traditional "Indian captivity," that was, for a time at least, the most entertaining thing in town.

"At Fort Marion [San Marcos] we were hungry all the time," remembered Eugene Chihuahua, an adolescent when he arrived in 1886, the son of an Apache army scout. "So we began making things to sell—bows and arrows, lances, moccasins, and bead work. We made anything for which we could get materials. Many people came to the fort just to look at us, as they might look at wild animals." The Apaches remained for almost a year before they were sent to Alabama, during which time some twenty of them succumbed to dysentery, bronchitis, epilepsy, and tetanus, the corpses interred on nearby North Beach. A fort handout states that only a few of the incarcerated Apaches were army scouts, when in fact dozens of them were, the decision to confine them creating great controversy in its day. The flyer also takes pains to reassure us that the Apaches were well fed—probably not a claim that would have impressed Eugene Chihuahua.

I'm relieved to find that St. Augustine offers more than the "man the barricades" mentality of San Marcos. Off the bustling pedestrian mall of St. George Street is the restored Spanish Quarter, maintained since the 1960s by the state-owned Historic St. Augustine Preservation Board. Visitors walk through a half dozen buildings—original and reconstructed—that recreate garrison life in the 1740s. A soldier explains how barter works. A blacksmith hammers at a forge. The wife of an artillery sergeant, brewing an "Indian stew" in her kettle, peels an onion grown in the adjacent garden. Tourists get a sense of domestic garrison life, even if they can look up from the courtyard in midtour and see a commercial sign for Tepee Town down the street.

I doubt the residents of colonial St. Augustine would recognize the Quarter today. By the 1740s, the town was filled with free blacks, Christianized Indians, and assimilated *mestizos,* none of which I would have guessed on my tour. The man who "plays" soldier Lorenzo Gómez tells me Gómez's wife is Indian and that intermarriage was common in the community; but in talking to a group of schoolchildren later, Mrs. Gómez alludes to Indians without mentioning she happens to be playing one. Black interpreters are conspicuously absent. In the Juan Sánchez house, visitors are shown the "mammy's room" and the space where the "servants" slept, but not until the end is it noted (in text only) that the family owned nine slaves. Walking through the Spanish Quarter, one would hardly guess the city was a magnet for runaway slaves escaping from the English colonies, a haven that predated the famous Underground Railroad by a century. In the Quarter, St. Augustine belongs to the Spanish more now than it did then.

The city has chosen its ancestors with care. While the Historical Society guide dismisses the native people as "savages," at the same time it notes that the execution of several hundred French Protestants by the city's founding father, Pedro Menéndez de Avilés (his statue stands before city hall), was "a matter of simple military expediency." Africans are hardly mentioned in the book, although Minorcan immigrants are given a separate chapter and lauded for their Roman and Carthaginian roots. Solid family trees are as much a part of old St. Augustine as the palms that line Avenida Menendez.

The decorum that ruled a society based on military and religious obedience has battled the commercial urge of this century with mixed results. While routing the fast-food restaurants to the edge of town on Highway 1 (Ponce de Leon Boulevard), boosterism has left some prominent reminders of the hard sell closer to home. A 208-foot stainless steel cross commemorating the first mass of 1565 towers above the harbor. At nearby Nombre De Dios is a reconstructed chapel where the first mission in the United States is said to have stood—advertised, not surprisingly, as "America's Most Sacred Acre." Here the mission modestly began within our borders over two centuries before those founded on the west coast. As elsewhere in the southeast, however, the surface remains have disappeared. Unless visitors retrace their steps, they conclude the holy tour by passing through the gift shop, a ploy used to good effect also in the Spanish Quarter.

St. Augustine practices "rootsmanship" with considerable backing. The spacious city and county Information Center near the castillo has as its main attraction *Dream of Empire,* an hour-long film produced by the Historical Research Center at Flagler College. In fact, the film's two-million-dollar budget was funded by St. Augustine Foundation, Inc., a private foundation whose major patron is the heir to the Flagler fortune. *Dream of Empire* is shown courtesy of a long-term sharing contract and will, I was told by a college official, eventually become city property. Thus is St. Augustine history wired on a closed circuit: Flagler money foots the bill for a historical film, a liberal arts college named for him produces it, and a comfortable city theater projects the results to tourists, all of whom have come to visit the town that Henry Morrison Flagler rebuilt.

Told through the eyes of Paco Ruiz, a Spanish farmer promised riches in the New World, *Dream of Empire* is a commendable contrast to the conquistador myth of strut and swagger. Ruiz encounters Indian resistance, a rebellious stepson, and indifferent authorities. But for all its shift in perspective, the movie holds fast to some old myths. Save for a few lines in a native tongue, no Indians even have speaking parts—their role, it seems, is to be seen and not heard. Once the commoner Ruiz has left the stage, *Empire* does its best to plead the case that Menéndez be honored as one of America's great founders. Not everyone in Florida, however, is so sanguine about his achievements. A state historical marker on Fort George Island, for example, refers to him as a cold-blooded murderer for his decision to execute some three hundred French castaways in 1565 to protect Spanish territorial claims. It's not a likely trait for a founding father, and a controversy the film doesn't engage.

St. Augustine is sitting on another site of great historical interest: Fort Mose, built in the 1730s as a settlement for free blacks and a line of defense against English attack. The original site is mostly under water, and though archaeological work has been done, it sits in limbo as a possible addition to the National Park Service. Currently owned by the state of Florida, it was declared a national landmark in 1994. The oldest community of free blacks in the colonial South, it represents a way to deepen understanding of the city's ethnic past, even if Mose was an effort by the Spanish to segregate a population that wasn't completely welcome in the city.

The ghost of America's first mission is in romantic company. With its alleyways, its public spaces, and its horse-and-carriage tours, there's no denying that St. Augustine has charm. A visit to town can make for an extended saunter through the good old days. But the city champions a kind of "I Got Mine" exoticism. Trumpeting a multilayered past, it privileges some communities as more marketable than others. The statues to Ponce de León and Pierre Menéndez downtown are reminders that the city, whatever its pose, tells a conventional version of the past. For English-speaking tourists, St. Augustine is a painless substitute for Oaxaca or the Yucatan, a weekend in the sun where the selling of the Spaniard is a profitable stock-in-trade.

A FRANCISCAN CONDOMINIUM

Inside Mission Nuestra Señora de la Purísima Concepción de Acuña, Father Balthasar Janacek of the San Antonio, Texas, archdiocese is about to conduct an experiment in the separation of church and state. To impress on me the acoustics of the chapel completed by Coahuiltecan Indians in 1755, he comes to a halt in the nave and asks me to join him in a rendition of "God Bless America." We stop after only one verse—badly mangled, I'm afraid. If he's surprised I know so few of the words, he's too kind to let on. "They're great for singing," he marvels at the acoustics, "terrible for preaching." And Father Janacek, archdiocesan director of the Old Spanish Missions, should know.

Today, Concepción serves as a chapel for a largely Mexican American parish in San Antonio, where Mexican Americans are a majority citywide. His choice of song, incongruous at first, seems only apt as he recounts Concepción's recent past. Pressed by a lack of funds for retarding the decay of historic properties, the archdiocese struck a partnership with the National Park Service in 1978 to maintain its four missions—Espada, San Juan, San José, and Concepción. Today the government keeps up the grounds and provides visitor services while the archdiocese ministers to the church-owned buildings—a preservation odd couple if there ever was one. I can still hear Kate Smith singing "My home, sweet home" as the father leads the way to the mission altar.

"God-awful," he dismisses the electric votive candles at the front. A former priest of the parish, he fondly recalls the weddings he's performed at Concepción. But Father Balty, as he's known to locals, is partial to many traditions. Fluent in Spanish, he speaks the language of his Czech grandparents and currently administers a city parish of largely Italian descent. The Concepción tour, then, begins with a bow to the Old World: "This is probably the closest you're going to get to a castle in this country," he says—a boast that never disappoints.

Concepción was built as a place of worship and defense, a testament to the cooperation of church and state on the Spanish frontier.

The Franciscan fathers came to the San Antonio Valley in the early 1700s, he tells me, bringing Tlaxcaltecan artisans from the Valley of Mexico—Indians who knew the secrets of working stone. In effect they were role models, teaching their trade to the local Coahuilte-cans, a group of hunter-gatherers more accustomed to building brush huts than a fortification that would come to have walls nearly four feet thick built from rock quarried nearby. Thus a self-assured vision of "civilization" was brought to the valley, with only a few Spaniards in the nearby fort of San Antonio de Béxar to enforce it. "The Fran-ciscans worked with the Indians," Father Janacek says of the church—some ninety feet by twenty, with twin belfries and a tower-ing facade—"and the Indians built it."

Though I expect a cold and forbidding place, Concepción is a sur-prise. Father Janacek shows me the detail of a floral pattern super-imposed on the facade that would have been, historians believe, painted in bright colors during the eighteenth century—the drab walls are too fragile to repaint today. The convento's restored interior reveals the stencil work of Indian artists who used root dyes to paint on one ceiling a sun with a human face. Windows are sculpted in a shell pattern that "people say could be right out of the casbah," he says of a Moorish niche. Although graffiti has sprouted in corners, some rooms still have their original plaster. Concepción, abandoned by 1819 at the end of the mission period, has had many uses. During the Mexican War it was a supply depot; in 1850, a visitor reported finding cattle dung a foot deep in the church. By 1861 it had been re-stored to its original function.

"[People] think that the mission is only the mission church," the father begins, explaining how the place of worship was the center of a much more complex community. But the mission, as he puts it, "was an idea." By teaching the Indians to speak Spanish, practice a trade, learn to handle arms, and perform a limited form of self-government, the fathers hoped they would one day be absorbed into Spanish soci-ety. Ideally, the mission holdings would be "secularized"—the land and other assets distributed among its occupants when they were ac-culturated. "Missions were not intended to remain missions," he ex-plains, "they were intended to self-destruct," adding that they offered occupants a standard of living equivalent to that found in many areas of Spain. "The Franciscans were like the caretakers of a condo-minium."

*Rock of ages: Mission Concepción, with stone quarry in
foreground, San Antonio, Texas*

A charming analogy, even if it turns out that not everyone was satisfied with the accommodations. Scores of local mission Indians ran
away, more than two hundred each at San Juan and Espada in 1737.
Father Janacek acknowledges the problem—"just as we've got people
[now] who don't stay in the night shelters because they like to be outside." Despite panels in the *convento* on mission life, an explanation
of *why* they ran away is nowhere in sight. While no doubt protected
from marauding enemies, they were subject to a life of rigid discipline
enforced by a strange and demanding culture. It's hard to understand
the mission without grasping this paradox. At night the entry doors to
the compound were securely locked—as much to keep Coahuiltecan
converts inside the gates as keep raiding Apaches out.

"From time to time the missionary should journey to the coast and
bring back the fugitives, who regularly leave the mission," instructions from about 1760 told Concepción personnel, "trying at the same
time to gain some recruits, if possible, so that more conversions are
realized and the mission does not come to an end because of lack of
natives." The fathers went in search of escaped "neophytes," often

under military guard. Appropriations depended on the number of converts they could maintain, a reminder of the fiscal realities of empire.

"We know how easy it is for the upper hand to oppress," says the father. "We don't have to even do anything and we're oppressing in many ways." Perhaps the early Spanish would have understood. Land distribution became untenable with the onset of epidemic disease. Numbers bear out the disaster that struck native populations in San Antonio, as elsewhere. At Concepción, a community of some three hundred Indians in the 1730s had dwindled to thirty-eight by 1794, partly due to epidemics. When few Indians remained, mission assets were sold to Spaniards who farmed and ranched the land for themselves. The pious plan of the Franciscans was undermined by invisible pathogens as much as by cultural hubris. None of the local missions managed to record as many births as deaths.

San Antonio may sound like an early round of cowboys and Indians, a ten-gallon hat traded in for a Franciscan habit. But the Spanish mission defies easy stereotypes. "There are certain places in Texas that claim to be the birthplace of the cowboy," says Rosalind Rock, Park Service historian for the San Antonio Missions since 1991. "But if you want to know the truth, the evolution of the cowboy in Texas began on the mission ranch." Like the fields maintained through an elaborate network of irrigation ditches, the ranches were major sources of income to the Franciscans. In 1762, the Concepción ranch owned over 300 horses, 600 head of cattle, and 2,000 sheep and goats. The *vaqueros* who herded them were a dark-complexioned people who, a few generations before, wouldn't have even known what a horse was.

At the missions, the cowboys *were* Indians. The first *vaqueros* were part of a religious system that shared wealth communally—not exactly the popular image of the lone cowpoke riding fence. To demonstrate that the mission was more than a place of worship, the Park Service is acquiring the Espada Mission ranch, twenty-five miles from San Antonio. All that remain today are a corral complex and small chapel, both buried recently by archaeologists because so many of the stones had been carried off by locals—a problem that has reduced many mission walls to rubble. An unfortunate overall result is that—except at San José, rebuilt by the federal government in the 1930s—the habitat of the original Indian community is hard to visualize.

Rock agrees that interpretation isn't as advanced as she'd like, acknowledging that social history can be forgotten in a sacristy tour or a stroll along ruined mission walls. Corporal punishment, for example, would have been common for the time, but they haven't found any evidence yet that it was practiced on neophytes in San Antonio. The fathers strove to teach them Spanish, she says, but few were given instruction in literacy. Reading and writing were considered separate skills, and some children were permitted to decipher their names without receiving instructions on how to write them. Through all the depositions and court suits she's uncovered, she has yet to find an example of a woman who could sign her name—a fact that doesn't surprise her.

"The employment of women could lead to disorder with single men in the kitchen," warn the instructions to Concepción personnel. But the greater threat to women, says Rock, came from outside. The shortage of Spanish females inspired a rough and tumble ethos of matchmaking on the frontier. Sometimes native women were purchased; sometimes they were taken by force. No wonder the padres saw the confinement of women to the missions as a "blessing." But Rock raises another point: regardless of status or race, the women in New Spain possessed a legal right to royal protection, a legacy of Roman and Moorish traditions largely absent in British common law. This medieval vision, however paternalistic in spirit, helped sustain women in civil and criminal cases in the colonial period.

As the eighteenth century progressed, marriage became less a question of conquest and more one of mutual arrangement. "Indian" and "Spaniard" had become identities difficult to separate, more cultural than racial. In his 1778 census of San Antonio, Father Augustín Morfi counted 324 Spanish, 268 Indians, 16 *mestizos,* and 151 people of "broken color," or mixed race. Whether by force or consent, the cultures were becoming "creolized"—a mixing that never happened to the same degree in the British colonies. "Those folks are scattered out in the blood around here," Father Janacek says of the mission Indians, a testament to the Mexican—*mestizo*—heritage on both sides of the Rio Grande.

The San Antonio missions thrive on a delicate balance. The Park Service has free rein in interpretation, says Rock, who foresees little interference from the diocese "as long as we don't come out with something that's totally anti-clerical." The tradeoff is that Washington can hardly complain when the diocese dresses a church with "garish" decorations for a fiesta. For his part, Father Janacek is glad that locals ended up not putting a catechistical center next to San Juan, though it was hard to convince them of that when they'd seen the Park Service build a visitors' center within a few yards of Concepción. He's thankful that the Park Service, known for its commitment to wildlife, has made the "people life" of the churches accessible without charging admission.

With weddings, fiestas, masses, and funerals, the San Antonio missions don't need an excuse to do "living history." The San José chapel hosts a mariachi mass every Sunday to standing-room-only crowds. Next to Espada is a parish-run Head Start school, continuing the tradition of mission education. As the churches have endured, the makeup of the parishes may have changed: San Juan served a Hispanic community at secularization, and later became German, Italian, and Alsatian French. Today, once again, it is Spanish speaking. "It's a place for the young Mexican-American to be able to take some pride in his heritage," says Father Janacek of the missions—even if that heritage is mixed in more ways than one. What became an intolerable form of oppression for some—the mission runaways—is a comforting symbol of the past for many of their descendants on a Sunday morning in south Texas.

REMEMBER THE ALAMOS

A useful piece of advice, "Remember the Alamo" isn't as easy as it used to be. The question asked by people in San Antonio is more complicated today: "Whose Alamo are we going to remember?" Some propose the Spanish one, founded as mission San Antonio de Valero more than a century before the famous battle of 1836. Others suggest the Indian Alamo, for it was native people who built the chapel that has become the most popular tourist attraction in Texas, and who are buried in front of it today in the midst of continuing controversy. There's also the Alamo of legend—Davy Crockett, swinging Old Betsy as he goes down before a horde of charging Mexicans. Before you remember the Alamo, it's usually a good idea first to find out what kind of neighborhood you happen to be in.

Nestled in the heart of downtown San Antonio, the Alamo church, begun in 1758, is America's answer to the ancient wonders of the

A contested shrine: the Alamo chapel, San Antonio, Texas

world. Like the Sphinx, its exterior is familiar to most everyone, although the insides remain about as visible as the caves of Aladdin. To see the interior you have to go to San Antonio, where a mystery play has unfolded to the great delight of downtown business. Every year three million people make the pilgrimage, passing through the large wooden doors into a time when, in 1836, some two hundred patriots withstood a Mexican army of thousands before being overrun after a thirteen-day siege. "The cradle of Texas liberty," the Alamo became the symbol of the Texas Revolution and the struggle for independence from Mexico.

No doubt the Mystery explains why Alamo protocol in the chapel is more elaborate than anything I found at Concepción. Bathing suits, of course, are prohibited. In front of me an armed guard asks a boy to remove his baseball cap. Another advises me that photography of the interior is forbidden, and recounts how, at Dachau once, he had his own camera stripped away by an angry policeman. It's not the kind of Alamo lore I was expecting, but I melt into the growing crowd that, in a few minutes, has made it hard to wander.

A herd instinct takes over. Most visitors join the tours that meet every few minutes in the transept. Sporting an Alamo tie, our guide stands above a scale model of the mission, detailing the campaign against the brutal Mexican leader, Antonio López de Santa Anna, with a blackboard pointer. After a ten-minute resume of the battle, he solemnly concludes, "out of respect for people who died on both sides, we request that you do not applaud." Applauding at that moment seems about as likely a response as if the crowd were to burst forth chanting the Nicene Creed, which would actually be a more fitting gesture for the building's original purpose. Bustling and crowded, the Alamo chapel is host to a strange ritual—one part civic piety, one part exalted camp.

What the Mystery can't condone, I discover, is survivors. Near the front door a plaque recalls that the Alamo, unlike Thermopylae, had no witnesses to tell its story. But barely twenty feet across the nave, another plaque describes where the women and children of the garrison hid during the battle—and were later spared by Santa Anna. A third sign recounts the cowardice of Louis "Moses" Rose, the only man said to have deserted during the siege ("One of the most pathetic days of time," it scowls). The names of Alamo heroes appear on the inner walls—all, that is, except Joe, a slave of Colonel Travis who fought the Mexicans and was later spared by them. I ask a guard why Joe isn't listed. He sighs, a bit peeved that I could have missed the whole point of the shrine, and says, "because he survived." (Father Janacek, it turns out, has a different spin: "His slavery turned out to be a blessing," he told me later).

The adjacent Long Barrack museum further pursues the Mystery. A short film muses that most of the men who died in 1836 probably never knew anything about the Alamo's history—a fact equally true for most visitors today. The museum, after all, devotes more space to the Daughters of the Republic of Texas—caretakers of the Alamo since 1905—than it does to the mission's Indian inhabitants. Once the film concludes, a guide appears to reassure us that General Santa Anna (for many Anglos, the Genghis Khan of Texas history), was later to die "blind, one-legged, and poor" in Mexico City—presumably an act of poetic justice intended to warm the hearts of Alamo patrons.

The Alamo takes pride in honoring its fallen. The names of the defenders appear in the chapel shrine. They're listed again in the museum—officers twice—and on the front plaza they're engraved on the cenotaph by Pompeo Coppini. No less devoted to their memory, the IMAX theater in the Riverwalk Mall a block away showcases the list after its forty-five-minute epic film, *Alamo: the Price of Freedom,* a six-story-high battle reenactment preceded by a bouncy rendition of "Auld Lang Syne." The only people whose names you're likely to see more in downtown San Antonio are either running from the authorities or running for public office.

If one digs deep enough, the Alamo has all kinds of martyrs. In 1745 San Antonio might have been plundered by a force of 350 Apaches, had it not been for a hundred Indians from the mission (only later was it called "the Alamo") who rushed to its defense and put the enemy to flight. Some of the rescuers, no doubt, are buried in the holy ground (*campo santo*) beneath the plaza today. Even the early period of the Alamo is dogged with tragedy. In a sense, the mission was a fatal gesture from the start. The first three Indian baptisms in 1703—years before the mission officially relocated to San Antonio—were recorded not for healthy converts, but dying children.

Mission San Antonio de Valero moved several times, in fact, before settling on the site we know today, built at a remove from the original city to keep the Indians from being "corrupted" by townspeople. The famous chapel was the second church at that location, and at the time of the battle in 1836 was without a roof. Only when the U.S. army added a pitched roof in the late 1840s, finishing what had become a quartermaster's depot, was the chapel, in an architectural sense, finished. Today the remains of the Alamo are situated in a four-acre public park lined with pecan, live oak, juniper, and mescal trees, an irrigation ditch snaking its way across the well-manicured grounds. But not only have the buildings and grounds been severely altered: the meaning of the Alamo, in recent years, has come under full assault.

In early 1994 the Inter-Tribal Council of American Indians, based in San Antonio, asked that the street in front of the chapel be closed to automotive traffic, offering evidence that the thoroughfare traversed the mission cemetery. While the Daughters of the Republic of Texas protested, the city, which owns the plaza that fronts the Alamo, ordered it closed. For some, it was an added insult that the Battle of Flowers parade, annually celebrating Sam Houston's victory over Santa Anna at San Jacinto, traversed the same street and the cemetery below it in its official tour. The parade was rerouted by city authorities and the street (Alamo Plaza East) remains closed to this day.

Much of the controversy seemed motivated by ethnic pride, but racial definitions are ever slippery. Is San Antonio mostly Mexican—

or Native American? It depends on who you talk to. Many locals who descended from the mission Indians are "masquerading as Hispanics," claims Gary Gabehart, president of the Inter-Tribal Council. Gabehart, who is Catholic, knows something about mixed identities: three-eighths Indian, he's an enrolled member of the Chickasaw tribe and says the Choctaw branch of his family "rode into Texas with Sam Houston." Indians, he says, have never had much status in Texas, so the designation of "Native" is commonly refused. The clash over ethnic claims leads him to identify the *campo santo* as a "multi-ethnic dedicated Catholic cemetery"—not just an Indian burial ground.

Composed of Indians and non-Indians, the council, Gabehart says, is opposed to digging up the cemetery as the University of Texas at San Antonio has proposed. Having consulted mission records, council members believe they already know what's there—the remains of nearly a thousand Indians, with a few Spanish and "African Spanish" thrown in. The council wants to see the site marked for what it is, and to have streets on the plaza closed in recognition of its original purpose. "This is hallowed ground," Gabehart says of the *campo santo,* "not the church." He goes so far as to add that it may be the "oldest integrated cemetery in North America," a claim, of course, impossible to prove.

"It's a *mestizo* society," agrees Gilberto Hinojosa, Dean of Humanities and Fine Arts and professor of History at Incarnate Word College. But "it goes beyond racial mixture," he says, noting that in a culturally diverse city even the most powerful symbols have dual identities. Some people celebrate the Battle of Flowers parade because of the Mexican defeat at San Jacinto, he says; others in the Latino community do so because it's a *fiesta,* a feast day. Even the early mission Indians performed burials at the *campo santo* that may have "looked Catholic, but could have been Native too." But one place in San Antonio hasn't been won over to the idea of sharing history, he says—and a little of the power that goes with it.

"I grew up with the sense of 'Forget the Alamo—that's their story, it's not our story,'" Hinojosa says of his boyhood in south Texas. "I didn't want to go to seventh grade because they were going to do Texan history," he remembers. The rest of the missions give a sense that "we were here a long time ago," Hinojosa adds, while by contrast, "the Alamo [story] has been told merely as a means of singing the praises of Manifest Destiny." A member of the city's Alamo Plaza

Commission, he supports the idea of opening the whole plaza to interpretation, explaining that the battle took place in front of the
chapel, not inside it. The founding epic that the Alamo offers Anglo
society can be transformed, he thinks, into a shared symbol—one
that includes Indian, Tejano, and Anglo—and that allows "local historians to have a say in telling the story."

Some people aren't sure how anyone could see the Alamo in a negative light. "It's a symbol of freedom all over the world," says Madge
Roberts, fifth vice president general of the Daughters of the Republic
of Texas. Dismissing complaints of some Mexican Americans, she
notes that Tejanos (Texans of Mexican descent) were among the
Alamo defenders; a whole company of them, she says, served with
Sam Houston at San Jacinto. After all, she reminds me, she *is*
Houston's great-great-granddaughter. Roberts was the official mascot
of the Texas centennial in 1936, going as far as Richmond, Virginia, to
unveil the statue of her ancestor that stands in the state capitol.

"We are certainly open to change," she offers, claiming the Daughters can't really do much on their own anyway. The organization has
no official stance on digging the *campo santo;* it's up to the city to decide what to do with the Battle of Flowers parade, she says, though
the Daughters once opposed rerouting it; as for criticism that they
minimize interpretation of the mission period, she counters, "The
state has entrusted us to honor the Texans who died there," claiming
that, in effect, their interpretive hands are tied. A fourth-generation
member of the Daughters, Roberts adds that "considering what we
have, we've done a pretty good job."

The Daughters, it turns out, have quite a bit. Hardly innocent of the
market forces that guide relic-hunting, the shrine operates by a time-
tested commercial principle: the loss leader. Admission to the chapel is
free, but a visit to the gift shop (built in 1937) is part of the Alamo experience. In a recent year, the *San Antonio Express News* reported, the
Daughters sold over fifty thousand dollars' worth of coonskin caps and
almost five hundred thousand dollars' worth of Alamo T-shirts. Profits
for 1992 and 1993 each exceeded a million dollars. Funding for upkeep
is necessary since the organization receives no state or federal
money—it is, as Roberts tells me, their only source of income. But the
Daughters maintain a large fund for emergencies, and recently purchased property to increase storage facilities and parking. At the
Alamo gift shop, even a wooden nickel goes for fifteen cents.

The Alamo dispute has its ironies. The very organization that has so resisted change is the same one that prevented part of the site—the *convento* "barracks," at least—from being sacrificed to the wrecking ball in the first place. As at Mount Vernon, a conservative group devoted to preservation has at least provided a place for the discussion of what history means. Meanwhile, the city is flush with development plans for an urban park that would redesign the plaza to interpret the mission more completely. No doubt they're trying to amend for the town council decision of 1847 to sell stones from the plaza wall by the wagon load, thus razing the mission walls that Woolworth's, A&H Burritos, and a tattoo parlor have come to rest on today.

So who "owns" the Alamo story? Gabehart says the owner of the *plaza* hasn't even been decided. The church sold the Alamo buildings to the state, he says, but not the mission property itself. A quitclaim deed filed by the city in the 1970s may be invalid under state law, he adds, noting that the church probably still owns the land, though it may not wish to have it back. "You can't sell a cemetery," he concludes despondently. But selling an exalted notion of death is what the Alamo has been doing for decades.

Whatever else can be said, the Alamo attracts a bewildering array of devotees. Father Janacek recalls the time he pulled up with a tour group to find a chapter of the Ku Klux Klan using the plaza for a demonstration. Rock troubadour Ozzie Osbourne urinated on a wall in 1982 and was banished from playing in San Antonio thereafter. Of course, some people are too busy to care very much either way. "You can keep the Alamo," runs a local Mexican American joke, "we'll take Kelly Field"—a reference to sought-after federal jobs at the nearby Air Force base.

For such a shrine, an epitaph is only fitting. "The sharp reports of the rifles, the whistling of bullets, the groans of the wounded, the cursing of the men, the sighs and anguished cries of the dying," wrote eyewitness José Enrique de la Peña of the battle. "The shouting of those being attacked," continued the Mexican officer, "was no less loud, and from the beginning had pierced our ears with desperate, terrible cries of alarm"—and here he added a most crucial detail—"in a language we did not understand." That is what I would like to see above the front door of the Alamo, something that could have been written by anyone who was there.

THE GOLIAD MASSACRE AND MY OWN PRIVATE ALAMO

The coattails of the Alamo stretch at least a hundred miles. At Presidio La Bahia, near Goliad, a reconstructed garrison—"the world's finest example of a Spanish frontier fort"—interprets another event dear to the hearts of (many) Texans. Though the original fort was put up at the same site in 1749, its rebuilt version recalls a different era. Here, in 1836, a museum brochure scowls, took place "the darkest day in Texas history"—another wrenching display of public grief in the heart of the Lone Star State.

The tale of James Fannin is the stuff of a rather sad martyrdom. Having been outmaneuvered by the Mexican army in March of 1836, he surrendered his force of some three hundred Texans, assured by General José Urrea that everything within his power would be done to grant the prisoners clemency. The promise, unfortunately, was not to be kept. Santa Anna rejected the request out of hand, citing a government decree that stated that any armed rebel taken on Mexican soil was to be executed as a pirate. Though a struggle among the officers ensued, Santa Anna prevailed. "There was a great contrast in the feelings of the officers and the men," wrote Colonel Nicolás de la Portilla only hours after handing down the orders for execution. In the end, he recalled, "Silence prevailed."

Just what their silence meant—shame? fear? indignation?—isn't explored at the "massacre site" today. (The Alamo is described as a "massacre" in its museum too.) Trumpeted as part of a "war of extermination," the Goliad incident is meant to stir deep passions instead. Visible from the fort walls is the towering Fannin Monument, with, as one would expect, the names of the dead inscribed at its base. An atrocity? No doubt. But the historian at nearby Mission Espíritu Santo, Luis Cazarez-Rueda, told me it wasn't so much a massacre as an execution, a defensible military act given Santa Anna's overextended position and his rank as Urrea's commanding officer in defending Mexican territory.

That seems like hairsplitting to many a Goliad devotee. "I don't think any military rules were followed here," scoffs Newton Warcheza, La Bahia director, who prefers to call the event a "senseless execution." Warcheza explains to me the reenactment of the massacre held every year in March, which he calls "the largest living history event in the state." Mock skirmishes are held in front of the fort; an evening

candlelight tour visits the enlisted men's quarters and the chapel
where the wounded prisoners were held; the next morning, the massacre is reenacted on part of the actual ground, preceded by a chapel
memorial service presided over by the bishop of the local diocese. "It
is partially religious," says Warcheza of the ceremony that begins and
ends with a prayer, capping events that drew three thousand people to
Goliad for the weekend in 1994.

Do many Hispanics participate in the festivities? "I have a hard
time with people who divide Mexican Americans from Anglo Americans," he replies. "We're all Americans. We're all Texans." While
Warcheza claims that the presidio is restored to 1836 because it was
"the last period of occupation of the fort," he concedes that the Texas
Revolution is an even more compelling draw. He'd like to have more
on the Spanish period, he says, but hasn't yet had the time or resources to follow through. Owned and administered by the Diocese of
Victoria Catholic Church, the site survives on donations and admissions alone. "We don't make the history," he tells me of his limited
role as director, "we just tell how it happened."

Goliad, Texas, is the inverse of balmy St. Augustine. Instead of
placing a statue to Menéndez (the executioner of several hundred
Frenchmen) before city hall, the memory of Santa Anna is revived as
a permanent memorial to infamy. Rather than admire the Noble
Spaniard, here the public is offered the specter of the Depraved Mexican instead, architect of a massacre in which, the museum repeat-
edly reminds us, more than twice the number of those who fell at the
Alamo met their Maker. The only story that leavens the critique of
Mexico is that of the "angel of Goliad," a certain Señora Alvarez who
saved several of Fannin's men the night before they were to be shot.
It's not a museum that prides itself on southern exposure. "Two great
nations confronted each other at the presidio," says a display on the
colonial period. "Today only one survives on this continent—the Comanche nation located in Oklahoma."

In short, a Spanish colonial fort has been restored in order to remember the Goliad of James Fannin. One can walk through the buildings—few of them interpreted—and wonder just what the garrison
was like. In 1778, the presidio had more than five hundred occupants,
male and female, of various ages. Their lives seem even more of a
mystery today than those of Fannin's men, buried nearby in what is

said to be the largest mass grave in the country. Like the Alamo, the fort is interpreted as an event, not an institution.

Though a presidio rather than a mission, La Bahia's aim is no less religious: as Warcheza put it, it is "to preserve a piece of history like no other." Built as an outpost of Spanish civilization, the fort becomes the symbol of "a war of extermination" waged by its descendants. The presidio is restored as an excuse to celebrate a horrible, if sacred, memory. "Give us the head of Generalissimo Santa Anna," the prevailing sentiment seems to have it. And Goliad does, on a platter.

Skirting the Rio Grande Valley in the days to follow, I find garish yellow signs pointing to a place called Alamo Village near Brackettville. I wonder if I should even bother, burdened as I am already with an advanced case of Alamo-itis. A fifty-mile detour later, I pay a five-dollar admission fee at the gate, then follow the winding two-track path across windswept pasture until, mounted on a rise ahead of me like a mirage from *Beau Geste,* I see a prairie clone of Mission San Antonio de Valero—the most literal expression of "Remember the Alamo" you'll ever want to see. One Alamo, I think to myself, isn't enough for Texas.

I pull up next to the plaza wall to admire the life-size replica of the mission. A plasterer waves me off, pointing to a small adobe village down the road. When I finally park—the only car in the lot, I note suspiciously—a watchful older fellow eyes me from the village. Fitted out in straw hat, workshirt, blue jeans, and waders, a red kerchief tied around his neck, he looks like a hand at a dude ranch enjoying the off-season. Times must be tough at Alamo Village, I think—so far, the help outnumber the tourists. "You must be Colonel Travis," I say with a smile. He approaches at a bowlegged mosey.

"Happy Shahan," he offers, poking out a weather-beaten hand. At first his words have the ring of a Celtic greeting—or maybe a local variant of "Happy Trails"—until it finally dawns on me that he's just introduced himself. He pegs me as being from north of the Mason-Dixon, and we shake on the idea of our standing there on a hot May afternoon in the shadow of one of America's most famous symbols—or a pretty fancy imitation of it. I have the odd feeling he's been waiting for me all day, a sentiment that Happy, long on personal charm, is expert at conveying.

Shahan sets me up to an iced tea in the Alamo Village cantina, where the Hispanic girls behind the bar defer to him as "sir." James T.

"Happy" Shahan is, I learn in the hours to follow, a big-time rancher, music publisher, former mayor of Brackettville, and Texas film booster extraordinaire, the man who masterminded the rebuilding of the Alamo in the late 1950s for a movie about to be made by John Wayne (a close personal friend), and who's been inviting film crews ever since to use the nearby adobe village—for a consideration, of course. The mission of Shahan's Alamo is hardly to "self-destruct," as Father Janacek said of Concepción. "This is a movie set," my souvenir brochure cries. "No refunds!" There's not even a phone on the set; Shahan communicates with people by walkie-talkie.

Having heard so much about how the first Alamo fell, I was curious to learn how this one was built. With the approval of U.S. immigration authorities, Shahan tells me, he began busing hundreds of Mexicans across the border in 1957, once Wayne had chosen the location of the set. In what was a good deal for both sides, he insists, he paid them a dollar a day. Texas laborers would have asked for twice that amount, while Mexicans would have been lucky to earn fifteen cents south of the border. For the mission and nearby village, over a million adobe bricks and thirty thousand square feet of imported Spanish roofing tile were used. It took them almost two years to finish—less time, I note, than it took the Indians who raised the original in San Antonio.

When it came time to start shooting *The Alamo* in 1959, director Wayne decided to bring in hundreds of extras, mostly to play soldiers—Mexican and Mexican American both—in the battle scenes. Casting calls went out for types such as "40 males, unkempt in appearance, must be willing to let hair grow," and "12 to 18 Mexican women . . . Must weigh over 160 pounds." Those who crossed the border spent their days charging the Alamo in what has been called a Cold War allegory about the struggle against communism. But even the lucky ones didn't get to say much more than a spirited *Fuego!* or *Adelante!* on camera.

Built to Wayne's specifications, Shahan's Alamo is more accurately restored to 1836 than the original mission. Gone are the Woolworths and fast-food joints atop the old plaza walls in San Antonio. Gone is the famous round top put on the chapel facade by the U.S. Army in the 1840s. Gone are the cenotaph, the disputed path of Alamo Plaza East, the nearby Crockett Hotel. The chapel is even left without a roof, just as it was during the battle. One employee tells me that Mexicans even come up to see it, "common people," he says, not the intellectuals involved with the controversy at the Alamo. The other Alamo, that is. The real one. The Alamo near Brackettville seems to have been purged of its demons.

In the past thirty-five years, Alamo Village has become a place where filmmakers play out different versions of history. There was Wayne's paean to embattled democracy; the noble portrayal of the Alamo's Tejanos in *Seguin;* Raul Julia's complex Santa Anna in *The Alamo: Thirteen Days to Glory.* On the Shahan HV Ranch, a sacred symbol is pretty much for rent. Several more Alamo films are soon to be in production, I'm told, so the future looks good. I ask Shahan how he feels about possible revisionist stories being played out in his own backyard. "It's just movies," he shrugs.

To hear his people tell it, Happy is a big-hearted patron who convinced Hollywood that Texas rangeland was a good place to shoot the most memorable western of them all—and then some. He gets up to go after a long day. "If you don't like what you see here," he says with a twinkle in his eye, "don't tell them anything about it." You can say that again, Happy. Finally I feel as though I can leave the Alamo, having seen how John Wayne imagined it.

ROMANCING THE MISSION

No one understands better the romance of the Spanish mission than California, where twenty-one missions were founded in the eighteenth century, each one a day's distance by horseback, and today major tourist attractions in the old Bear Flag Republic. "While colonists in other parts of the world tried to expropriate and exterminate the natives," reads the brochure for Mission San Luis Rey de Francia, near Oceanside, "the Franciscan Padres and the Spaniards sought to save them." Owned by the Franciscans of Santa Barbara province, San Luis Rey has an airy grandeur. Decked with bright geometric and floral frescoes, the sanctuary is possessed of a festive mood in contrast with the somber icons that inhabit it.

Mission life is interpreted as an act of simple devotion at San Luis Rey. A furnished leather workshop, kitchen, and spinning room, reminders of everyday life, adorn the museum that was renovated in 1979. Indians and Mexican soldiers raised the church walls from 1811 to 1815, using experience accumulated from years of building structures habitually rent by earthquake. Aside from the crucifixes and stations of the cross, however, there is little sense of the sacrifice or strain that would have driven daily life at the mission. "It is not unusual to see numbers of [Indians] driven along by *alcaldes* [Indian overseers]," wrote visitor Alfred Robinson of San Luis Rey in 1829, "and under the whip's lash forced to the very doors of the sanctuary."

A monument to the San Luis Rey Indians was erected in 1830 in the mission cemetery, though there's a good chance other bodies are scattered far and wide, buried in the fields if they happened to die there. Local Luiseño Indians come to celebrate an annual day of memorial and are consulted, I'm told by the mission curator, before any archaeological dig. The impression is nonetheless striking: the neophytes of San Luis Rey are remembered most conspicuously in a cemetery memorial, a testament as much to their staggering mortality rates as to the new faith they practiced in the largest of the California missions.

Up the coast in Santa Barbara is the queen of the missions, where carved stone skulls sit atop a doorway at the entrance to the mission cemetery. Founded in 1786, the mission, damaged by earthquakes, has been completely rebuilt, the present church dating from 1820. Nearly 5,000 Chumash Indians converted to Christianity at Santa Barbara, some 4,000 of them buried in the vicinity of a giant Moreton Bay fig in the church cemetery. "All are infected with [syphilis] for they see no objection to marrying another infected with it," wrote Friar Ramón Olbés of the Chumash in 1813. "As a result births are few and deaths many so that the number of deaths exceeds births by three to one." Their dwellings once relegated to a street extending away from the church, the anonymous Chumash were welcomed back to the center of the fold when they died, the garden plot where they're buried surrounded by the elaborate mausoleums of later settlers.

Inside the museum, I find no mention of venereal disease. The Indians are portrayed as hunter-gatherers contentedly converted to the trades, even if the workshop area in the cloisters is closed to the public. Although the first of the fathers is said to have been accorded a warm welcome by the Chumash, no mention is made of the revolt of 1824 in which some neophytes were killed and large numbers of them ran away. On display instead are sculptures by an Indian called, simply, "Paisano"—the only Chumash I find mentioned by name in the museum.

"The number of deaths exceeded births by three to one":
the cemetery wall, Santa Barbara Mission,
Santa Barbara, California

Unseemly behavior, then as now, is discouraged. "These Indians have no fermented drinks whatever of their own but they hanker after ours," complained Olbés, "wherefore we keep them securely hid." Anxious to avoid graffiti in the men's room, the owners have hung a blackboard and piece of chalk for compulsive scribblers. "The Franciscans did not own the mission," the Santa Barbara brochure says. "They administered the mission for the benefit of the Indians." There is little doubt, however, who owns it today. Santa Barbara is the only mission in the state to have been under Franciscan control since its founding.

Not all the California missions have remained in church hands. Near Lompoc, La Purísima Concepción de María Santísima was rebuilt in the 1930s by the Civilian Conservation Corps, its 900 acres given by private donors and the Catholic Church, and is today a part of the California state park system. Over 1,500 converts recorded on the mission rolls in 1804 had dropped to some 600 in 1824. That year La Purísima was the site of the bloodiest Indian revolt in the California system, sparked by the whipping of a neophyte in nearby Santa Ynez. Today oriented toward social history more than most missions, La Purísima has accorded a momentous effort to rebuilding the church, soldiers' quarters, workshops, and friars' residence. But the labor was never quite finished. The buildings farthest from the church, two Indian barracks 572 feet long in total, are unexcavated, a mere rope surrounding the site. The tape-recorded tour for visitors doesn't bother to mention them.

A county road over the site once prevented the rebuilding of the barracks, explains Joe McCummins, interpretive ranger for the state park. Little reconstruction has been done since the county abandoned the road in the 1950s, he says, though money currently being raised would seem destined not for the barracks, but for a new visitors' center. McCummins says interpretation at La Purísima is "center of the road," explaining it's hard to make moral judgments of the Spanish fathers by current standards. The nearby Chumash reservation in Santa Ynez has little to do with the site, he admits. "They look back at their ancestry and believe the mission system destroyed it," he says a little glumly.

Visitors on the candlelight tours in October or the Mission Life Day festivals scattered throughout the year will watch activities performed by costumed volunteers: weaving, soap making, blacksmithing, and pottery making. Those who come the rest of the year won't be so lucky. Though a guidebook tells of the 1824 revolt, there's no mention of it on the signs that mark the self-guided tour. Taking control of the mission for a month, sixteen neophytes died in the assault by Mexican cavalry to retake La Purísima, which they did after a short battle; seven more Indians were executed later. Though the tape tour acknowledges that some of the Chumash were known to run away, it spends more time recalling that mission meals were *muy delicioso,* and that Indian girls were given to gossiping while a dashing *muchacho* serenaded them.

The tour and impressive rebuilding at La Purísima raise more questions than they answer. Did women as well as men become literate? Did the soldiers take Indian wives? How well did the Indians speak Spanish? What did the majordomos (overseers) give up in return for their privileges? Were young Chumash women confined to the *monjerio* barracks for fear of indiscretions by their own men—or Spanish ones? Was the 1824 revolt an exception—or a culmination of all that La Purísima stood for? What happened to the Chumash? Where are their descendants? If so many of them died, can La Purísima even be considered a "success"? If not, do most of the 160,000 people who visit every year sense the celebration of the mission as a paradox?

The Indian past is remembered differently at San Antonio de Pala mission, near Escondido. Not a full-fledged mission but an *asistencia,* Pala, on one of the Luiseño Indian reservations, is the only one of the California missions still serving a primarily native community. Administered by the diocese of San Diego, the mission and its school provide a private education for one hundred local students, most of them Indian. A reservation of some one thousand inhabitants, Pala is half native, half non-native; with its proximity to the international border, identities can be still more complex. "It's hard to be Luiseño and not be [ethnically] Mexican," says one resident, referring to longstanding mission ties. Thirteen hundred neophytes lived there until the mission was secularized in the 1840s, though some of the locals aren't too enamored of the memory now. In more ways than one, Pala is off the beaten path of the mission trail.

Popping wheelies on a bicycle in front of the mission museum, a boy with a rat-tail haircut—part Samoan, part Indian—offhandedly tells me that "the Spaniards enslaved my people." An elder from the Pechanga Reservation nearby isn't any more sanguine about the matter, saying that San Luis Rey had failed to mark the place on its premises where five hundred Indians were "murdered," boasting that he'd been up to Carmel mission of late to dance on Father Junípero Serra's grave.

Inside the Pala museum, I ask about local opinions regarding the proposed canonization of Serra, founder of the California missions. My question is met with embarrassed silence. Later, Sister Mary Yarger, a teacher at the Pala mission school, concedes that making Father Serra a saint would be an insult to many Indian people, given the destructive legacy of the missions. She personally would prefer the canonization of Kateri Tekakwitha, an Iroquois woman (born, of all places, in the Mohawk village of Ossernenon), who would be the first American Indian saint in the Catholic church. She's not at all sure it will ever happen: they're awaiting proof of an undisputed second miracle. "The church," Sister Yarger says enthusiastically, "is for all people."

Half Luiseño, she grew up next door to Pala and is a graduate of the mission school herself. "We're still serving the people that the church was originally intended to serve," she says, "[though] maybe not in the same way," explaining that sage is sometimes burned instead of incense at local services, and that the priest is making an effort to include elders in the liturgy. Having visited a few of the other missions, Sister Yarger says their purpose is to show "how wonderful the Franciscans were," perhaps displaying a few token arrowheads on the side. The missions, she contends, address themselves to the people they believe they're serving. Even the financial troubles of her own school reflect the community that surrounds it, in stark contrast to upscale cities such as Santa Barbara. "Indians here are present, they're not history," she concludes proudly.

A few days later I go up to Carmel mission, near Monterey, to find the grave on which my Pechanga acquaintance danced. If he wasn't exaggerating, he would have had to scale a low railing in the San Carlos Borromeo mission sanctuary to do the deed. If by the "grave" he meant the sarcophagus located in the *convento* wing of the museum, he would have had to climb several feet on top of a sculpted stone and commit a balancing act worthy of Nijinsky. Either way, such a contrary pilgrimage would have required a valiant effort, what with such nearby relics as Father Serra's cell and a piece of the live oak tree under which he sang a mass—the same place where Sebastián Vizcaíno had landed in 1602, commonly called "California's Plymouth Rock."

There is more of hero worship than social history at Carmel mission. One finds a statue of Father Serra, a sign marking the spot where he raised the mission cross, and museum text that notes his vow of poverty while adding that he wanted the best furnishings possible for the mission churches, of course. Meanwhile, the neophytes are most clearly recalled in the cemetery, adorned with a monument to the three thousand Indians buried there. As elsewhere, the peace-

"The church is for all people":
San Antonio de Pala mission school, Pala, California

ful place of repose implies that their conversion to Christianity was complete. But such was hardly the case. "As a sign of mourning, the [afflicted] cut off their hair," Father Juan Amorós wrote of the Carmel neophytes in 1814. "If scissors are lacking they burn it bit by bit. Moreover they throw ashes over their entire bodies, weep bitterly, abstain from food, and the old women smear their faces with pitch. . . . It is also their habit to go to the woods to drown their sorrow." Whatever the goals of the padres, many native customs persisted, a fact one would hardly guess when going through the more popular Franciscan missions today, filled as they are with a dazzling array of church vestments and relics.

For the public at large, the restored mission (California and elsewhere) shares much in common with the plantation. Although the Indians once dominated the site in terms of numbers, one would be hard-pressed to know it today. The buildings most likely to be restored are the church and *convento*—the "big house" of the mission—the center of power (then and now) that bespeaks the paternalism of the church. But a reconstructed mission convert's home, like a slave quarter, is an unlikely sight. At San José in San Antonio, a bleak quarter is restored. At Espíritu Santo in Goliad, Texas, a fine diorama and exhibit give a sense of domestic life that most mission visitors never glimpse. Though exceptions like these exist, they underline the lack of similar efforts elsewhere.

While the museums typically devote a display to native culture—usually to emphasize the warm welcome extended the padres—the exhibits rarely address what would seem to be fundamental questions. How were the Indians brought to the mission in the first place? Were they hunted down? Were they willing volunteers? How often was resistance encountered? The exhibits I saw hardly attempted to account for reasons behind native "mobility," both in and out of the mission. Estimates suggest that 10 percent of California Indian converts became permanent fugitives during the mission period. Such is the reverent mood at many missions that if one isn't careful, it's easy to think that the only good Indian was a mission one.

Many romances of the institution still abound. One holds that the padres, benign and gentle, blessed the natives with the gift of civilization—a look at the burial registers and runaway lists is enough to remind us that their "blessing" was a mixed one. Another argues that the natives were simply "corrupted" by the church, an idea that makes native cultures seem more naive than they really were. In places such as Texas, for example, the mission provided protection against enemies, a refuge many Indian people found attractive—though the hard realities that guided their acculturation are rarely mentioned. Then, too, if the paternalism of the fathers could be selfish, the further disappearance of Indians and the theft of mission land after secularization was a sign of how destructive Mexican and Anglo settlers could also be, not to mention the governments that sponsored them.

America's missions provide the best example of how ownership can dictate public history. At Carmel (owner: Catholic Diocese of Monterey), visitors read that Junípero Serra came to California to teach "the better way of life to a pagan race." At Purísima Concepción (owner: state of California), more space in the museum is spent crediting the Civilian Conservation Corps that rebuilt the mission than the Chumash Indians who put it up in the first place—not surprising in a public institution funded by taxpayer money. At San Esteban Del Rey (owner: Acoma Indian tribe) in New Mexico, visitors are told of the time that ten Indian children were traded as slaves to Mexico City in return for a new mission bell. Tourists also learn of the times

A question of balance: a ruined church and pueblo kiva,
Pecos, New Mexico

pueblo men were sent to Mount Taylor to cut pine timbers for the church roof, threatened by their Spanish overseers that, should any timber so much as touch the ground, the man responsible would have a foot chopped off.

Lacking an edifice worthy of the name, other sites are spared the temptation of presenting an "edifying" story. One peculiar advantage of Pecos National Historical Park in New Mexico is that both mission churches—the first destroyed in the Pueblo Revolt of 1680—are now in ruins. Thus the crumbling Spanish walls stand next to those of Cicuye [Pecos] pueblo, not towering above them—on equal footing in the realm of material culture. The trail unfolds on a rise atop a 360-acre site, traversing the Indian ruins that, when Francisco Coronado saw them in 1540, were a sturdy four stories high. The path unfolds chronologically, continuing to the church *convento,* where the Indians defiantly built a ceremonial center (*kiva*) after the revolt, later buried by the returning fathers. One has the sense of walking through layers of history.

The Park Service museum offers a clear narrative on the Indian, Spanish, and Anglo phases of settlement, and their subsequent blending. The museum text notes that two good horses could have fetched an Indian slave girl plus "trifles" in 1745. Objects range from parts of the old mission bell to a Spanish spur, pieces of Indian pottery, an Anglo hair curler, a wooden church corbel, and a cactus picker. A bulletin board titled "This Month at Pecos" explains that May was when *encomienda* payments came due, the mission community providing a levy of animal hides to Spanish authorities.

Yet Pecos misses the chance to say more of the complex rapport between native and Spaniard in the pre-mission years. The muster roll of the 1540 expedition that set out from Compostela (Mexico), listing only European members, obscures the fact that the Spanish were accompanied by a force of almost one thousand Indian allies. In terms of sheer numbers, if nothing else, Coronado rode at the head of an Indian *entrada*, not a Spanish one. The "rainbow coalition" that visited the Southwest is an unsettling image for those who would understand the missions as a simple conflict between Indian and Spaniard. "The people of this town pride themselves," chronicler Pedro de Castañeda wrote of Cicuye, "because no one has been able to subjugate them, while they dominate the pueblos they wish." So it was at Pecos that the native people came to outlive the mission sent to convert them, even as they no doubt recognized its objective as a familiar one.

OUR MEN IN BROWNSVILLE

The National Park Service has made a beachhead in Brownsville, Texas. Housed in a nondescript concrete block building on the corner of Washington and 14th (*taquerías* down the street, a taxi stand next door, the Mexican border just around the block), local rangers are deliberately keeping a low profile. In fact, they don't even wear their uniforms downtown. With tempers running high about immigration, one of them explained, they'd just as soon not be mistaken for border patrol guards. The Interior Department has come to Texas to commemorate a war that isn't a very warm memory for our neighbors to the south. Here, the colonial frontier that the mission and the presidio protected finally reached the flash point in the nineteenth century—decades after the Spanish had granted independence to their colonies.

The proposed 3,400-acre boundary established in 1992 for Palo Alto Battlefield National Historic Site will interpret the first battle of the Mexican War, fought on 8 May 1846, on a field eight miles north of the Rio Grande, two miles north of the Brownsville city limits. Historians claim the event has many unique features to commend it. Palo Alto was the first military engagement whose results were reported by telegraph. War correspondents made their appearance on the field of battle, as did the daguerreotype. Ether was introduced by U.S. surgeons as a battlefield anaesthetic. Thirty-three participants were to become generals in the American Civil War; Zachary Taylor, Ulysses Grant, and Mariano Arista later went on to serve as presidents of their respective countries.

In some ways, Palo Alto was America's first "modern" battle, a symbolic struggle between the technology and tactics of two centuries. Hand-to-hand combat was virtually absent in the encounter; the massed Mexican cavalry charges were brutally repulsed by American artillery. While General Arista's vintage cannon fired projectiles that the Americans were able to sidestep as they rolled by, the Yankee cannonades had a withering effect. The Mexican troops were enjoying the strains of "Los Zapaderos de Jalisco," played by an army marching band, when "the right section of Duncan's battery opened with cannister and shell," remembered correspondent Thomas Bangs Thorpe. "At the first discharge the musicians were completely annihilated; a shell exploded among them, piling them in one promiscuous heap of frightfully wounded and dead." American casualties at Palo Alto were 9 dead, 43 wounded; between 100 and 400 Mexicans were killed. It was a sign of things to come in a war where Mexican losses, usually not even estimated, would be several times those absorbed by the United States. By 1846, Washington was already possessed of a high-tech advantage over its southern neighbor—and one it has never relinquished. "Their instruments," wrote Thorpe imaginatively, "were rent as if of paper." The battle was over in a matter of hours.

"The whole United States doesn't give two hoots in hell about the Mexican War," gripes Bruce Aiken, a retired army colonel who's done his best to fight a plague of public apathy in recent years. Executive director of the Brownsville Historic Museum, where his dress blues hang on prominent display, Aiken regrets that the Mexican conflict has been overshadowed by the Civil War, and has lobbied hard to have the nearby battlefield preserved. Even locals, he says, tend to confuse Palo Alto with another encounter: Palomito (1865), the last battle of the Civil War, was also fought in the vicinity. Barely a few miles from where the battle happened, "Remember Palo Alto" doesn't summon a lot of civic pride.

Besides, some locals resent Aiken's enthusiasm. "There are a few people who share a Mexican sentiment that 'We got our tortillas stomped out there and it was an unjust war and we should give no recognition to it,'" he concedes. But Aiken writes off such thinking to bad history and a lot of sour grapes. The Mexican War, he says, was a pre-emptive strike by the United States over a legitimate border dispute. It was justly fought by the U.S. Army north of the Rio Grande, and only became a shady affair when reckless elements enlisted and started to plunder after crossing the border. "It's when the volunteers came in that the picture changed," Aiken insists, a defender of military regulars to the last. "I could see where Mexico would be a little upset," he allows, without belaboring his sympathy.

He's crossed the border to Matamoros to convince Mexican merchants that, whatever their differences in 1846, they all stand to profit from remembering them now. "You guys stomped us good at the Alamo," he likes to tell them. "You totally wiped us out. That thing draws more tourism than you can even imagine." The merchants, he says, are coming around. "Slowly they're beginning to take their feelings off their sleeves and say, 'What's past is past. I wasn't there, you weren't there. There's nothing we can do about it, so let's move forward.'. . . It has taken us too long to beat down this antagonism between the two countries." The wall calendar behind him, marked in detail for several months to come, suggests that retired Colonel Aiken, whatever the local sentiment, has a strong mind to march on.

Both sides stand to benefit from a memorial, agrees Yolanda González, librarian at the University of Texas at Brownsville. But she has different ideas about what will attract people to the site. "If we advertise [Palo Alto] nationwide, [people] will come and visit the site because that is where their great-great-grandfathers fought," she says, a genealogist and historian by avocation. "The park should be respected like a cemetery because lives were lost there," she adds, explaining that cultural attitudes might encourage traffic on both sides of the border. "That's the custom over here," she says of Mexican cultural habits, "to go visit a cemetery."

González admits that interpretation will depend on "who is there to tell what happened." One side has an older claim than the other. "Who was the founder of Brownsville?" she asks goodnaturedly. "This was Matamoros. We didn't care about the river." A member of the historical associations in both cities, González is a classic Valley dweller, her ancestors among the first Spanish families that settled Matamoros. "I'm between the two flags. My father was from Matamoros, my mother was from here." If you go back far enough, she says, the two sides of her family are probably related anyway. "I respect both nations, both flags," she insists, adding with an extra hint of pride, "My family was from Mexico."

By the usual standards, the Palo Alto battlefield is in pristine condition. Composed largely of salt flats, the grazed-over area has never been developed. In fact, a friend of Aiken's who calls it "bald-assed prairie" isn't far wrong. The current mesquite, yucca, and prickly pear cactus is much like the terrain described in the original battle accounts. But postcard shots for tourists will be hard to come by. Arista's Hill, the commanding ridge where the Mexican line took its stand, is all of twenty feet above sea level—you need a pair of binoculars to see the grade from a hundred yards. The Park Service is still awaiting appropriations to buy the land, and local owners are said to be anxious to sell. Our men in Brownsville are building the story of Palo Alto from the ground up.

Their enthusiasm is daunting. Park superintendent Tom Carroll calls the battle a "point of reunion," a kind of Civil War story of brother versus brother. For the Park Service, it's a NAFTA-age stab at binding old wounds. The Mexican government has been invited to help engage in joint research and interpretation at the site, a way of ensuring balance on the international border. For Carroll, the story has come full circle: the Interior Department, established after the Mexican War to administer the new treaty lands, has finally come around to interpreting the conflict that created it. "Its international authority is extremely unique for a National Park Service area," he says. That's what makes Palo Alto so difficult.

"It's a part of our history that we're ashamed to remember because we lost," says Alma Guerrero-Miller, a regional historian and Mexican national who resides in Brownsville and has acted as a consultant to the Park Service. Guerrero-Miller, who specializes on border issues, foresees formal participation by her government as very slow in coming. While lauding Carroll's conciliatory efforts, she adds of the park, "It is very difficult to get everyday people to see it [positively]. . . . Mexicans see it as a way to Americanize the Mexican American population." Nor does the tourism argument impress her: Matamoros has had its fill of spring-break students from the north who sometimes behave outlandishly, she says. "We still don't know what to do with the winter Texans."

Guerrero-Miller, who works for CIMTA, a nonprofit research organization based in neighboring Tamaulipas, stresses border above nationality in the making of local identity, a comment I heard from many people in the Valley. Mexico City, she notes, can be as nationalistic in its motives as Washington. "I don't see why we have to confront each other," she says of the local population. "I believe people at the border have a different way of seeing things. We have a common history."

Palo Alto is intended as a way to bridge the rift between neighbors possessed of a deep mutual mistrust. Even the language of the park legislation—Public Law 102-304—calls the conflict "the Mexican-American War," the most neutral of terms for what is hoped will be an even-handed portrayal. What most Americans call "the Mexican War" is referred to, south of the border, as "the War of 1847" or, even more tellingly, "the North American Invasion of 1846–48." "You have to understand," Guerrero-Miller says, recounting her country's attempt to make America a common enemy in order to pull people together, ". . . we have had to make you the 'other.' "

Although no Spanish mission ever stood in Brownsville, the mission of the Park Service today is no less earnest. The legislation requires that the battle be interpreted from both sides—that such a provision should even be necessary is worth noting. The Park Service, of course, has a history of interpreting battles according to a proud, national tradition. But Palo Alto is not like Horseshoe Bend, or Little Bighorn, or Gettysburg, or Yorktown. This time the government is depicting a sovereign "adversary" who is crucial to our economic future, a country of one hundred million people with a long series of grievances against their Yankee "cousins." Now the Park Service is going to tell both sides of the story—from the start. The reason it will do so has less to do with high principles than the hard political facts of the age.

Hearth and Home

THE RELATIVE ABSENCE of public memorials to women in this country is best explained by a chronic case of culturewide amnesia. True, a handful of women have fared well in the realm of public history. There are several interpreted sites devoted to the life of Mary Baker Eddy, founder of the Christian Science movement. Sacajawea, the Shoshone Indian guide for Lewis and Clark, has more memorials than do many a legendary mountain man: statues from Virginia to Oregon to Idaho, two gravesites, and inclusion in the Cowgirl Hall of Fame. The numerous "Madonna of the Trail" monuments, raised by the Daughters of the American Revolution, testify to the ease with which women have been portrayed as ideal figures ("liberty," "victory," "the pioneer mother") rather than flesh-and-blood human beings. Overall, America has been more likely to put women on metaphorical pedestals than marble ones.

PURITAN SKINHEAD OR PIONEER MOTHER?

This country's first public monument to a woman is said to be a twenty-five-foot marble obelisk erected in Haverhill, Massachusetts, in 1861. It honored Hannah Duston, a native of the village taken captive in 1697 by attacking Abenaki Indians. Having recently given birth, Duston helplessly watched as the attackers killed her newborn infant, dashing out its brains on a tree before escaping with their English captives in tow. As Frances Slocum, Mary Rowlandson, and hundreds of others could attest, white females were commonly taken as prisoners by Indians, whether to raise ransom money or replenish diminishing numbers. What makes Hannah Duston different from the others was how she dealt with her predicament.

Encamped with her Abenaki captors on an island in the Merrimack River two weeks later, Duston rose up on the night of March 30 with a vengeance. Enlisting the aid of two fellow captives, she killed and scalped ten Indians while they slept, the threesome effecting their escape down the Merrimack to Haverhill. They were later to receive the princely sum of fifty pounds from the General Assembly—paid, presumably, as an Indian bounty. After relating her saga to Puritan minister Cotton Mather—who published it in a collection titled *Humiliations Followed By Deliverances*—she settled back into everyday life. During a later Indian raid on the settlement (1707), it appears that Duston was not disturbed by the attackers.

New England literati wrestled over Duston's grisly tale for centuries. Mather lauded her courageous stand against Catholic- (French) inspired "idolators" and saw her deliverance as evidence of God's mercy. Henry Thoreau, floating down the same Merrimack by which Duston had fled, thought her exploits worthier of the Dark Ages than an enlightened modern era. Haverhill native John Greenleaf Whittier cast her as an avenging angel acting in a fury of passion. And intent as always on revealing a stain in the Puritan soul, Nathaniel Hawthorne dourly offered in *The American Magazine of Useful and Entertaining Knowledge,* "Would that the bloody old hag had been drowned in crossing Contocook River."

Not only did Hannah's bravery go in and out of literary fashion, but her monument suffered a similar fate. When public subscriptions for the monument lagged during the Civil War, the obelisk was repossessed and shipped off to Barre, Massachusetts, eventually to honor the Civil War dead of that town, its legend rubbed out and replaced with a new one. Hannah was gone, but not forgotten. In 1879, funded by a local millionaire, a bronze statue of Duston on a granite base was erected on Haverhill Common. There the Puritan mother stands today, a raised tomahawk in her right hand, her left one pointing with the intensity of a wartime Uncle Sam. The morning I saw her in Grand Army of the Republic Park, her finger was gesturing toward an

Homage to "Saint Hannah": the statue of Hannah Duston, Haverhill, Massachusetts

abandoned shopping cart—declaring war, it seemed, on an offending domestic totem.

"Had she not tangled with the Indians, she would be this great heroine," offers Greg Laing, special collections curator at the Haverhill public library, within eyeshot of the statue. Lately, Laing has heard a lot of grousing about Duston because she doesn't fit the prescription of political correctness—not when she scalped ten Native Americans. "If she just got murdered by the Indians, it would probably be OK," he muses. He walks me through the history of "Saint Hannah," as he ironically calls her, from her inclusion as a heroine in early school primers to her current reputation among skeptics as an

Indian ax murderer. In the later nineteenth century, Laing says, her image was downplayed to emphasize the role of her husband, who rescued the remaining children—an example of Victorian attitudes about female propriety. Duston is proof, if anything is, that heroism has its fashions.

Pamphlets on Hannah are a best-selling item in the library gift shop. "Hannah Duston draws people from all over the United States," Laing explains. "For whatever reason; that's their problem. The point is they end up here, and we may as well sell them something." An attempt to sell a T-shirt emblazoned with Hannah and her hatchet was nixed a few years ago when a local Native American objected. Laing guesses the shirts would outsell the John Whittier ones by fifty to one—so much for the enduring legend of literati. What does he think of native complaints about publicity from the Duston story? Not oblivious to the problem of stereotyping, Laing gives a philosophical shrug of his shoulders anyway: "It happened."

Many visitors to Haverhill are touched by Hannah's story. She must have had a lot of descendants, the shop cashier tells me, because just about everyone who comes in claims to be family. There's a whole range of Duston collectibles, from sterling silver spoons to Wedgwood tiles to "ax jewelry"—earrings and tie tacks. Laing shows me a commemorative porcelain Jim Beam bottle commissioned by the New Hampshire Alcoholic Commission in the 1970s. Hannah appears to be holding flowers in one hand—on closer inspection they turn out to be a couple of scalps. The linen she was said to have wrapped the scalps in is on display at the local historical society, as is the famous hatchet—not authenticated, and definitely not for sale.

For traditionalists, New England has other stories of pilgrim mothers who killed when Indian invaders crossed the threshold, but none so bloody. For revisionists, Duston seems more like a John Wayne in drag with ten notches on her hatchet. Then too, Hannah just as well answers the feminist call for engagement in a male-dominated world: she told Mather she was promised the prospect of running the gauntlet "Strip't and Scourged" when the captives reached their destination, not a pretty fate to imagine. The Duston captivity has about as many "victims" as it does players, which explains why Hannah's image has been sullied and rehabilitated more times than that of Czar Nicholas. Although the statue in the park has never been toppled, the tomahawk has been broken off many a time.

The Duston statue is a rare kind of monument to the Indian massacre—the victims, after all, were Indian. Another Duston statue, dedicated in 1874, stands near Boscawen, New Hampshire, where she performed the deed. But the fact that the statues are more celebratory than somber no doubt makes them typical of tradition. Both monuments, however, omit a significant fact in Hannah's original story. Among her victims were two women and six children. "Onely one Squaw Escaped sorely wounded from them, and one Boy. . . ." wrote Mather. "But cutting off the Scalps of the Ten Wretches, who had Enslav'd 'em, they are come off." Just about everyone in the Duston case can scream bloody murder, a rather strange beginning for the public history of American women.

TROUBLE IN RIVER CITY

To grasp the image of women in U.S. history better I went to the heartland. Here the myth of the small town and the emerging cult of womanhood came together in a number of nineteenth-century communities that proposed, in principle at least, that women were the equal of men. Overrepresented among restored sites, America's utopian communities are hardly typical of how the mass of women lived in our history. Still, they offer a telling glimpse of how far reality can fall short of rhetoric, a common pitfall for the very act of doing historic preservation. If Hannah Duston was a deranged exception, I wanted to find how women safely moored in a larger community were depicted.

I found that place in New Harmony, Indiana, where the rhetoric of equal rights was the cornerstone of a nineteenth-century community that is still fondly remembered. Whatever rights it accorded women, however, New Harmony advertises itself as the story of its adopted sons. The most famous of these was Robert Owen, a transplanted Welsh-born industrialist who saw America as fertile ground for an experiment in communitarian living. New Harmony would be a place where, as his own rhetoric claimed, women and men could live in . . . well, perfect harmony. Credited by some with having coined the word *socialism,* Owen might not have foreseen a time when the word would bring a scowl to the face of many a heartland inhabitant.

In 1825, Owen purchased the land and buildings of New Harmony from the German Lutheran visionary George Rapp. In the way shrines are often erected on the sites of older, abandoned ones, Owen's Harmony took root in the very town the Rappites had left after a decade of successful communitarian life. Nor was Father Rapp the first to break Harmony ground. The old cemetery on West Street was laid out on a burial ground whose mounds, a thousand years old, are still visible today. The German graves are unmarked in accordance with the beliefs of the immigrants, succeeding a culture we describe today, with still more humility, as simply "Woodland Indian."

The operative word in this friendly town on the banks of the Wabash River is still *harmony*. A nonprofit organization run jointly by the state and the University of Southern Indiana, Historic New Harmony, Inc. has fashioned an impressive welcome for the thirty thousand people who visit every year. The official brochure avows how the Rappites "perfected a cosmopolitan and efficient community"; it notes that the Owenites contributed toward "a golden age of innovation in American science and education." If these sound like large claims for a town of barely one thousand people, New Harmony does seem to be one of the few places in America where tourists looking for a historic bargain can find two utopias for the price of one.

Visitors begin by climbing a series of ramps to visit the plush 200-seat theater in the visitors' center known as "the Atheneum," built at a price of $2.8 million in the 1970s. With a sudden hush the sun disappears, the windows covered by sliding wall panels. We settle in to watch *The New Harmony Experience,* a seventeen-minute history narrated in the voice of a farmer who unblushingly admires the people who have come to build a model town. "People were living as well here—or even better—than anywhere [else] in the United States," we learn of the Rapp years. Lauding even the failed Owenite experiment, the narrator concludes with a piece of trademark New Harmony rhetoric: "Will this treasured town continue to inspire," he asks, "energize, focus, teach, contribute, fulfill?" New Harmony has taken the task of being a model town to heart.

I leave the Atheneum, a three-story modernist design faced with white porcelain, 15,000 square feet of space that towers above the town like a mother ship. And I'm left with a doubt. Given the successes of Rapp and Owen, why didn't their communities endure? I find the first clue at the Harmonist (Rappite) cemetery, bordered with bricks from the church torn down in the 1870s. A sign explains that

"A cosmopolitan and efficient community":
New Harmony, Indiana

230 Harmonists (out of a peak figure of a thousand) died during the community's ten-year stay. Most of these were consumed in the first year or two by malaria, a mortality rate that would have rivaled that of some of the earliest European colonies in America. "It was efficient and it was beautiful," the film said of Father Rapp's experiment. The graves are unmarked, though a burial list I find later makes clear the victims were diverse: "Steiger's daughter," "3 Trautweins," "Zundel he and she." New Harmony was also a pestilential trap.

Lutheran separatists who immigrated to America in 1804, the Rappites adhered to a strict core of values: property was communally owned, labor was equally distributed, loyalty to the patriarchal Father Rapp was required, and eventually a commitment to celibacy—in expectation of Christ's imminent return—was an expected vow. It was a strange brew of beliefs, a mash of Biblical injunction, economic pragmatism, and utopian dreaming. Although their industry assured them of worldly success, the celibate status of the Rappites abetted their eventual disappearance, an irony that, given the lack of converts, would characterize other communal sects such as the Shakers.

The Rappites built a community characterized by rigid self-control and savvy entrepreneurship. In fact, they carried on a lively commerce with the outside world—selling hemp, tobacco, sugar, butter, flour, cattle, hogs, and furs—becoming the envy of many a less successful neighbor. Religious principles may have limited them to consuming wine and cider, but they produced copious amounts of beer and whiskey for sale downriver in New Orleans. Although my tour at New Harmony explains the lack of local markets as a reason for the Rappites' move to Pennsylvania, the broader implications of Harmonist trade are never considered.

What were the consequences of doing business with the outside world? "The Receipts of the last week was $259.42," wrote agent John Hay in 1824 from the Rappite store in Vincennes, "owing in some measure to the Execution of a Black Man on Friday last, which brought a great Concourse of people together. . . . I was enguaged from morning until dark and took $115." The accused, William Cox, was hanged for rape—a punishment the Rappites might well have abhorred as much as the modern visitor. But commercial success sometimes meant profiting from the ugliness of the world, a paradox from which the principled Rappites were not exempt.

Our guide at Harmony stresses the community's egalitarian principles. For example, a belief in celibacy removed childbearing and infant care as traditional female tasks, a fact that would have made women more independent in Father Rapp's plan. But there were limits to shared ideals, even so. Charles Nordhoff, who visited the later Rappite community of Economy, in Pennsylvania, noted that an elementary education was given to all children, but "as the boys learn also agricultural labors of different kinds, they are generally self-helpful when they pass into the world."

Even among Harmony women, equality was a hard promise to live up to. In 1820, the Harmonists indentured a seven-year-old girl—an apprentice to "the art and mistery of Housekeeping"—to pay her parents' passage to America. Philippina Regina Fegert was bound over for a modest period of six years and nine months. Meanwhile, "Henny a woman of Colour" was indentured to Rapp and associates in 1817, promising "well and truly to demean herself in all things," though her terms were not nearly so friendly. "The said Henny," read the contract, "hath put, placed, and bound herself as an indented servant . . . to dwell and serve untill the full end and term of forty years." Given the demands of the local climate, it wasn't a contract likely to come to term. Though our guide says of the Harmonists, on more than one occasion, that "they were a kind and loving people," the condition of their black servants could amount to little more than a state of permanent servitude.

By the standards of the community that followed, however, the Rappite experiment was a smashing success. Robert Owen's utopian plan for New Harmony, purchased from Rapp, officially lasted for only two years, though many members stayed on after the community was formally dissolved. Several hundred people resettled Harmony: curious Americans from back east, scientists brimming with optimism, celebrated European intellectuals. In the founding documents, "equality of rights, uninfluenced by sex or condition in all adults" is a basic principle. Owenite beliefs also included freedom of speech, the existence of communal property, and equal compensation for all work. But it was the gap between ideal and real that, even in a community founded by a philanthropist, was the source of many a festering complaint.

"I am unable to sustain the fatigue of hard work," complained Sarah Pears in 1826 from New Harmony, "without such complete exhaustion of strength that I have no power to sew, and scarcely to read in the evenings." Married with children, Pears complained bitterly in the privacy of family letters of the local New Harmony "aristocracy." The role of married women—expected to master domestic family duties while contributing to communal tasks—was, for many, a continual source of contention. New Harmony was less a utopian vision than, for Pears, "a place where the worth of a woman is so much hard work as she can go through."

The tour notes Harmony's claim to have established the first trade school and public kindergarten in America, an educational system where corporal punishment was forbidden. But not everyone was enamored of the Owenite system that took children from the home at the age of a few years. "The boys have learnt nothing," Pears complained of the Harmony school. "I have heard that the girls have learnt a little geography, and a little sewing, but plenty of bad language, disobedience and contempt for their teachers." She found it hard to fathom that boys and girls would be allowed to board in the same dormitories while attending public school. Should sickness come, the thought of having staff at the Owenite hospital attend to her—instead of her own daughters—seemed an equal affront to common sense. The public realm of Harmony, whatever its stated role, could also seem a cruel invasion of privacy.

At Harmony, the drudge of daily utopian chores isn't the stuff of guided tours. "The single men of this town were generally obliged to make up their own beds for their lodgings," complained resident Paul Brown, "carry their clothes to the wash, call for and recover them when they could, as much as if they had belonged to an army." Whether married men even bothered to make their beds Brown doesn't mention. But behind the "army" he belonged to was another one required to serve it—one that did the washing, performed kitchen duty, and was left behind when the expeditions led by Robert's son, David Dale, later went out to perform their geologic surveys of the Midwest. In the Atheneum film was a scene with the illustrious Mr. Owen presenting a geology lecture. All of the raptly attentive students, of course, were male.

Pears wasn't alone in lamenting the backbreaking labor that left her exhausted at day's end. Harmony had a heady profile that, even today, focuses on the achievements of a few intellectuals rather than the common labor that kept them afloat. "What harasses and torments the female population of Harmony, and no small portion of the males," wrote William MacLure, Owen's financial partner, "but that base sensation of attaching consideration to the action in proportion to its uselessness and extravagant cost, and disgrace and shame to all occupations that are positively usefull." Someone, MacLure well understood, would have to furrow, sow, harvest, bind, thresh, grind, knead, and bake, if, as Owen suggested in his speeches against organized religion, the men and women of Harmony could be expected to live by bread alone.

Such rancor couldn't be allowed to spread, especially in a town where equality was a professed ideal. So it was that the *New Har-*

mony Gazette, published for several years by Robert Owen and his son, Robert Dale, heaped sumptuous praise—of a sort—on the female sex. "The most inestimable blessing which the benign bounty of the Creator has bestowed upon man," crowed an 1828 edition, "is the possession of a virtuous, amiable, and educated woman." Just what "possession" meant the editors did not discuss at length. "It is in the midst of trying suffering," the paper went on, "in scenes of distress and anguish, that the finest qualities of the female . . . are displayed in all their characteristic grandeur." A sentiment custom-made for deflecting rebellion, it probably would have seemed cold comfort to Sarah Pears.

True to its name, New Harmony doesn't recognize any differences in the social roles of men and women. Frances Wright, early feminist and frequent visitor to New Harmony, isn't mentioned on my tour. The only place where women are singled out is the Fauntleroy House, birthplace of the Minerva Society, an early women's rights group founded in 1859 by the granddaughter of Robert Owen. The Society is an achievement, not an inconsistency, and so, according to Historic New Harmony, merits a (limited) place in public perception. The desire to reflect well on the community fathers is tempting. Owen family descendants—by blood and marriage—still reside in town, own some of the historic properties, and have been instrumental in restoring New Harmony from the start.

It seems odd that, in a community that witnessed two prominent social experiments, so little actual space should be given over to the public realm of early New Harmony. Only two of the original dormitories remain. One is converted into an opera house, the other furnished with a mix of printing presses, antique chairs, and Victorian four-poster beds. Our guide tells us that the Rappites who lodged there would have slept on cots, not interesting enough, she adds, to be artifacts for historic interpretation.

In fact, one can spend the day in New Harmony—shopping, enjoying the Atheneum, taking the three-hour walking tour, bunking at the Harmony Inn—and be ignorant of many aspects of its history, including the dissension that helped dissolve the Owenite experiment. Today a sleepy, well-kept Midwestern town, Harmony then was anything but a bucolic preserve. "The gardens and fields were almost entirely neglected," wrote Paul Brown in 1827, admittedly something of a town scold. "The weeds grew as high as the houses . . . and swine ranged at pleasure throughout." Even if Brown exaggerated, Historic New Harmony, Inc., has preserved the town so nicely that it's hard to grasp how its early incarnations ever failed. "With all this," said one of my fellow tour members, "I can't believe they left."

Still, Historic New Harmony is more than merely a staid restoration. Much to its credit, it invites visitors to think about history as a continuing process: original structures built by Harmonists and Owenites blend with newer houses in a restoration effort that links two centuries. An impressive display of landscaped public space— Tillich Park, the Roofless Church, the Harmony Labyrinth—gives the town a private, meditative cast rarely found at a historic site. There is much to be learned at Harmony apart from the tours; it is a place for quiet reflection that asks people to think about the forces that originally founded the community.

But the interpreted version of New Harmony seems quaint. Would it be fair, for example, to call the early residents "cultists"? Outsiders no doubt considered them strange; insiders were sensitive to the way they were depicted. "It is good for you if (as you say) you do not blaspheme the Harmonie," wrote Catherina Kant to her runaway son, "and you have no reason to do so, for nothing was done to you here that might have given you reason to leave me, your mother, or the community." In addition to runaways during the Rapp years, many Owenites also bristled under the yoke of authority. Why should we celebrate these people as visionaries and look askance at today's religious cults, commonly described as the work of extremists?

The political questions are even harder. Were early inhabitants of New Harmony "communists"? Is it ironic to take pride in communitarian philosophies of the last century that our national ideology has attempted to discredit in this one? Beyond admiring the commercial know-how of Father Rapp, how much of Harmony prosperity was owing to trade with a section of the country where slave labor was widespread? Were the Harmonists, bent on the noble rhetoric of equality, in any way responsible for perpetuating slavery beyond their borders?

I left New Harmony with still another question. I had to wonder what relations would have been like between these two communities had they been neighbors in space, rather than in time. While Rapp struggled to fulfill the oracle of Biblical prophecy, Owen and his colleagues dismissed religion as a dangerous superstition. Nowhere else, that I know of, do we have a site where such contradictory beliefs were put to work in the service of a similar communitarian ideal. It is as if the patriarchal bluster of John Brown had suddenly sold the family farm to a pagan socialist. If respectful in their early relations, these founding fathers would have one day—given half a chance—had each other by the throat. I wonder if, for the women involved, it would have made any difference at all. There is something about us in that story, something that Historic New Harmony leaves out.

MOVERS AND SHAKERS

Set in the hills of Kentucky are the remains of a Shaker settlement idyllically known as Pleasant Hill. Some thirty buildings in brick, limestone, and clapboard remain from the nineteenth century, scattered over 2,700 acres of bluegrass. Its borders are marked by a maze of fences—white picket, cobbled stone, cross hatch, brown-and-white four-rails—that follow the gentle roll of the land, recalling another people who tried to live in the world while keeping its temptations at arm's length. Founded in 1805, Pleasant Hill, in fact, had good relations with the early Harmonists. Like the Rappites, the Shakers practiced celibacy, were a separatist Protestant sect that subscribed to Christ's second coming, exported manufactures to the South, and were regarded with general suspicion by their neighbors. Founded by Ann Lee, an English immigrant who claimed to be a female incarnation of God, the Shakers were rare in our history for the doctrinal and social equality they accorded women. Pleasant Hill was to be patterned after no Old Testament patriarchy.

A nonprofit, educational corporation, the Shaker Village of Pleasant Hill has managed the site since the 1960s with touches of the famous plain style. Visitors find no introductory movie. Site tours are self-guided, with costumed volunteers demonstrating crafts in the outbuildings. Tipping in the public dining room is discouraged; alcoholic beverages aren't even sold in the county. Many of the original buildings have rented guest rooms furnished with Shaker reproduction furniture. And though the guest rooms do concede to being equipped with telephones and color televisions, they start at the eminently modest rate of forty-six dollars a night. Two hundred full- and part-time employees cater to some three hundred thousand visitors a year—half of them to tour the site, half to use meeting facilities in restored buildings. For the most part, the tone of the restoration would have pleased Mother Ann, a stickler for pious simplicity.

A stroll through the limestone Centre Family Dwelling (1834), now a museum at the heart of Pleasant Hill, bears out the egalitarian stamp of the Shakers. The believers toiled for sexual and racial equality, the museum text informs us. For every deacon of the church there was a deaconess; for every elder an eldress. The Shaker commitment to celibacy relieved women of the burden of childbearing; the rearing of adopted children was done by the whole community. The Shakers educated boys and girls alike, even if they practiced a conventional division of labor. Women were confined to such tasks as cooking, washing, dairying, and weaving, a strict segregation that minimized unsupervised relations between the sexes. "They lifted their hands to work and their hearts to God" (the words of Mother Ann) is the uplifting motto of the restoration. It seems a happy coincidence that, before the village was restored, the dormant building was used as a storage shed for Goodwill Industries.

A communal residence in its heyday, the Family Dwelling is well stocked with Shaker brooms, seeds, tools, beds, tables, and chairs. Its two-and-a-half stories and forty rooms showcase a community where wealth was shared and the cultivation of the human spirit was a priority. But Pleasant Hill is an oddity for a public site: the "Great Man" school of history is put aside for a "Great Body" of religious believers, recalled with a spare restoration that knows the appeal of a picket fence and a souvenir flat broom. More than anything it seems like "corporate" social history, with a dash of pastoral nostalgia thrown in. I seem to have found the country antithesis of the plantation, where even the privy for the communal West Family Dwelling is restored with painted seats, lids, and air holes for ventilation, well beyond reach of the Centre Family "big house."

Like New Harmony, Pleasant Hill assigns the causes of its failure to anything but its own doing. "The [Civil] war destroyed their southern markets," reads the official guide, "and exposed the Order to new and corrupting worldly influences." It was true that marauding armies laid waste the local countryside (in 1994, the site hosted a Civil War encampment). Legal squabbles with outside jurisdictions also made the Shaker enterprise a difficult one. But internal pressures made Pleasant Hill a hard enough place to live in even without the world spilling its bad blood over it. "The Shakers never recovered from the depletion of their stores," we read of the war, but the demise of this Shaker colony near Harrodsburg wasn't nearly so simple.

In fact, Pleasant Hill had known severe internal dissension long before the 1860s, a fact hardly to be guessed in the outbuildings where broom making, woodworking, and weaving are performed today. "Infidelity, pride, presumption, disorder and confusion took deep root. The contagion spread and grew into a plague," wrote Elder Benjamin Youngs of a visit to Pleasant Hill in 1828. "'Away with the Elders and Deacons but such as are of the Peoples own choosing' became the pretty general sense." The authoritarian grip that would not permit a brother to pass a sister on the stairs, or allow one to receive a letter without an elder reading it first, made Pleasant Hill a less friendly residence for many than its name would suggest.

The governing "millenial laws" of the Shakers bore witness that, at least in theory, the daily regimen at Pleasant Hill was like something out of a celestial boot camp, a fact lost on many an admiring visitor. For example, the 1821 laws proclaim that brethren and sisters "are not allowed to make presents to each other in a private manner"; "no believer is allowed to play with cats nor dogs"; "it is thought imprudent to eat bread the same day it is baked"; "when we clasp our hands together our right thumbs and fingers should be above our left"; "no one is allowed to go into the water to swim or bathe where it is over his head"; not to mention that when Believers walk together, they "should not let an undercreature, whether human or unhuman get between them if they can consistently help it." Such rules cast a quainter light on the "Society of Believers" than does a made-up bed with a row of wall pegs in the Centre Family Dwelling.

If more enlightened when applied by Shakers, "separate but equal" still had its disturbing costs. It's one thing to marvel that women and men had to enter the meeting house by different doors. But in a self-contained community where celibacy was a core belief, the sexual tension must have been palpable. "Leonard . . . has been admitted into one of the families of the young order of Believers," wrote resident William Byrd in 1827, "where I hope he can content himself without any more molesting the young Sisters in their duty, in order as he wrote you to ascertain what progress they are making in the work of God." Leonard Jones, in fact, had been disciplined by the elders for his indiscretions, even, as Byrd suggests, after cleverly trying to rationalize his behavior. It's no wonder that celibacy was referred to by Shakers with the respectful euphemism "bearing the cross."

Pleasant Hill, one of many Shaker settlements, had nearly five hundred inhabitants by 1830. But one could people another community with the adult members who deserted it, many of them after long residence. Adam Baty, one of the few black members, left in 1827 after seventeen years as a Shaker. James A. McBride was "expelled" in 1849 at the age of thirty, having spent over half his life in the community. While "winter shakers"—deadbeats who took advantage of hospitality during the coldest months and then absconded—were common, the Society as a whole was only able to retain 10 percent of the children it "adopted." Runaways were often actively pursued by the brethren. Elder Youngs lamented of apostates that "with all the labors that could be made numbers continued going off to the world leaving still their poison behind." The history of any community is partly gleaned from the stories of those who leave it, a testimony that goes unspoken at most restorations, particularly in one that would exhibit, as the brochure puts it, a "highly successful type of society."

Practitioners of a communal lifestyle, the followers of Mother Ann are not likely to be remembered as family breakers. But the strictures of the faith rent many Shaker families asunder, and women seem to have most often borne the burden. Shaker women were vulnerable to a set of beliefs that, as in the legal system of the country at large, was less than balanced. "I considered the scenes of trial and affliction passed through by many families," wrote Thomas Brown, a Shaker apostate, in 1812, "in consequence of only part of the family receiving the faith; especially when the husband believed and not the wife, which caused a separation." Even if full equality was promised, not everyone was anxious to be a follower of Mother Ann.

Though not a Pleasant Hill resident, Brown had wide experience with a number of Shaker communities. A wife whose husband did not accept the Shaker system, he wrote, was typically forced to reside with him and nurture her beliefs apart; a husband, on the other hand, was permitted to leave his wife and move in with the community, sometimes taking the children with him. "Many have forsaken their wives and children," added Brown, an appraisal attested to by other Shakers. "Many women," he concluded, "have been left desolate and destitute." Though accusations against the sect were often motivated by personal spite, there seems little doubt that the equality of sexes in Shaker doctrine made for a tidier picture in theory than it did in practice.

The Pleasant Hill Shakers persisted for over a century. With fewer converts entering the Society, the site was turned over in trust to the private sector in 1910, and the last local member died in 1923. It is only fair to note that Shaker ideals and realities did not always jibe. Granted equality with their counterparts, deaconesses wielded less political authority than deacons, having little say in affairs outside the domestic sphere. Shaker women were often described by visitors to be in worse health than the brethren and to have a heavier work load. Even so, by the turn of the century, 72 percent of Shakers were women, a reminder of the alternatives outside the Society of Believers.

The dignity of women at Pleasant Hill is dutifully asserted. Gender equality "was a tenet of Shaker beliefs," confirms Marcheta Sparrow, director of public relations. "The Shakers were such a singular group of people," she enthuses, citing their generosity, work ethic, architecture, and sense of order as enduring cultural contributions. The very reputation of the sect is imbued with purity. People will complain if they see a piece of trash on the road, Sparrow says, adding that "the experience [of Pleasant Hill] becomes a very personal thing to them." The handful of Shakers still living in Maine come to visit the site every couple years—and they like it, she adds proudly. It's a fact that doesn't surprise me. As the millenial laws put it in 1821, "All tattling, talebearing & backbiting are forbidden among Believers." This might still be a motto for today's Pleasant Hill, whose believers, at least among the public, are legion.

LATTER-DAY SAINTS AND SINNERS

New Harmony and Pleasant Hill enshrine the values of the heartland—hard work, cooperation, independence. What's more, their lesson is thoughtfully declared in a safe, nondenominational rhetoric. But if they obscure certain social realities regarding women, I took comfort I might find a more honest depiction further west. A week later, standing on the banks of the recently flooded Mississippi, I discovered the remains of a settlement where women, beyond mere equal footing, have been placed on something of a pedestal of late. What I didn't expect was that their tribute would have been fashioned by the Church of Jesus Christ of Latter-Day Saints, known in popular parlance as the Mormons.

Founded by Joseph Smith in 1830, the church subscribed to many beliefs that made it suspicious in the eyes of outsiders. Important to Mormon thinking, for example, was the role of revelation in creating new scripture (The Book of Mormon), the practice of baptizing the dead, and a strong ethic of communal sharing—including plural marriage. A central tenet of the church was that women were forbidden from becoming members of the priesthood. Though given a central role in matters such as childrearing and charity work, they were absent from the realm of high church politics. That the Saints were hounded from early settlements in Ohio and Missouri was an experience that only made them more clannish. Finally, in 1852, the church experienced internal division when the son of Joseph Smith (Joseph Jr.) led a schism creating a Reorganized Church, still in existence today.

The home of the Saints from 1839 until most were driven out by angry neighbors in 1846, the town of Nauvoo, Illinois, (at least that part of it owned by the Mormons), takes pride in remembering the role women have played in the church—popular stereotypes to the contrary. "Gentling a modern wilderness or stepping forward bravely beside a handcart, each woman raises her own signposts on a unique yet universal journey," says a publication in the Latter-Day Saints visitors' center. The civilizing mission of woman, advanced as part of the cult of female domesticity in the nineteenth century, has been reborn with a passion in Nauvoo.

The towering visitors' center is graced by the adjacent Relief Society Monument to Women, an outdoor sculpture garden unveiled in 1978. Some dozen bronzes depict female stations in the journey of life, including "Woman Learning," "Woman and Her Talents," "In Her Mother's Footsteps," "Teaching with Love," and an elderly lady in a rocking chair, contentedly titled "Fulfillment." Inspirational insights play at the push of a speaker button; scriptural passages accompany each bronze. Sponsored by the Women's Relief Society of the church, the garden is a reminder of the divine ideals that suffuse the Mormon vision of Woman—or, as the commemorative monument guide puts it, "Between the generations from a garden in Eden to a garden in Nauvoo."

Nor will visitors find women confined to some pious corner. The

*Family values: Latter-Day Saints visitors' center and
sculpture garden, Nauvoo, Illinois*

Relief Society, founded in 1842, is remembered at the home of its
founder, Sarah Melissa Granger Kimball, who later headed the Utah
Women's Suffrage Association in 1890. "There is so much to be enjoyed here in the city of Nauvoo," narrates a woman in the LDS visitors' film on the city's founding, "I can't tell it all on paper." At the
other end of town in the Joseph Smith Historic Center—run by the
Reorganized Latter-Day Saints—guides extol the exemplary life of
Emma Smith, wife of the prophet Joseph, who bore his children, lived
with him in the homestead cabin, managed the Mansion House across
the street, and is buried next to her martyred husband—killed by a
mob in 1844 in nearby Carthage—a few steps from the Mississippi.

Although the suffering pioneer wife is a familiar symbol, it's rare
that her icon is given the attention one finds in Nauvoo. To a layper-
son it seems strange that Mormon women are granted a high profile at
all. After all, females are still prohibited from entering the LDS priesthood in the Utah church; only since 1984 have they been allowed to
join that of the Reorganized Saints, based in Independence, Missouri.
The sumptuous praise of women exhibited in Nauvoo might be
viewed as a handsome form of compensation for the Mormons'

"other" half, the one that's endured a structurally subservient role in the church from its beginning.

I'm encouraged to take the guided tour of the Mansion House, where Emma Smith's handwoven coverlets are on display. Recalling a bit of Mormon history from my school days, as we pause in the parlor I make the unconscionable blunder of asking how Mrs. Smith might have felt about polygamy. An awkward silence settles over the group, most of whom are Mormon. Responding that we can discuss the matter later, the guide briskly moves us into the next room. Later, he privately allows that there were rumors that Joseph Smith had taken plural wives, insisting nonetheless that monogamy has always been the lifestyle of the Reorganized church. Though the Latter-Day Saints at the other end of town will talk about plural marriage only if asked, their reorganized cousins are even more diffident on the topic.

Polygamy is like a family secret in Nauvoo—everyone is pledged not to discuss it in front of strangers. Nowhere that I could find, in either the orientation films at the two visitors' centers or the voluminous tourist literature, is the subject even discussed. But the issue is historically important for the city, since the introduction of plural marriage by Joseph Smith (denied by the Reorganized Saints; confirmed by any number of scholars) was responsible for splitting the church during its Illinois period. Given the town's emphasis on the persecution of Mormons by intolerant neighbors, explaining such a doctrinal schism is embarrassing. One might as well ask about slave mistresses on an Alabama plantation as get a clear answer about plural wives in Nauvoo.

In a moment of weakness, I imagine how the town might be differently revealed if Nauvoo Restoration, Inc., and Restoration Trails Foundation—nonprofits controlled by the Utah and Independence churches respectively—were to provide an alternative "Polygamy Tour": This is the Mansion House where Emma Smith learned that Eliza Snow, a friend who lived under the same roof, was sharing the sexual favors of her husband, Joseph. This is the home of suffragette Sarah Granger Kimball who, approached by Smith to become one of his wives, later recalled of his proposition, "I asked him to teach it to someone else." And this is the site of the Erastus Snow house, whose second floor was alleged to have been the hiding place to which the wives of high church officials repaired when found to be pregnant under suspicious circumstances. An entrance by a separate staircase minimized contact with the family downstairs.

To ignore plural marriage at Nauvoo is to miss the drama of the Mormon story and the mores of the society that suppressed its practice. The point is not to condemn polygamy as a system that oppresses women and be done with it. There may have been reasons for its introduction by Smith that went beyond either the sexual gratification of the elders or the rationalization that what was good for Abraham was good for his chosen children. The extended mission of Mormon men required that husband and wife be separated for years at a time. Men found themselves far from home; women were temporarily without mates. Such hardship was felt on both sides, and may have been a motive for the church fathers in permitting some men to take plural wives, including women who were already married. But one would never guess during a visit to Old Nauvoo that some women in the community found the practice vile and repulsive from the start.

In fact, the irony of Nauvoo now and Nauvoo then is rich stuff. Joseph Smith's red brick general store, demolished in 1890 to build a meat market in the upper town, was reconstructed and opened in 1980 to the public. On the Reorganized tour we're told that the Women's Relief Society met regularly in the store's large upstairs room—my group is so enamored with the idea they pose for a picture on the premises. Never mind that the Relief Society was composed of members who were secretly wed to Joseph, much to the dismay of Emma Smith, who used the meetings as a pulpit from which to attack the institution she opposed even on her deathbed.

There were, it appears, more clandestine kinds of meetings in the Smith store. Martha Brotherton, a seventeen-year-old English convert, testified to a St. Louis justice of the peace in 1842 that she had been invited by Brigham Young into the small office adjoining the room where the Relief Society met. The room was marked, she later recalled, by an ominous sign that read "Positively No Admittance." Young closed the door and pulled the curtains, Brotherton testified, and Smith entered a short time later. Together, the affidavit claims, they tried to convince her of the doctrinal correctness of plural marriage, expressing their heartfelt desire that she be willing to observe its most sacred rite with one of them.

The promises flew like penny candy. Brotherton testified she felt herself "an insulted and abused female" by the veritable onslaught. She recalled Smith insisting, " 'for I know Brigham will take care of you, and if he don't do his duty to you, come to me, and I will make him; and if you do not like it in a month or two, come to me, and I will make you free again; and if he turns you off, I will take you on.' " The number of choices was staggering—even if they did all seem to lead to the same end. Brotherton begged a few days to think it over, then left the community, stopping in St. Louis to swear out the affidavit and have the story published in *The St. Louis Bulletin*. Although tabloid journalism was a staple of nineteenth-century life, similar eyewitness accounts suggest that, even if Brotherton was dissembling, other Nauvoo women told of remarkably similar experiences.

The Reorganized Saints have been "glacially slow" to talk about plural marriage at Nauvoo, admits Alma Blair, an advisor to the Joseph Smith Center who teaches a class for summer guides. A member of the Reorganized church, Blair says reticence to talk about polygamy is typical, especially when guides, anxious to avoid doctrinal disputes, may be leading tours that include members of both churches. Calling polygamy a "Pandora's Box" at Nauvoo, he acknowledges that the RLDS could talk about women in greater detail, especially given their importance when men went out on mission. His own mother is opposed to the idea of women in the priesthood, he says, a reminder that there are divisions within the Reorganized church itself. "Mormons like to push the idea that women were freer [than they were in the rest of society]," he says, "but I'm not really sure that's true."

Across town at Nauvoo Restoration, Inc., owned by the better-known Latter-Day Saints, opinions are more upbeat. "[Mormon women] were very instrumental in the early days of the church," says Elder Arthur Elrey, visitors' center director, ". . . and they have been ever since." The church vaunts the largest women's organization in the world, he says, offering training in homemaking and—he's quick to add—things such as career management too. He dismisses polygamy in Nauvoo as an aberration, saying it "never surfaced as a general practice here." If true, its rarity may have been owing, as much as anything, to women such as Brotherton who refused to partake. Such a dismissal also fails to explain how polygamy fueled the schism that rent the early church.

For all the exceptional history of Mormonism, Nauvoo, as restorations go, has its conventional side. Never mind that a major family secret is typically left to a few bookstore pamphlets for the hopelessly curious. That the founders built a bustling community out of what was "literally a wilderness" is a common boast of other frontier restorations—never mind that local signs admit there had been an Indian village on the site and several buildings remaining from an earlier settlement called Commerce. Nauvoo ("beautiful place" in Hebrew) was an archetypal American refuge from the world. In the LDS visitors' center hangs a painting, circa 1880, of a mob destroying Mormon homes, the type of image common at pioneer sites—except that this time the "savages" are white.

Religious and utopian settlements are ideal stuff for historic tourism. Self-contained and high minded, they play to the old curatorial agenda of edifying future generations. Whether secular or sectarian, they're accorded the status of "noble minorities," though, like people everywhere, they're a lot less noble upon inspection—and a lot more interesting. Something vital that was present at their creation is too often missing in their memory: dissent, repression, inequality, and human failings. In the same communities that lionize a revolt against the social order, the memory of personal dissent within their ranks is suppressed as an embarrassment. There was, they seem to say, no trouble in River City. After all, it takes an immense effort to reconstruct a community: to consider internal rifts seems contrary to the very instinct that would preserve it.

So it is that our myth of the small town presumes a happy consensus. Pleasant Hill, New Harmony, Nauvoo—these are inland avatars of an old story, that of the Pilgrims and the Jamestown colonists struggling to make a foothold in the world. They hark back to a pre-industrial age when work was still meaningful and human fellowship still possible. Although the enemy is no longer the wilderness or the natives who inhabit it, the world exercises a tragic pull nonetheless. If there are unfaithful individuals within the ranks, as there were in Nauvoo, let them be known as "opportunists." Otherwise, the seeds of destruction are sown by war, the hard laws of economics, the violence of persecution.

I stand with Elder Anderson under a plaid umbrella, admiring the ruins of the Mormon temple a few blocks from Old Nauvoo, whose spire once rose 165 feet. Signs at the temple site tell how Nauvoo was, among other things, "the largest and most progressive city in Illinois." A fine shower is falling around us as he describes how the mob took over the temple after the saints were driven out of town, how they held raucous poker parties downstairs and shouted obscenities from the towers. A few hours before, I remember, the LDS film had recalled Old Nauvoo, ending with images of a ball game, girls playing jumprope, and a pair of lovers by the river. Supported by the church, Nauvoo is a work of mission and nostalgia, a case of ancestor worship where the descendants still have much to prove. Though the temptation was great to cross the river and go further west, I decided I had finally had enough of the heartland, and turned back.

FACTORY GIRLS

A century and a half after Hannah Duston floated to freedom down the Merrimack River, its waters were being harnessed by a new industry anxious to lure the rural daughters of New England to its door. In her free-fall escape to Haverhill, she would have passed the future site of Lowell, the showcase city of America's textile industry in the early nineteenth century. Had she been able to glimpse ahead, the Pioneer Mother would have blanched at the changes: she would have seen a land full of canals and factories, almost emptied of Indians except for the odd literary romance. But Lowell, Massachusetts, was to be the witness of struggles no less important than the frontier.

In the Lowell textile mills, the forces of organized labor would confront those of corporate management; the industrialized North would link hands with the plantation South, even while decrying its brutality; the infighting of Yankee natives and European immigrants would sow disunity among the working classes as the century wore on. Yet some things had barely changed. "We did not recognize the grim features of the Puritan, as we used sometimes to read about him, in our parents or relatives," recalled Lowell mill worker Lucy Larcom. "And yet we were children of the Puritans." In a sense, they were the distant offspring of Haverhill's Saint Hannah.

A station wagon is parked on the mall outside the visitors' center on Market Street. A woman moves luggage into an apartment in a restored mill as a calypso tune wafts from an upstairs window. It's hard to tell if the surrounding brick buildings house a coffee shop, an apartment block, an office complex, or a National Park Service visi-

tors' center that greets about half a million people a year. As it turns
out, it contains all of them. "The museum as city," boasts a popular
local slogan, "the city as museum." First-time visitors to Lowell may
wonder whether they're visiting a relic of the last century or a har-
binger of the one to come.

Thirty years ago, there would have been no tourists. Suffering the
abandonment of textile mills that had once made it famous, the commercial heart of Lowell, by the 1960s, was dead. In a project aimed at
encouraging reinvestment in a decayed city center, an unusual alliance was born—a joint venture that came to include the city council,
the University of Massachusetts at Lowell, private banking and business groups, and, eventually, the National Park Service. Authorized by
Congress in 1978, Lowell National Historical Park has become a state-
of-the-art showpiece for the Department of the Interior—more famous
for protecting Western rangeland than the facades of depressed factory towns.

It may lack the vistas of Yosemite, but Lowell is a spectacle in its
own right. One of the Boott Cotton Mills, straddling the Merrimack
Canal, has been restored and outfitted with a fine museum. In the
Tsongas Industrial History Center, students learn how to weave on a
loom, design a community using urban-planning principles, or study
the ever-changing ethnic layers of Lowell: its population is almost 15
percent Cambodian today. Guides lead tours to ethnic neighbor-
hoods. Barge tours ply the extensive canal system built by Irish laborers in the nineteenth century. The 136-acre downtown district, an
experiment in mixed ownership and zoning, blurs the border between commerce and public history: hero sandwiches are sold on one
corner while the history of Lowell's huddled masses is told just down
the street.

Named for industrialist Francis Cabot Lowell in the 1820s, the city
was incorporated with hopes of being an urban model. Dignitaries
tromped through at the behest of its corporate owners to see how
Lowell had avoided the excesses of England's squalid factory towns.
Davy Crockett, Andy Jackson, Abe Lincoln, Henry Clay; later Teddy
Roosevelt and Henry Ford—many extolled the enlightened methods
of the Lowell system. None less than Charles Dickens, that nemesis of
industrial blight, would write in *American Notes* that "from all the
crowd I saw in the different factories that day, I cannot recall or sep-

arate one young face that gave me a painful impression." Lowell was a successful company town with a vision.

For the first quarter century, the textile looms were largely staffed by young, unmarried women from rural New England. This, in fact, was part of the Lowell plan. Quite simply, mill owners hoped to avoid the creation of a hardened proletariat. Women, it was believed, would be more malleable than men; they would marry and move on after a period of employment, thus recycling jobs. The corporation intended to direct their lives with a paternalist bent. Workers were required to stay on the job for at least a year; reside, if not with family members, in a company boardinghouse; attend church on a regular basis; comport themselves in a respectable, ladylike fashion. Regulated by the ringing of bells from five in the morning to ten at night, their habits marched to the daily rhythm of what might best be called life in an industrial monastery.

Most "mill girls" stayed for a few years and left. Paid monthly cash wages, they could save enough money to finance an education or fund a dowry—a freedom otherwise hard to obtain. The owners went so far as to offer an enlightened after-hours environment that included lectures by the likes of Whittier and Thoreau on issues ranging from temperance and anti-slavery to phrenology and mesmerism. "It was kind of like a college dorm," explains one Park Service guide, searching for an analogy to the boardinghouse experience. If so, imagine a dorm from the 1950s—not the 1990s—where conduct unbecoming a lady could result in instant expulsion.

The mill "sororities" had a sorrier side. Standing for fourteen hours in a weave room where the windows had been nailed shut in mid-summer, deafened by the roar of machinery, breathing air filled with dust and cotton motes was, for many, a stressful and unhealthy experience. As competition with other cities increased, the vision of the founders unravelled. The Lowell bosses cut wages, placing greater demands on mill "operatives." Walkouts and strikes marked the 1830s and 1840s. When demands for a ten-hour workday were refused by the state, many women decided to walk. But it wasn't hard to replace them. By the late 1840s, other groups such as the Irish were clamoring for a chance. Eventually French Canadian, Polish, Jewish, and Greek immigrants came to the Lowell factories, giving the city a cosmopolitan, if sometimes divisive, character in the years to come.

Today the Park Service portrays how the profits of an industry were bought at a grim cost. Rather than a technology museum devoted to mechanical wonders, the park gives industrialism a human face. "The noise of machinery was particularly distasteful to me," remembered Larcom. "But I found that the crowd was made up of single human lives, not one of them wholly uninteresting, when separately known." A bittersweet observation, it's one the Park Service has taken seriously. In the weave room at the Boott Cotton Mill, some ninety power looms have been reassembled—many in working order—so the visitor (equipped with ear plugs) can visit the machines in full tilt to get a sense of the roar that disturbed Larcom. In the museum, a floor above, one can still hear the pulsing of the looms that, in full operation, required their operatives to use an improvised sign language if they were to communicate despite the din.

Also true to Larcom's spirit, the story is told through the eyes of many workers. Pull-out quotes from the writings of mill girls highlight the Weave Room and Boott exhibits, expressing a complex attitude toward the machines that, while enslaving some to the rhythm of work bells, liberated others. "You ask why we work in the mill," read the words of Josephine Baker in the Weave Room. "Because the time we do have is our own. . . . our work, though laborious, is the same from day to day. We know what it is, and when finished we feel perfectly free, til it is time to commence it again." The testimony at Lowell features a chorus of voices, including twentieth-century workers on video—one of the latter recalls the day a woman had her long hair caught in a machine, and describes the shrieking of the victim who died of her injuries two days later. It is a living link with the tragedy that was often a part of mill life.

For the most part, Lowell frames its story as a struggle between Labor and Management. This is hardly a surprise, given the wealth of public sites (especially forts and battlefields) that are told through narratives of conflict. That Labor is given a major voice at all is long overdue. But as with any conflict, dissension is not always between the main antagonists. The ranks of one side, thought to be unified, sometimes reveal interesting divisions. Thus Lowell, in the story of workers and bosses, attempts to deal with the bugbear of slavery, a hallowed topic in the heart of old abolitionist New England.

The Boott Mill slide show (*Wheels of Change*), for example, links southern "lords of the lash" with northern "lords of the loom," acknowledging the devil's bargain cut between cotton planters and tex-

tile owners bent on a profit. It is one of many places where the plight
of northern workers is seen as parallel to that of their more unfortunate brethren in the South. Some mill owners were violently opposed
to abolition, we learn. Women operatives, powerless to resist, were
sexually abused by Lowell overseers. Of a cargo of Scottish women arriving in 1865, five ran away before they could serve in the mills. If
this was not slavery, it was a condition that existed somewhere in the
precincts.

The mills, to be sure, were knee-deep in the cotton trade. "Us
slaves didn't wear nothing but white lowell cloth," recalled Willis
Winn of Texas years later. "We had straight dresses or slips made of
lowell," echoed Jenny Proctor of Alabama. Thousands of other slaves
might have echoed the same memory, for Lowell and other northern
cities sold vast amounts of "Negro Cloth" below the Mason-Dixon line
for a handsome profit, a point noted, if in passing, in several exhibits.
But the visitor to the Boott can come away thinking that pro-slavery
sentiments were limited to only the grasping mill owners, intent as
they were on wrenching every penny they could from a blood-stained
bale of cotton.

At the Working People's Exhibit in the Mogan Cultural Center—a
restored boardinghouse built in 1837—visitors hear an imaginary discussion on audio tape between several mill girls. One criticizes a recent lecturer for failing to sufficiently denounce the crime of the
South: "I could make a better argument against slavery right now,"
she says, "without any preparation at all." It's a heartwarming sentiment, further cementing the bond between oppressed labor of North
and South. Organizer Sarah Bagley seconds the motion in a displayed
quote upstairs: "A father's debts are to be paid, an aging mother is to
be supported, a brother's ambition is to be aided. . . . to my mind it is
slavery."

But what do such analogies really prove—worker solidarity or self-
aggrandizement? "Our country will be but one great hospital," complained a Lowell worker in 1845, "filled with worn out operatives and
colored slaves." The mill women made constant use of such metaphors to describe worsening conditions in the 1830s and 1840s. Although "wage slavery" was a common complaint of northern workers,
it by no means ensured a sentiment of solidarity with blacks. Some
workers worried their jobs might be threatened by emancipation;
others sought, in the rhetoric of "white slavery," less to critique the

*"To my mind it is slavery": Boott Cotton Mills Museum,
Lowell, Massachusetts*

horrors of bondage than to publicize their own complaints. For those
in the textile industry who stopped to consider the matter, their jobs
were dependent on raw materials picked by slaves—and, to a lesser
extent, on those among them who wore the finished product.

The visitor might assume that northern labor was united in its opposition to slavery—and for the best of reasons. There is a sense at
Lowell that the "right" people were on the "right" side of America's
most divisive issue, a patch of stereotypes about North and South
that answers a need to have conflict explained in conventional terms.
But the reality was more complicated. In 1844, for example, an edito-
rial in the *Lowell Offering and Magazine,* a publication written by
mill employees, conceded that "Should we write against slavery, perhaps a thousand subscribers would 'please discontinue,'" a telling
point considering that the *Offering* was most heavily subscribed in
states such as New York and Massachusetts, states with strong abolitionist movements.

Lowell women may have been low on the industrial ladder, but
they didn't have to look far to find others who were even more de-
based. Worker Harriet Robinson remembered the Irish immigrants of
the 1830s. "The fourth class," she called them, "lords of the spade and

the shovel, by whose constant labor the building of the great factories was made possible," lived, as she pointed out, not in boardinghouses but squalid shanties. As fine a job as is done describing common laborers at Lowell, I hardly remember seeing a word about how the mills were put up—and by whom. In short, if Sarah Bagley and her friends were "slaves," then what were the Irish?

Even the labor press could be hard on the immigrant proletariat. In 1849, Eliza Cate wrote of Irish women in *The New England Offering,* "Even the middle class of our New England girls, will not be seen in the street with them, will not room with them, cannot find them in the least degree companionable. One can see then that it is incalculably better that the native girls fill the mills. How much better for the future!" Ethnic hostility doesn't reflect well on the laboring cadres and their struggle against management, and so is scrupulously kept in the background at both the visitors' center and the Boott Museum.

Aware of the popular tours the city associates once offered, the Park Service fashions its own cheerful epilogue to Lowell. Both its impressive multiprojector slide shows incisively critique the Industrial Age, only to end their cases on a false note. "Voices of rage," concludes the Boott Museum show, "voices of despair—voices of hope—voices of America!" Given the tenor of the rest of the show, this seems a hollow finale. At the visitors' center, a bouncy electronic score underlines *The Industrial Revelation,* a slide show in which Lowell is congratulated for its "remarkable revival in the local economy." So the rise and fall and rise of the city is dutifully chronicled. Lowell has turned the memory of a failed nineteenth-century experiment into a high-tech display of history that, once again, has made it a public flagship.

The fact that freedom, for many Americans, was less a self-evident truth than a market commodity or piece of good fortune is brought home at Lowell in the story of industrial workers. Laborers such as the Lowell mill girls, given the freedom to earn cash wages and imbibe the wisdom of public lectures in their free time, were reminded upon leaving that they could not vote, could not own property in most states if they were married, could not even sit on a trial jury. If "wage slavery" is an exaggerated description of their plight, the "pursuit of happiness" seems to be an equally overblown conceit.

Life at Lowell was a progressive experiment that became a trap of long hours, broken strikes, and accidental deaths. The conflict inherent between a rural life ruled by seasonal changes and one that turned on clock time and turbines represented the leap from the premodern to the modern world. That women were among the first to participate in the industry en bloc is noted with compassion and imagination at Lowell. What was for some a liberating chapter in their lives was for others an indentured bondage, an industrial captivity that, until Lowell Park, had precious little public recognition.

In the beginning, Lowell was a manmade frontier worked largely by women. But it wasn't a frontier that lent itself easily to myth or romance: no Indians, no abduction, and no redemption by a Puritan God. The struggle, for all that, was no less difficult. "My life and health are spared while others are cut off," wrote Mary Paul from Lowell in 1845. "Last Thursday one girl fell down and broke her neck which caused instant death. She was going in or coming out of the mill and slipped down it being very icy. The same day a man was killed by the cars. Another had nearly all of his ribs broken. Another was nearly killed by falling down and having a bale of cotton fall on him." Then, with a nonchalance that comes when the observation of death is a commonplace, Paul adds, "Last Tuesday we were paid."

OVER THE RAINBOW: WOMEN'S RIGHTS

Since before the Civil War, women have been engaged with the politics of public history. The Mount Vernon Ladies' Association bought General Washington's home in 1858, a purchase that would set in motion a tradition of women's historic societies. The most famous of these was the National Society of the Daughters of the American Revolution, founded in 1890, an organization that erected memorials to generals, veterans, presidents, and pioneers—most of them men—that still proudly adorn our public spaces. Patriotic and self-effacing, the women put family, God, and country as concepts worthy of public homage before any consideration of gender.

The conservation ethic of the nineteenth century came to be synonymous with a conservative vision: tradition as an act of national faith. Although women were partners in raising funds or wording a monument's inscription, when it came time to select the figures who would stand before town hall for all eternity, they were rarely the ones asked to pose. In large part organized by women, early public history was rarely about them, a trend that persisted well into the twentieth century. In the last decade, however, one town in western New York state has been fighting to change that, even if it means talking about subjects that most sites don't even dare mention—rape, abortion, harassment, domestic violence.

The town is called Seneca Falls, a name that doesn't leap from the tongues of most American schoolchildren, even if it is a kind of Cooperstown, Independence Hall, and Mount Vernon all rolled into one. In this small town of seven thousand people, the National Women's Hall of Fame occupies a storefront on Fall Street—even though it seems a token space for such a big idea. In the town's Village Park the monument to the Civil War dead is crowned with a woman—even though it is only Lady Liberty at the top. Here Elizabeth Cady Stanton, a leader of the early women's rights movement, lived in a house on Washington Street—even though it's so modest you could almost drive by without knowing it. Seneca Falls is the home of a groundbreaking idea built to a diminutive, almost cozy, scale.

Authorized by an act of Congress in 1980, Women's Rights National Historical Park celebrates the formal beginning of the national women's movement. The centerpiece of the park in downtown Seneca Falls is the Wesleyan Chapel, where the Women's Rights Convention organized by Stanton was held in 1848. The building—roofless when I visited—has been rescued and restored by the Park Service from its less respectable incarnation in recent years as a coin-op laundromat. Consisting of only five acres, the park properties are dispersed, including the restored Stanton home and the home of fellow organizers Mary Ann and Thomas M'Clintock in nearby Waterloo.

Next to the chapel stands the former village hall, home of the NPS visitors' center and a new exhibition that opened in 1993. The park makes its central motif the link between women and minorities in their struggle for liberation. A group bronze in the foyer depicts the most famous members of the 1848 convention—most conspicuous among them is Frederick Douglass. Upstairs, the exhibits advance the alliance between abolitionist and suffragette. We learn that men could advertise for "runaway" wives, that Harriet Tubman was a member of the National Woman Suffrage Association, that Sojourner Truth is as good an example as any of "true womanhood." The scope widens further, including everyone from cartoon characters Betty Boop and

Nancy to the photo of a Navajo woman casting a vote: a rainbow coalition raising its voice against the (largely white) patriarchy.

The exhibit avoids a common pitfall of public history. What might have been a simple celebration of women's rights is a more ambivalent look at the tortured path the movement has followed. It comes as a surprise to learn that American women were better represented in the medical and legal professions in 1890 than they were a century later; or that women's property rights in the early nineteenth century actually *diminished* in some parts of the country. "It's celebratory with warts," says park historian Vivien Ellen Rose of an exhibit that includes frank mention of topics such as abortion rights and spousal battery.

The Women's Rights exhibit was contracted by the Park Service to Chermayeff and Geismar, the design firm that did the highly acclaimed display at Ellis Island, New York. The first draft, says Rose, was marked by "an uneducated conception on the part of the contractor that there was continual progress, that . . . there would always be progress, that at some point in nirvana we would reach total equality." Because that is a common misconception, she understood the problem immediately. "Sometimes," she says, "the Park Service has that same line."

An exhibit on "True Womanhood," for example, proposed to describe how much sewing and baking Elizabeth Cady Stanton did in a single day, but didn't say enough about the living conditions of women as a whole. For that matter, says Rose, another contractor—hired by the Park Service to provide illustrations—was reluctant to draw a picture of a battered mother. Motherhood, she thought, was an image too special to defile—although she was finally convinced to do it in the end. "It's really not the beautiful picture of women's rights that are totally achieved," says Rose, underlining the park's role in challenging complacent assumptions about progress.

The warts to which Rose refers are real enough, although others seem hidden from the public gaze. A twenty-minute video celebrates the 1848 convention and its link to the abolitionist movement, hardly bothering to mention, for example, the attitudes of southern women. Not all of them were entranced with the idea of being liberated by the peers of Harriet Beecher Stowe. "They live in nice New England homes, clean, sweet-smelling, shut up in libraries, writing books which ease their hearts of their bitterness against us," complained

southerner Mary Boykin Chesnut in 1861. Not all women were be-
holden to the abolitionist cause. Some, like Chesnut, supported
women's rights and still benefitted from slavery.

The alliance between suffragettes and abolitionists is suited up in
its Sunday best at the visitors' center. Nowhere did I see it mentioned
that there were no black women who signed the 1848 Declaration of
Sentiments, even if Douglass did; nor are we sure that any even at-
tended the convention at all. Although a strong supporter of women's
rights, Douglass argued that the quest for women's suffrage be subor-
dinated to that for black men, a rift that rippled through the early
women's movement—and one that is acknowledged in the museum.
But the venom that sometimes characterized the struggle is hardly
evident. "Not another man should be enfranchised," Stanton was
cited as saying in the official minutes of the American Rights Association in 1869, "until enough women are admitted to the polls to out-
weigh those already there. [She said] She did not believe in allowing
ignorant negroes and foreigners to make laws for her to obey."

Anglo and native women are also portrayed as natural partners in
the struggle for freedom, an unusual reading of our history. "In missionary schools," one display reads, "native American women were
sometimes forced to give up their own language and cultures to learn
English"—but fails to say that many of the missionaries who made
them do so were women. That the ladies of Seneca Falls were, after
all, the descendants of victors in a war against the Iroquois of upstate
New York is not clearly noted as an irony of the struggle. "If they had
been forced to keep [Africans] in New England," teased Chesnut, "I
dare say they would have shared the Indians' fate; for they are wise in
their generation, these Yankee children of light."

Rose has had to parry criticism from a number of sides already.
Right-to-lifers have complained they're not represented in the exhibit, she says, while underlining the distinction between rights of the
pre-born and rights of women—the latter subject explicitly endorsed
by park legislation as the focus of the site. Lesbians have protested
that they're not recognized, but Rose counters that no one in the display is identified by race or sexual preference; even Jane Addams, she
says, didn't describe herself as a lesbian. One prominent photograph
in the exhibit—a woman holding a sign that says "Lesbian Feminist
Mother"—took a week's worth of heated debate with Park Service authorities before they conceded it was acceptable for public view.

The lack of national sites that interpret women's history makes Seneca Falls a crucial addition to the Park Service, but you wouldn't know it from its "poorer sister" status. Site parking facilities aren't much more than one would find for a small gift shop. The operating budget—about eight hundred thousand dollars for 1994—may have tripled in the last eight years, but is still smaller than appropriations for Klondike Gold Rush National Historical Park, the Vanderbilt Mansion, or Dinosaur National Monument. Women's Rights receives about half the money allotted to Civil War battle sites such as Petersburg and Vicksburg, a reminder of long-standing bureau priorities. "The Park Service does a much better job at dealing with conflict between armies," Rose says, "than they do at dealing with conflict between groups of our peoples."

The first superintendent at Women's Rights recalls the resistance she met over the very idea of doing women's history. While perusing a Park Service list of historic sites in 1978, Judy Hart realized that some groups were barely given a token status in the schema. "What really struck me," she remembers of the list, "was that at the bottom [of the page] there was an asterisk that said 'black history is incorporated in all of the above'"—thus relegating the African American past to something of an afterthought. But that wasn't the worst of it. "There *was* no asterisk for women," she continues, barely able to contain her astonishment. "We didn't even get an asterisk!"

Hart, at the time a legislative affairs specialist in the bureau, made it something of a mission to get Seneca Falls on the Park Service map. When Washington expressed tentative interest in the town, the locals "came out of the woodwork," she says. "They were so excited that we were there they just piled onto the car when we pulled up," she says of the preliminary visit. Their enthusiasm rubbed off—the bureau began a reconnaissance study to consider its inclusion in the park system. "There were thirty or forty [people] who were excited," Hart remembers of Seneca Falls, "and they appeared to be about five hundred," making phone calls, drawing up agendas, even sending roses— in short, lobbying everyone from the mayor to their congressman.

Though blessed with volunteers for doing the spade work, the site would never have been approved, Hart stresses, without the efforts of the Elizabeth Cady Stanton Foundation and congressional support in Washington. Once the area study was completed in 1979, the site passed preliminary congressional hearings the following year. "And then it just got lost," she remembers. "It's not a huge park. It's not a lot of money, and just disappeared off everybody's screen." But help came after all. "Senator [Daniel Patrick] Moynihan just pulled it out of the basket and got it enacted in 1980," Hart recalls, still a little awed by what must have seemed at the time like an act of divine intervention.

Things began to fall into place. The Stanton Foundation, owner of Elizabeth Cady Stanton's house, agreed to donate it to the Park Service on condition that it be renovated. With a much smaller budget than anticipated, Hart went to work as the superintendent in 1982, not expecting that other hurdles awaited her. Another test would be overcoming public preconceptions about what a historic site is even supposed to look like.

"It happened to me dozens of times," she remembers of her trips to show visitors the park sites. "We would drive up to the Stanton house and . . . I'd stop in front and they'd say, 'Oh.' And then we'd go over to Waterloo . . . and we'd drive over to the Hunt house," the former residence of convention co-organizer Jane Hunt, privately owned. "Richard Hunt was probably the wealthiest man in Waterloo. [Here's] this great big house that looks like *Gone with the Wind* with these big pillars out in front, this big circular drive and this big green lawn, and they'd say, 'This is more like it.'" The lesson wasn't lost on her: the Hunts had more money than the Stantons, and their public memory was all the more impressive for it.

It got her thinking about how historic parks are conceived in the first place. "We started out as a collection of grand views," Hart says of Park Service sites such as Mount Rainier and Sequoia. "And that's really all we were doing—breathtaking, overwhelming, awesome, grandiose. . . . It's a fairly easy step to go from there to the grandest people. . . . Of course presidents are grand, and of course generals are grand." She halts to savor a bittersweet truth about the woman who led the early fight for equality. "Elizabeth Cady Stanton—for all that she was—was not a grand person."

That Seneca Falls made the cut at all seems a miracle of legislative evolution. Involved with park legislation for several years, Hart witnessed how few sites ever make the political grade. The culling process of reconnaissance and area studies means that only a tiny fraction of sites even reach the level of formal legislation. Of those formally proposed as bills, she estimates, only about 10 percent ever get a hearing. She's seen enough infighting to know that "Congress is not designed to pass legislation, they're designed to stop it," adding that "If [the bill] has a lot of political power behind it, it doesn't matter how bad it is."

In the past few years the Park Service has become more open to sites that deal with women and minorities, Hart believes, although she cautions that obstacles still abound. She denies any conscious bias in the process of selecting sites, but admits that "it favors people who know the system." Women's history sites "don't tend to attract the corporate lawyer or the head of the corporation in town," she says, or people who have access to fax and copying machines, mailing privileges, discretionary office income. Without local organization and money, she concludes, a site will never even come to the attention of Congress.

Other factors may be weighted, too. Director of the National Coordinating Committee for the Promotion of History, a nonprofit historical and archival organization, Page Putnam Miller led the Women's History Landmark Project that began in 1989. A Park Service study intended to identify more women's sites as national landmarks—a designation that sometimes leads to park status—the project spent several years culling and proposing women's sites for recognition. Today, Miller estimates, in spite of new additions, only about 5 percent of all landmarks focus in any substantial way on women. The very criteria for recognition—among them that a specific site have "national significance"—seemed inherently exclusive in her view.

"I remember arguing [with the Park Service] about a woman in the 1820s who founded a school in Connecticut," Miller recalls. "They said, 'Oh, but she's not a national leader,'" a response that struck her as anachronistic. "There *were* no national platforms for women in the 1830s and '40s," she explains. "There was no national teachers' organization for her to be president of then. In other words, you have to rethink what potential there was for a national leader." After considerable debate, the Prudence Crandall school was finally admitted as a landmark, but a southern California site where women had been involved in a strike was rejected as too "regional."

In the preservation field, Miller continues, "a large number of people still think of what women did as trivial." After a few are noted for special accomplishments, the story of women comes to a halt. Of some fifty nationwide sites with public programs on women, Miller says, six are dedicated to Christian Science Church founder Mary Baker Eddy. The most popular—the home of seamstress Betsy Ross in Philadelphia—is visited by more people than all the others combined, though there's no documentary evidence that Ross made the original flag or even lived on the premises. "The most-visited site is a site that lacks authenticity," she groans.

Social history wouldn't appear to have been the main concern of national landmark designation, even from its effective beginning in 1958. "I'd say six to seven hundred of the two thousand sites that are landmarks are on there purely for architectural reasons," Miller estimates. The Park Service criterion of "architectural integrity," she adds, has favored the restoration of buildings that have been protected from excessive alteration, thus reenforcing a gentrified view of the past. After all, it takes a lot of money to keep up the "integrity" of a building over the long haul. "You're left," she concludes, "with an elitist approach to history."

For historic preservationists, it seems a woman's place is still in the home. The houses of educators, writers, and religious leaders are about all that end up being restored, says Miller. "Maybe that isn't as bad a picture as we think," she allows, "but you certainly don't see women as workers." She'd like to see preservation efforts move in another direction—such as the Triangle Shirtwaist Factory in New York, where a fire in 1911 inspired a quest for labor reforms by organized women. She notes that the house of Madame C. J. Walker—black entrepreneur in the cosmetics industry—became a national landmark before her corporate headquarters did, although the latter probably tells more about this woman of politics and business. The early Park Service reaction to making the headquarters a landmark, says Miller, was that " 'There's already a building for Madame C. J. Walker,' " an example of the resistance she has found so common.

It may be that limitations imposed on women long ago have simply come back to haunt them. "Respectable women were not to be seen outside of their houses or their friends' houses," Hart explains of a certain class. "Women were not supposed to be seen with men—except their husbands. And they weren't supposed to speak in public. So it's not too surprising that there are no [public] buildings particularly associated with women." Of the few that were, many simply haven't survived. She mentions the building in Seneca Falls that housed reformer Amelia Bloomer's newspaper, a structure demolished long ago.

The new feminist history is only starting to be felt at Seneca Falls, where the role of women was challenged in 1848. For now, however, the park finds itself trapped. As one of the only national sites devoted to women's history, it has been stretched to tell a story that ranges from suffrage to temperance to abolition to domestic violence—all this in a densely packed space. In such cramped quarters, the park can hardly suggest the complexity of gender as a social variable. Conflict, although obvious on the battlefield, is harder to admit when it derives from the heart of a group whose presence has been ignored, especially when the terms of restoration still seem designed to obscure that presence.

The Railroad

JOHN HENRY was a steel-drivin' man. His wife, Polly, they say, could drive too. A tribute to Henry stands on a winding curve outside Talcott, West Virginia, a strapping bronze commissioned by the Hilldale Talcott Raritan Club in 1972. Visitors have left their mark on the man reputed to have had a race with a steam drill in the 1870s at nearby Big Bend Tunnel. The top of the statue is shot up with bullet holes. An empty Pepsi bottle stands at its feet. A few disposable diapers are strewn in front, and a bandanna is tied to the monument's base. Off to the side, the Raritan Club sells souvenirs in-season from a parked caboose. John Henry is standing between strokes, bent at the waist, his hammer down around his thighs. For the ex-slave that whipped a machine, it's a strangely inert pose, a steel-drivin' man in the grip of fatigue.

Our legends revere big feats of brawn and muscle. Paul Bunyan felled timber and ruled from the blue spring to the China winter. Mike Fink, half-alligator, half-horse, wrestled a grizzly and dueled a Mississippi steamboat to a draw. John Henry won the race against a steam drill in West Virginia. It's as though we really believed the stories that America was the work of giants, a Herculean labor of local pride. What our mythology neglects to mention is that it took a whole army to cut the tunnel at Big Bend—a thousand men and boys, most of them black. Who laid the track, held the drills, drove the steel, died in the premature tunnel blast? The work of hundreds stands silent in one swing of John Henry's hammer.

*Workin' on the railroad: the statue of John Henry
near Talcott, West Virginia*

In a few decades the railroad industry brought vast changes to American life. Developed in Britain, the technology of the steam locomotive had crossed the Atlantic by the 1820s. The railroad quickly outpaced turnpikes and canals in swiftness, creating the first industry to exist nationwide in the United States. By 1869, one could ride the rails from coast to coast, a journey that would have been inconceivable a generation before. The railroad employed over 400,000 people by the 1880s; in 1890, the Pennsylvania Railroad alone had 15,000 more employees than the federal post office. But the achievement of grand scale didn't come without cost. In 1881, it's estimated that some thirty thousand trainmen were killed or permanently disabled from accidents with hand brakes and coupling pins. Congressman Henry Cabot Lodge was to note that railroads were the cause of more annual casualties than the Duke of Wellington absorbed at Waterloo.

The railroad has almost lost its epic glow. What began as a spectacle—from Wall Street investors to Omaha engineers and Chinese laborers with pickaxes in the Sierra Nevadas—seems little more now than a mundane fact of life. As a public work, the railroad ranks with any of the world's wonders, giving up nothing to the engineering precision of the pyramids or the meandering scope of the Great Wall. But it fails as a monument, barely managing—except for bridge and trestle—to rise above its deference to the earth's grade. It can hardly even claim permanence. In the past century and a half the early iron rails have been replaced with steel, the line built and rebuilt—as though the pyramids had been dismantled block by block and raised again without anyone even noticing.

Not all of the mystery has been lost. Passenger stations at major urban hubs have become major renovation projects. Restored town depots are the last link with a past many locals are reluctant to give up, the buildings a source of communal identity. Railroad museums from the east coast to the west are as common as pioneer monuments, utopian villages, and frontier forts. Although such museums showcase the accomplishments of an industry, most are hardly at the cutting edge of public history. Celebrating a technology that has long seemed on the verge of extinction, the railroad museum seems permanently stuck in time.

There's no mistaking the typical Iron Horse exhibit, mired as it usually is in the public history of the 1950s: dusty display cases with fine-print text, scale model locomotive reproductions, and displays of punched ticket stubs and old timetables. Out back, a collection of rolling stock from the Age of Steam gathers more dust than grit. The museums rarely have a human scale, ranging as they do from the epic gloat of diesel engines to the miniature H&O models in the basement exhibition for kids and confirmed enthusiasts. In fact, railroad museums are no more likely than the local genealogical society to explain how the phalanx of people known as "John Henry" went about their lives working on the railroad.

For public historians, there's a paradox in studying the railroad: not only were the rails a part of our history, but from a very early time they were in the business of preserving it. America's first commercial railroad, begun in the 1820s in Quincy, Massachusetts, started by hauling granite blocks to build the Bunker Hill battle memorial. The Northern Pacific Railroad agitated for the creation of Yellowstone Park in the 1870s, standing as it did to gain from the influx of tourism. Indians were hired by many lines out West to give their depots an authentic feel for rubbernecking passengers, and the Spanish mission became a popular depot style, an architectural advertisement for Old California. When the Union Pacific convinced the Pawnee to stage a mock Indian raid in 1866 to impress junketing congressmen, it was already straddling the line between making history and manipulating it.

The railroads, of course, were deeply enmeshed in national politics. By the time of the Civil War, Uncle Sam wasn't only riding the Iron Horse but keeping it in oats, an investment in national security. Many railroads obtained the necessary construction capital through federal bond issues and land grants. In return, the government benefitted from reduced freight rates, not to mention having a country where improved transportation made the task of governing that much easier. When federal troops went into Pennsylvania to crush the railroad strike of 1877, a gondola car mounted with a Gatling gun ran ahead of the locomotive, one of many times that the politics of corporate management would coincide with what Washington perceived as "the national interest."

It should therefore come as no surprise that the railroad museum is a tribute to the American Way. The scandals of corporate financing and congressional bribery, common in the early days of the industry, are not likely to be mentioned. It is rare to find a display that questions the most fundamental of sacred cows: Manifest Destiny, the Happy Homestead, the Dignity of Free Labor, the Inevitability of Progress. This may be one reason the federal government has not been more involved with protecting railroad sites—local enthusiasm would seem to make such labors redundant. Though railroads were not born in this country, the narrative of nation-making seems hollow without the call of the steam whistle racing across the prairie to open the wilderness.

The railroads were a paean to another American icon, the melting pot. People of virtually every ethnicity in nineteenth-century America ended up working somewhere along the line. Slaves were firemen, brakemen, mechanics, and track-layers in the antebellum South,

while blacks above the Mason-Dixon during the same period were almost entirely excluded from the industry, a casualty of discrimination. The Irish and Chinese have long been the stuff of transcontinental legend. Navajo men were working on the line before the turn of
the century. Grading or laying track for a rail contractor was an
entry-level position for native and immigrant both, while a bona fide
company job was regarded as among the most respectable modes of
employment in the country. Of all America's industries, none was
more inclusive of minorities than the railroad, although jobs were
handed to a workforce that was rigidly segregated from the start.

John Henry, in short, couldn't have been an engineer if he'd wanted
to. But the Iron Horse did bring many Americans a regular wage. "I
digged pits out, going along front of where the tracks was to go," recalled former slave Boston Blackwell in the 1930s. "I get one dollar a
day. I felt like the richest man in the world!" But for all its virtues, the
industry brought in its wake an unscrupulous element. Will Ann
Rogers, the daughter of former slaves, remembered a man who came
through her hometown in Arkansas after emancipation, selling five-
dollar tickets for a train that was going to Africa. Her parents sold their
possessions, bought tickets, and turned out with the rest of the crowd
on the appointed day—and every day thereafter for a couple weeks.
"The depot agent, he told 'em he didn't know 'bout no train going to
Africa," Rogers recalled. "The tickets was no good on his trains."

Even if it couldn't fulfill every dream, the railroad was central to the
growth of nineteenth-century America. William Cody, who hunted
buffalo for the Kansas Pacific before going on to impress the crowned
heads of Europe with his Wild West show, had an important lesson to
teach his former employers, if they hadn't already grasped it. One
could become a full-fledged player in the story of America—Cody,
after all, had participated in many real Indian battles—and still be el-
evated to the status of being one of its storytellers. To be both part of
the tale and its teller was a chance that many of the railroads—and the
museums that remember them today—couldn't refuse.

A TALE OF TWO MUSEUMS

In Washington, D.C., the Railroad Hall in the Smithsonian Museum of
American History is a study in still life. The locomotives, like steel be-

hemoths, stand at rest. The finished products of the great railroad age repose in inertia: headlights, semaphore signals, link-and-pin couplers, builders' plates, and the boiler of the Sturbridge Lion, that dates to 1829. The only sense of movement is the sound of a charging locomotive—from what turns out to be a recorded tape loop. Hearkening after a whiff of grand nostalgia, the Hall is a kind of Gilded Age Jurassic Park. The great engines of the Smithsonian give the impression of having been stuffed for public display.

That's just the way it was supposed to be, it turns out. The Hall was conceived some thirty years ago in "a kind of classical evolutionary model," explains William Withuhn, director of the Smithsonian transportation division, who admits to being a little tired of the display himself. "Here's the evolution of a dinosaur . . . from rheohippus to the great mammoth. It's a kind of natural history approach to the specimens," he jokes. "The idea of telling personal stories didn't occur to anybody."

Those stories, Withuhn says, should be the heart of any exhibit, although this would have seemed a strange opinion when the Hall was designed in the 1960s. "You've got these big, powerful-looking objects that tend to overwhelm when you try to put them in a museum setting," he continues. Displays that sought to explain solely through technology "were deadly years ago when people were probably a little more attuned to them," says Withuhn. "They're even more deadly now. . . . If you're going to have an effective exhibit about technology," he adds, "I think you have to begin and dwell on people."

In the Railroad Hall, labor is invisible—the memory of machines has won out over those who built and drove them. The glistening locomotives, in fact, hardly seem to have come from human hands. Looking at the artifacts, I think of Thoreau's remark that it was the railroad that rode us, not the other way around; or the comic image of Buster Keaton in *The General,* absentmindedly perched on the drive rods of a locomotive as it chugs away, a passenger with the ultimate illusion of ease. In Washington, the dark comedy of the Iron Horse that hints at our ambivalence about Progress is scrapped for a fascination with grand toys.

Withuhn has some ideas about what could be done to change the "sculpture garden" at the Smithsonian: take out the trolley cars, use first-person accounts (such as diary entries of people who rode by train), "even some Emily Dickinson poems," he muses. "I'd use graphics, models, try to create the feeling of being in a station . . . the whole thing would be, 'What did you do when you took a train ride in 1920?'" He'd also like to deal with modern public policy issues concerning transportation, he says as an afterthought, then shrugs as the dream of a different Railroad Hall passes by. "It's an embarrassment to me, but there's no money to do anything with it."

Since congressional money dried up in the early 1980s, the exhibit has stood virtually still. "We basically have to go out and shill," says Withuhn, referring to the recent trend at the Smithsonian toward private funding. "And I haven't found anybody interested in an old-hat, parochial sort of topic like railroads." The history of flight at the nearby Air and Space Museum is, for many visitors, a more central and exciting story in the unfolding of the twentieth century. "Railroads have disappeared into the plumbing of society," admits Withuhn. "The trains don't come to the front door of America, they come to the back."

It wasn't always that way. Some of the best American architecture in the last century proves that the railroads had a powerful pull on the public imagination. Some of our grandest buildings still, then the big city depots were like temples," says Withuhn. "They were consciously contrived to present an image of power and economic hegemony," he argues. "They were intended to be more than utilitarian. They had to be big Roman-style statements of the power of the owning railroad." The temple where the iron behemoths took on passengers, coal, and water was bound to be an edifice lavish beyond compare.

The awe that accompanied a visit to a major terminal was carried over into the philosophy of the railroad museum. The impression for the uninitiated today is a sense of wonder—if not befuddlement—at the spectacle of silent machines both bigger and smaller than life. Created by experts for other experts, the railroad museums assume that visitors have a ready grasp of technology, something that has proven, if anything, to be a self-fulfilling prophecy. Though the curious are always welcome, the average railroader's collection is for the pure at heart.

For the great unwashed, the rail museum qualifies as something less than a shrine, a fact that isn't lost on many people in the profession. "A number of people have come in here and get up on our locomotives and want to know where the steering wheel is," laughs John Ott, executive director of the B&O Railroad Museum in Baltimore,

Maryland. "When [these] people get up into the cab of a locomotive, they might as well be staring at the console of a jet aircraft." Since his arrival in 1991, Ott has been overseeing a change in exhibits that will attract a new kind of visitor. He credits his persistence, in part, to an unlikely revelation. One day, early in his tenure, he overheard the front receptionist respond to a friend's inquiry about what kind of exhibits were in the museum. " 'It's just a lot of railroad stuff,' " she responded matter-of-factly. " 'Nothing for you.' "

Although the sentiment may have been familiar, it came from very close. Still not satisfied that their one hundred thousand annual visitors were being given the right things to look at, Ott began to articulate further what the museum was missing. Visitors, he says, "lose sight that these [locomotives] were all built by men and women," adding that the public shouldn't hesitate to see railroaders in a contemporary context. "How long you stare at a [computer] screen is no different from how long a person looked at a welding torch and burning lights. . . . What we have to do are make some of those comparisons."

The "old" B&O museum, which opened under company management in 1953, was a classic period piece: extinct locomotives herded in the roundhouse corral, soup-to-nuts display cases with tiny labels, an elaborate miniature gauge railroad on the second floor. The exhibits showed the evolutionary change from horse-drawn railroad cars to steam power and diesel. But aside from the presence of a lone handcar and the cornerstone that Charles Carroll, a signer of the Declaration of Independence, laid at the 1828 B&O groundbreaking, you wouldn't have known that human sweat had anything to do with it. Like many museums of the genre, the B&O created more awe than understanding, reeking as it did of iron and steel-plated taxidermy.

For many enthusiasts, the B&O site is an object of veneration. The land where the museum stands was donated to the company in the 1820s by James Carroll. The original station, built in 1830, is somewhere beneath the current parking lot, while the second, rebuilt in 1851, serves as the museum entrance today. "We think the B&O was the first railroad that realized one thing it had to trade on was its history," says Ott, noting that the company had already commissioned a history by 1853, displaying an early concern for its place in the annals of American railroading.

The museum separated from the railroad in 1987, coming under independent management four years later. Today it's run by a private nonprofit entity—the B&O Railroad Museum, Inc.—which grants it substantial independence from the usual corporate strictures. "We can deal with labor," enthuses Ott, "we can deal with strikes, we can deal with wrecks—things that went wrong," a perspective rarely afforded technology museums, where celebrating the gains of industry is more common than exposing human costs.

Despite its independence, the museum has a symbiotic relationship with railroad conglomerate CSX, says Ott. Although it doesn't provide funding, the company donates rolling stock, old B&O records, and track materials to the museum: not surprising since the conglomerate came to encompass the B&O after a series of corporate mergers. CSX has no say in interpretation, says Ott, but he adds that "we try to be sensitive about things." A new exhibit on railway safety, for example, stresses the stringency of industry safety standards.

The B&O museum—before and after—has yielded mixed results. Renovation of the entrance hall in 1994 produced a more uniform, better lit, stylish display that's more oriented to kids, who can now send a message in Morse Code on a mock telegraph. In a wing called "Railroaders," section gang workers and office employees are recalled with assorted paraphernalia: union literature, steel-toed boots, old typewriters, a worker's lunch pail. As if in revenge against the antiquated style of the old Iron Horse museum, the exhibit uses hands-on educational devices, even if they do seem aimed at the very young.

Much in the display still claims bragging rights for the industry, however. Almost all the entrance hall photographs depict locomotives, not people, an appeal to industrial macho. Panels marked "A New Technology," "Building the Nation," and "The Great Road" are cut in the typical mold of the "Railroad as Benefactor." While it's noted that African Americans worked for the early B&O, for example, nothing is said of the fact that many were slaves. One exhibit also informs us that railroad life could be "brutally hard, dirty, and dangerous," while quickly adding that rail workers, after all, were still considered to be the "aristocrats of labor." There is still more at the B&O about physical and technical barriers than human and social ones.

Exhibit designers explained to me that many stories about the hardships of railroad life were deleted due to "limitations of space." One concerned a B&O engineer from the 1890s who, having worked fifty-two hours straight, signed off with a warning not to be disturbed for at least eight hours. Forty-five minutes later, a work call came in.

"Go to hell," was his uncompromising response, for which he was handed a month's suspension by the company. If they hadn't been able to find another crew, he probably would have lost his job, a parable about the twenty-four-hour pressures of the industry. There is, instead, a small panel in the "Workers" section dedicated to the engineer as romantic hero.

Even more telling, one of the most dramatic events in company history gets only a small paragraph. In 1877 the most famous strike in the history of American railroads occurred, sparked by B&O management's announcement of a 10 percent wage cut. In the course of several months, over a hundred people died and five hundred were wounded nationwide when angry mobs, comprised of strikers and sympathizers, clashed with federal troops and militia. B&O management was bitterly anti-union at the time, and proposed lowering wages while stock dividends remained constant. "From [the strike]," the new exhibit tells us, "railworkers learned the power of solidarity and united action," what seems a perfunctory moral for one of the most violent labor disputes in American history.

On balance, museums like the B&O and the Railroad Hall in the Smithsonian seem engaged in a losing battle with their traditional audience. Enthusiasts would probably have them continue in much the old way. But to draw too much attention to technology is to prepare the way for disappointment. "Progress," after all, was the rallying cry of the early railroads and "progress" has threatened to render them obsolete. The spirit that saw the steam engine replace the horse-drawn carriage would, in turn, make steam power seem quaint after the invention of the airplane and the automobile.

So the B&O, in full transition, is battling a paradox. "In fifty years, railroad technology itself may be gone entirely," admits Ott, emphasizing the importance of making the museum relevant in other ways. "The less people know about something, the less reason there is to remember why it was important to begin with, and therefore people don't feel compelled to come here, they just go down to the aquarium to see porpoises jump in the air." The competition is stiff—and getting stiffer. Just how should the railroad market itself in a world of multiplying entertainments? "People don't really understand what museums are about," Ott complains of the mothball stereotype that still dogs them. It's an image the new B&O is still trying to live down.

THE LARGEST RAILROAD IN THE WORLD

At the Railroaders Memorial Museum in Altoona, Pennsylvania, visitors are asked to break a professional taboo at the front door. An open notebook is scrawled with a message asking if anyone can identify the artifacts in a display case below, the museum having been unsuccessful. Well, that's an auto brake handle, someone has written; another allows that a lump of chalk is, just maybe, a lumber crayon; yes, those alphabet bits are the cut-out letters from sleeping-car berths; yet another item, no doubt about it, has got to be a piece of chalk to mark steel plate. Though I catch a whiff of the old railroad hodgepodge at the entrance, this time the curators are asking for help sifting through it. For the time being, the Railroaders Museum has about as many questions as it does answers, a rare thing for any museum to let slip.

"We're not afraid to admit our ignorance," says R. Cummins McNitt, collections curator since 1992. "We'll be the first to tell you that we're not the end-all and know-all of railroading history." Their ignorance, in fact, is something of a story. When the Pennsylvania Railroad (Pennsy) went bankrupt in 1968, he says, many company records were simply tossed. As scavengers salvaged what they could, much of Pennsy history came to reside in the private collections and memories of former employees—a "loss" that the museum, opened in 1980 through the efforts of community volunteers, has since tried to turn to its advantage. A display of photos from the grimy Altoona machine shops asks for help in identifying workers. An exhibit on train disasters has an accompanying sign, "Can you identify any of these wrecks?"—which is exactly the way photos of the Mount Union accident, in which twenty people died in 1917, were finally fingered.

A folklorist by training, McNitt has family roots in the industry. His grandfather owned some small timber railroads in the early part of the century. He brags that the old man was one of the first to drive an automobile cross country, financing the trip by hustling pool games. McNitt's father ran away from home and became a railroader of a different stripe, he explains, the kind that rode the rails for free. Before I can jump to any conclusions, he's quick to point out the difference between a "bum" and a "hobo," his father aspiring to the latter class. After earning a meal by doing a few chores, the hobo would wash his hands before sitting down to eat; the bum wouldn't bother. "This was

Tools of the trade: Railroaders Memorial Museum,
Altoona, Pennsylvania

before the depression," McNitt adds, visibly proud of his father's calling, "it was a choice, not a layoff."

With its emphasis on people, the Railroaders Museum lends itself
to stories. Visible in the entryway is its stated mission "to honor the
railroad workers . . . for the enrichment of present and future generations," a commitment it takes seriously. Docent tours are given by retired railroaders. Current and former workers come to adjacent
Memorial Hall to lecture on horns and whistles, the impact of the
change from steam to diesel, or what it was like being a Pullman porter
in the old days. For one hundred dollars, one can sponsor a plastic
plaque engraved with the name of a favorite railroader to hang in the
hall—two thousand people have already contributed. High-school students are given exhibit space to display artwork (any subject), a deliberate touch of amateurism that gives the museum another tie to the
community.

Altoona's museum, like many of its genre, is filled with the spirit of
someone ministering to a once-powerful but now ailing relative. I feel
as if I'm standing in a small barn, a sloping ceiling with exposed

rafters above me. An old baggage wagon is piled high with suitcases; a Track-Construction exhibit displays a broad axe, tie pick, adze, scythe, rail tongs, ballast pick, and driver's hammer—an array that would rival any dentist's armory for sheer scope of imagination. The displays seem to have been added to by fits and starts, the work of informed volunteers more than professionals.

The place gives off the impression of a well-organized attic. There are the usual small-print labels, the hodgepodge organization, the miniature train set, the musty air. But the human scale of the industry is graspable. A video, *Working the Mountain,* remembers the pain and romance of the famous Horseshoe Curve, located a few miles from town. A worker recounts a wreck on the curve, while another describes the trackwalkers who checked the joints where the rails grew brittle in winter. From the Irishmen who laid track in the 1850s to retired workers who still live in the community, the museum offers, however jumbled, a sense of history in the present. As McNitt puts it, "It's just as important to document what's going on in 1994 as . . . 1904."

The Railroaders Museum is gearing up for its move to an empty brick edifice a couple hundred yards away, scheduled to open in 1996. Built by the Pennsy as a storehouse in the 1880s and since used as a test lab, train dispatch, medical lab, and police headquarters, the building is one of the few extant from the days of the Altoona yards where 17,000 people were once employed. Financed largely with state money, the new museum plans to show a car under construction, a display of engines with sculptured human figures working on them, and a cutaway house exhibit that portrays the domestic lives of railroaders. At computer terminals, visitors will even be able to access biographical data on rail employees. The day I visit, McNitt hears from a docent who's willing to donate film of the Penn test department in action during the 1930s and 1940s—shot in the same building that will house the museum.

The plans for development start to sound like another celebration of big industry. "They did philanthropic work," McNitt says of the Pennsy, "sports teams, bands, built hospitals." And on a personal level, "If a man was killed, a spouse would be given a job for life." But Altoona isn't encumbered with the burden of being a company museum. "There are other stories of a man being killed on the line," he says. "The woman [has] to pull her children out of school so that they live at home with her all of the time and they spend every waking minute [walking] up and down the tracks looking for pieces of coal . . . in order to make enough money to stay alive."

That story is on tape, part of an ongoing oral history project to document the lives of rail workers. The museum has over two hundred video and audio interviews with Pennsy employees, some of whom had parents who worked on the line a century ago. "The Pennsylvania Railroad was not this huge, benevolent, sweet, loving, trusting entity that took care of its own," McNitt cautions. The new museum, he hopes, will give the industry a human—and not always benign—face. He interviewed the family of Mary Adams, a train signaller in the last century at Horseshoe Curve, who long ago chided her children for thinking that two-income families were an invention of the twentieth century. "We want the people to tell their own stories," he says.

To hear McNitt, that story will be more than the predictable one of man versus machine. "You show a tool—fine," he says of the current exhibit, leading me to a case where an "allegator wrench," named for its large jaws, is displayed. "How was that tool used?" he asks rhetorically. The attached label doesn't say very much of interest. But the men on the line carried them everywhere they went, McNitt explains, so they could conduct repairs on the spot. (Some of the larger wrenches were almost the size of a man.) But the mechanics in the shops didn't take to that, McNitt continues: they were there to do repairs, and if the machines weren't brought in, they were the ones who risked being furloughed. When linemen took money away from mechanics, bad blood arose. "I want people to understand that tools have history," says McNitt.

Executive director Peter Barton admits he feels "a little blessed" that the museum will have no pressing need to raise corporate railroad money. Such independence will permit them, in the new museum, to show a 3-D representation of the Pennsy boardroom—with the backdrop of a hospital ward behind it, a reminder that, even if the passenger safety record of the company were sterling, employee accidents were common. "Here in Altoona an army of railroad workers designed, built, and maintained the largest railroad in the world," Barton says proudly, adding that their exhibits will be marked by the stories of people, not a bare display of artifacts.

Barton wants those stories to deal with ethnicity and race. Yes, the Italians were typically trackmen. Yes, the Germans were tradesmen, WASPS were administrators, blacks were given menial jobs as cleaners, cooks, and waiters—"The Pennsy didn't treat them any differently" than other railroads did, he says. As for women, Altoona had a high percentage of single-parent families, what with accidents or extended periods of absence on the part of working husbands. Women, too, will have their place in the museum, if sometimes an ancillary one. One resident recalled that when women crossed the Twelfth Street city bridge that straddled a powerful air vent, country girls would hold their dresses while city ones grabbed their hats—an anecdote they plan to use in the front entryway, despite some chivalrous objections that it doesn't show women in the "right" light.

One still has to wonder if the museum will lose its sense of community by going high-tech. "I'm sure that the complexion of the animal will change a bit," says Barton, who hopes to entice a younger audience by offering curriculum programs through the school district. The notebook in the entryway, useful but quaint, will probably disappear, though there's always the possibility of doing its work on computer.

Too much nostalgia may not be a good thing for Altoona, anyway. "With all its beautiful environment," recalled a man who grew up here in the mid-nineteenth century, "Altoona was deadly uninteresting and almost squalid. Outside of a dozen or so houses that the railroad built for its officers and higher workmen, the dwellings were all makeshift wooden affairs, most of them painted a dull drab, unrelieved by any trimming. . . . Workmen carried planks to throw across the mud holes on the way to work." Although the museum plans to focus on the early twentieth century, the very low-tech roots of Altoona are a further reason to tell the human story of the Pennsy.

Before leaving the area, I have to pay my respects to Horseshoe Curve, what Barton calls "the earliest successful use of switchback" in American railroading, five miles west of town. It's the place where 450 Irishmen with hand drills, picks, shovels, sledgehammers, and blasting powder moved considerable parts of Mother Earth between 1851 and 1853 for the whopping sum of twenty-five cents a day. Over 2,000 feet long, rising 122 feet in elevation, the curve was fashioned, in part, by human—not natural—forces. An invisible monument, an embankment of packed earth that made a trestle unnecessary, the curve still sees sixty to seventy trains a day.

Not content with working conditions, one year the men from County Cork who built the curve decided to lay down their tools for better considerations. "The Contractors we are told have been working them from day-light to dark," remarked the *Register Inquirer* of Hollidaysburg in 1852. "The laborers claim from sun up to sun down as a day; and they're right. It is barbarous to require more." Between first light and dawn, the paper suggests, many an extra barrow of earth could be moved for the company, anxious to increase its margin of profit. Though McNitt says the museum isn't certain what happened to the strikers, he adds that the local militia was called in to quell a small war between different laboring factions among the Irish in 1851, taking thirty-three "prisoners" as a result. Clearly, the industry was the proving ground for a complex set of loyalties, even among laborers. The railroad crossed the Alleghenies before the Civil War, coming down into the flatlands of the Midwest and what would be its most formidable challenge—building the wonder known as the transcontinental.

A CHINAMAN'S CHANCE

In downtown Omaha, Nebraska, the Union Pacific Railroad Museum, located on the ground floor of corporate headquarters, is a public history version of the company store. Owned and operated by the UP since 1922, it claims to be the oldest corporate museum in the country. Over the intercom rolls the company jingle, "We're pullin' for America, that's what we do the best," while exhibits take us on a wild shotgun ride on the coattails of notorious legend. Visitors admire the scalp of William Thompson, UP worker who had his topknot removed by the Cheyenne in 1867, prominently displayed after its preservation in salt water. There are sleek and shiny Winchesters, Henry rifles, Colt revolvers, and photos of the "Wild Bunch": Butch Cassidy and gang, who used to hold up Union Pacific trains for their amusement—and today, for ours.

The UP museum is about the romance of railroading. Mixed in with old travel brochures, baggage checks, and portraits of the company fathers sporting muttonchops and beards is an array of memorabilia worthy of "America's Most Wanted": a piece of rope used to hang killer Tom Horn, and part of bank robber Big Nose George's skull and skin. It's no surprise that this museum is also a study in the showmanship of the West. We see tickets to one of Buffalo Bill's Wild West

shows and the original script for the 1939 Cecil B. DeMille extrava-
ganza *Union Pacific*—replete with Cheyenne attack, smooth-talking
Joel McCrea, and Barbara Stanwyck bleating in a broad Irish brogue.
Omaha, after all, was where the UP started laying track for the
transcontinental epic.

But this is one desperadoes museum that chooses the comfortably
notorious. I don't find any mention of the Rock Springs Massacre of
1885, for example. In the company town of Rock Springs, Wyoming
Territory, Chinese laborers were called in to replace white workers on
strike at a UP-owned mine. Tensions were rife until a dispute erupted
between workers from the two camps. Chinatown was burned to the
ground; some forty Chinese were killed; no one was ever indicted for
the murders. There's the Wild West, I suppose, and there's the West
that's a little too wild. Rock Springs isn't a good yarn for a company
store.

All is forgiven when I lay eyes on the museum's prize—a diorama
model of the interior of President Lincoln's funeral car, the original
purchased by the UP for its directors but destroyed in a fire early this
century. Like so many sites and museums, this one, displaying some
of the car's original furniture, claims a Lincoln relic as an authenti-
cating patriotic gesture. The buffalo robe spread out on a davenport is
symbolic of yet another icon dear to Americans. A few steps away, a
stuffed buffalo on display is meant to allay our fears about any destruction the railroad might have occasioned. Extinction? The buffalo? "Now there are ample herds which are managed much as a
rancher manages cattle," the text reassures. "Buffalo stew is a popular dish at Nebraska state parks."

Though sidetracked in Omaha, a thousand miles later, as I approach Golden Spike National Historic Site on Utah 83, I feel as
though I'm finally in the Old West—the park road signs have been
shot full of bullet holes. The land is filled with sage, cheatgrass, rab-
bitbrush. Near ghostly Great Salt Lake stands Promontory Summit,
the place where the Union Pacific, building from Omaha, and the
Central Pacific, from Sacramento, came together in 1869 in a mad
rush to cross the continent. A few miles from the park are the futuris-
tic grounds of the Thiokol Corporation, builder of the space shuttle
booster rocket, just a newer version of America's leading-edge technology. Once the linchpin of Manifest Destiny, today Golden Spike
seems a long detour from Interstate 84.

The other side of the tracks:
Golden Spike National Historic Site, Utah

Promontory is something of a ghost town—a reconstructed ghost town—with wooden facades for the old bakery and hotel. Along with a small visitors' center is an engine house where replicas of the Jupiter and 119 locomotives from 1869 are kept in storage and brought out for display in summer. The site looks like the remnants of a Hollywood set that was struck in a hurry—which isn't far from the way it was. Railroad towns were commonly built with tents behind wooden storefronts that could be packed up and moved down the line as the crews went through, grading and laying track.

The town that was known to some as the "Sodom and Gomorrah of the West" could hardly be imagined by looking at the storefronts today. Gone are the saloons. Gone are the labor camps that furnished them with many an unruly customer. Gone are the two-bit hustlers, the petty con men, the bullies, the snitches, the prostitutes. A patch of land not very far from the middle of nowhere, Promontory became the focus of national attention for a time before settling into the comfortable retirement of a historical symbol.

Although the Great Railroad Event happened here, there are few relics to prove it. Rail buffs will scoff at the repro locomotives; the originals were scrapped early in this century. The iron rails laid in twenty-eight foot sections were replaced with steel ones, later torn up in the 1940s for the war effort. Even the proverbial Golden Spike was taken to California; a cast replica is all that remains. But Golden Spike is about much more than just the railroad. "Our reason for being is not steam locomotives," emphasizes Randy Kane, chief site ranger and historian. "Our focus is the impact of the railroad on the West and how it changed things." He leans back in his chair and intones what I realize only later is the Promontory mantra: "It eliminated the frontier."

Sure enough, the railroad eliminated many a cherished symbol: the Pony Express, the Oregon Trail, and the lifestyle of the Plains Indians and the buffalo they hunted. Starting with the passage of the Pacific Railroad Act in 1862, the government was the agent that made this elimination possible. The Union and Central Pacific railroads were heavily subsidized with federal bonds and land grants, provided a generous right-of-way from the time they began construction in 1863. The effect of their labors, accomplished in a few short years, was staggering. "Before . . . it took six months to go by wagon from Missouri to California," brags Kane, "now it took four days and seven hours."

It's the seven hours—the precision of the new timetable—that strikes me. "Railroad fashion," as a visitors' center display notes, was nineteenth-century slang for doing something with great efficiency. The standard time zones first proposed in 1883 were, after all, the work of the railroads. Given such regimentation, it's not surprising that the Golden Spike story is infused with a paramilitary glow. Kane tells how a lot of UP track was laid by Civil War veterans, their ex-officers hired as bosses. Among the first transcontinental passengers of 1869 was a contingent of soldiers—complete with regimental band—bound for San Francisco. A veteran of several NPS military sites himself, Kane is dressed in ranger brown and Smokey-the-Bear hat, emitting the efficient aura of a G-man in uniform.

But Promontory exudes more the romance of battle than the labor of frontline grunts. A visitors' film recounts that "the Indian harassment began not far from Omaha and continued all the way to Utah," a good description of Cheyenne behavior, but unfair to the Pawnee scouts who protected UP workers and the Indian women who helped build the grade out of Omaha for fifteen cents a day. As for the Chinese workers on the Central Pacific—Kane tells me they accounted for over 80 percent of the labor force—they fare somewhat better, praised as "an army of coolies" who sometimes made eight inches of daily progress blasting through the Sierra Nevada mountains while the Union Pacific workers swept across the Plains surveying and laying track. It's hard to fathom that this epic feat could have been the work of, as narrator Royal Dano puts it, "these diminutive Chinese."

Evidence of the Chinese at Promontory is, as Kane admits, rather sparse. A plaque in front of the center, dedicated by the Chinese Historical Society of America in 1969, pays tribute to their "indomitable courage." On the east side is a more imposing obelisk in concrete built in 1919 by the Southern Pacific Railroad to commemorate Golden Spike, and moved to its current location in 1981 by the Daughters of Utah Pioneers. The new inscription, by the Daughters, honors the pioneers who died along the trails—instead of the railroad workers who would eventually make such a sacrifice unnecessary. On one of the few NPS sites dedicated to the railroad, it seems incongruous that the most visible monument, even in part, should be a memorial to fallen pioneers—not to track layers, graders, blasters, and cut-and-fill men.

The human cost of the transcontinental was enormous. Although there are no precise numbers for the workers who died building it, Kane estimates that it was close to a thousand for both the UP and CP—from avalanche, Indian attack, blasting accident, and disease. To get through the Sierras, for example, the CP was using as much blasting powder in one week as generals Lee and McClellan did at the battle of Antietam. The labor gangs, after all, were the size of small armies. "The rugged mountains looked like stupendous ant-hills," wrote Albert Richardson of the Sierras in 1865. "They swarmed with Celestials, shoveling, wheeling, carting, drilling and blasting rocks and earth, while their dull, moony eyes stared out from under immense basket-hats, like umbrellas." By any other name, these *were* pioneers.

There is a monument to the Chinese, in fact, that predates this 2,700-acre park established in 1965. For that matter, it was there long before the grading gangs came through and raced past each other in wild abandon in early 1869. A modest limestone formation on the park's east automobile tour—Chinaman's Arch—was so named in the 1880s for workers who inhabited the nearby camps. "Although the arch was created by forces of nature," a more recent Park Service sign reads, "it testifies to the strength and durability that the Chinese workers demonstrated during their assault on the Sierras and throughout the construction of the CP railroad." That the Chinese "assaulted" the mountains is accurate as far as the military parlance of Golden Spike goes; that their labors resemble an outcrop of rock seems like a page pulled from a bad volume of Greek mythology.

What happened at Promontory was no wonder of nature. What appears to an undiscerning eye to be the lay of the land is, in part, a built landscape. The Big Fill of the Central Pacific can still be seen, where ten thousand cubic yards of dirt and stone were dumped by hand to "make the grade" to Promontory. Unlike our legendary pathways—Cumberland Gap or Natchez Trace, passages carved by natural forces and later by Indian tribes—the way to Promontory was forged in recent times. Although early Europeans failed to find the Northwest Passage, the closest thing to it was hacked out by railroad grunts in the 1860s to achieve "the spanning of the continent by iron rails," as the park film puts it. No simple act of nature, the way to Promontory Summit was clawed by hand.

The way was blown with blasting powder, chipped with picks and shovels, driven with hammers. The Central Pacific, for its part, was a labor intensive operation that refused to employ steam drills or dynamite in its epic course eastward, preferring more tried and true methods. A sign on the west auto loop reminds us that one CP group laid ten miles of track in a single day to win a wager for a company official in 1869. A correspondent from the *Alta California* newspaper wrote that the largely Chinese gang that day was laying two hundred feet of rail every minute and a half. "This is about as fast as a leisurely walk," he noted, "as fast, in other words, as the early ox teams used to travel across the plains."

Yet a labor of immense cost completed at Golden Spike becomes obscured by a landscape, or somehow entangled with it. This may seem fitting for the Park Service, inheriting as it did the stewardship of natural sites such as Yellowstone, which was established as a park not long after the breakthrough at Promontory. But a visitor can drive away thinking that the Chinese were something like a force of nature—a tornado under harness, a swarm of worker bees, a span of limestone. In a sense, California's "John Chinaman" started the labor that John Henry was said to have finished at Big Bend Tunnel a few years later, paying a heavy cost again to beat the untiring steam drill of legend.

That men of many races died in the doing gets barely a nod at Golden Spike. That whiskey and opium were in widespread use, or that the Chinese—largely indentured laborers—were paid a smaller wage than Caucasian workers on the CP doesn't merit much attention. That Chinese were injured—if not killed—by Irish gangs blasting without warning, a visitor would never guess. And that opposing Chinese clans working on the line could engage each other in violent conflict seems antithetical to the Golden Spike spirit. "The battle cry, when they charged on the Imperialists yesterday afternoon," wrote the *Alta* correspondent of the clans, "beat anything I ever heard in Apacheland, and would have done no discredit to a division of Longstreet's rebels."

Other than "man versus nature," conflict is not a part of the Promontory epic. When some two thousand Chinese tunnelers went out on strike in 1867 for equal hours and wages, they received little support from other workers. The CP, ever alert, wired for black replacements—a reminder that it was a buyer's market for pick-and-shovel men. When the company cut off their food supply, the Chinese were back at work within a week, having been granted a modest wage increase. But it's not a crack one can see in Chinaman's Arch, or hear in the reassuring voice of Royal Dano.

That the railroads rigidly segregated ethnic groups is still less a part of the Promontory tale, which has nicer myths to extol. "The idea probably is beginning to dawn on the mind of the white laborer," wrote the correspondent, "that John Chinaman, instead of competing with him or pulling him down, is shoving him up the social scale. John has to do the hard work, while Patrick generally commands and directs." One of the few remaining reminders of railroad laborers, Kane tells me, are some of the caves that provided the men with temporary shelter.

The famous company publicity photos of 10 May 1869—the ones that show up in standard American history texts—don't even reveal a Chinese face. Kane speculates that they may have arrived a couple days before the celebration and been sent back to shore up the line. Or, he adds thoughtfully, maybe they'd already been laid off. Another story has it that the official photographer yelled, "Let's shoot!" and the Chinese, misinterpreting the command, scattered. A more likely account is that they were simply muscled out by those aware that May 10 was going to be a historic day—the *Alta* notes on May 11, after all, that the last few ties were laid by Chinese. After the ceremonial golden spike had been tapped, an iron one was brought out for Leland Stanford, president of the Central Pacific, to drive home. He tried and missed. A few sniggers passed through the crowd. Finally, a real railroad man stepped up and drove home the spike. Nobody I've talked to has ever been able to tell me his name.

THE ULTIMATE RAILROAD MUSEUM

At every stop on my travels someone was bound to pull me aside and ask, "Have you been to Sacramento?," the question almost brimming with awe. In Old Town Sacramento, it turns out, is the California State Railroad Museum, founded in 1976, and by most accounts—including its own—the most impressive interpretive museum of railroad history in America. "Go to Sacramento," people practically begged me, giving experienced advice to the equivalent of a Gold Rush greenhorn.

"Few other artifacts in American history and culture have been so pervasive," begins senior museum curator Stephen Drew, talking about the industry that helped make Sacramento famous. Drew is less taken with the big locomotives than the more humble items that have become classic pieces of Americana. "You can buy OshKosh B'gosh coveralls from the cradle to the grave," he says, without so much as cracking a smile. In what other industry do you have popular folk icons, he asks, ticking off the names of John Henry and Casey Jones before I can even put in a word for "Smokestack Lightnin'" and the Little Train That Could. "We don't have that kind of thing with folks who run eighteen wheelers."

Attired in pressed white shirt and plaid suit, Drew looks more like someone headed for a corporate board meeting than a crawl through the roundhouse with the local OshKosh crowd. Notwithstanding California's current financial woes, the museum is going strong. Its 1994 operating budget was $3 million, and the state is well along with plans for the final phase, a 114,000-square-foot Museum of Technology due to open in 1998. Even if it does ride the crest of folklore, the railroad museum of California has the sheen of state-of-the-art.

Sacramento still has the problem of rail museums everywhere, however. The status of "Chattanooga Choo Choo" seems demeaned in a culture that virtually worships high-tech; Casey Jones pales next to space shuttle pilots or the folks who fly AWACS. "Part of our message has to be that railroads are alive and well," Drew responds, explaining that California is shoring up inner-city rail transport even as we speak, and that, in this day and age, most products still make part of their journey to the American consumer by rail. Reports of the death of the American railroad—a popular species of obituary for decades—are, to hear Drew tell it, premature.

The hard thing is reaching the skeptics. For many people, "their only encounter with a train [may be] waiting at the freight crossing while this mile-and-a-half-long freight train goes from horizon to horizon," Drew says, breaking into a sudden smile, "and they cuss a blue streak." But although the technology seems antiquated, he adds, the effect can still be magical. The kid who's never seen a piece of rolling stock up close knows what a train whistle sounds like—chances are he's been haunted by one far away, blasting out the midnight special. So the formula of other rail museums still applies: high nostalgia rubs shoulders with high-tech. The only difference is that they're not preaching only to the coverall choir in California.

Most of America's more than 250 rail museums, Drew explains, are run by "foamers"—an affectionate name for hobbyists whose devotion to railroads sometimes gives their museums a parochial slant. It was a group of foamers, in fact, who helped start up the California museum in the 1970s. But, from the early planning stages, the museum set out to have a broader appeal—a luxury not afforded the typical train barn run on donations and lots of volunteer effort. With 75 percent of its budget paid by the state, the four-building complex in Sacramento had a bigger audience in mind.

"The mythical eighth-grade mentality" is how Drew puts it, the consumer profile that museums traditionally target. In designing exhibits that would appeal to retired couples, vacationing families, preschoolers, post-graduates, and fourth graders doing units on American history, however, they discovered that the classic profile wasn't much help. A paradox began to emerge. Sacramento would be a specialty museum serving a general audience, a publicly funded site that would have to interpret what is, for all but the most devout, an arcane technology. In the rarefied world of railroad hobbyists, public history was finally going public.

The founders of the CP Railroad would have recognized the solu-

tion the museum settled on: a labor-intensive industry to be interpreted, in part, by a large volunteer staff. In 1993, over ninety thousand hours were donated by costumed docents, who were given sixty-
hour training courses before hitting the museum floor. The morning I
start my tour of the Museum of Railroad History, opened in 1981 as
the centerpiece of the complex, a graying man in coveralls is demonstrating to a group—all of them blind—how long a ninety-foot rail
feels from end to end, explaining it would have taken ten men with
tongs to lift and set it in place. It's as tactile an introduction as anyone
will get to railroad heavy metal.

A celebration of the Age of Steam, Sacramento also pays homage
to the human sweat that made it possible. A life-size diorama depicts
Chinese laborers preparing for a black powder blast in the Sierra
Nevadas. A wooden snow shed stands next to the Governor Stanford
locomotive—which plied its way only a short distance from the site—
giving context to machinery, showing a necessary adaptation to railroading through the mountains in winter. In Truckee in 1866, "An old
[shed] collapsed and killed four Chinese," remembered worker A. P.
Partridge. "A good many were frozen to death"—a reminder of seasonal hazards that made crossing the Sierras a costly feat.

At 100,000 square feet, the History Museum tries hard not to lose
sight of human scale. A postal car—not the usual star of rolling
stock—is open for inspection, a costumed mail sorter on duty. Window displays on a Santa Fe dining car show the evolution of passenger
travel over the years. A cutaway diagram of a steam engine stands
near a life-size mannequin of a railroad hobo. Over twenty pieces of
rolling stock are displayed, but function as borders between exhibits
as much as the objects of curiosity. In the People Gallery, mannequins gesture: there are a black waiter and Mexican American laborers on a handcar. Sacramento remembers that building the railroads was, for the Gilded Age, the first Hands Across America.

A temporary exhibit, "They All Wore Hats," explains how laying
rails on the transcontinental was as intricate a labor as it was ex-
hausting: first, joint tie men bed the ties; fillers shovel dirt; lifters with
tongs clamp the rails into position; gaugers align them; spikers drive
the bolts; backspikers bolt fishplates; backfillers shovel dirt between
ties; tail-piece men gather loose spikes; and the carriers, entrusted
with the most essential task as the CP crossed the arid climes of the
Great Basin, perform the delicate balancing act of bearing water to

the members of the "anvil chorus," that raffish gang of unsung Patricks and Johns. "If there's ever been a museum to the dignity in manual labor," enthuses Drew, "it's this museum."

But the costs incurred for that dignity aren't equally exposed. The Chinese are shown to have paid a heavy price on the railroad, a fitting tribute to their contribution—and, one would think, a pragmatic acknowledgment of the large Chinese American community in Sacramento. Groups from mainland China have even come to the museum to lay wreaths and observe a moment of silence, says Drew.

Yet discrimination against the Chinese is the only kind we learn about in detail. "Three generations of African Americans worked on the rails," the museum's big-screen orientation movie says, "and encouraged their children to do the same." But the kind of jobs they were given are not discussed. Were they happy being Pullman porters, for example—a job considered beneath the station of white people? What should we think of an industry where being a porter was a top-line occupation for a black employee? Whatever their differences, the Chinaman named "John" and the porter called "George" had a world of discrimination in common.

The same film opens with a shot of a Plains Indian on horseback taking in a grand vista—the railroad going through the valley. For his people, of course, it was the end of an era, not the beginning. The Union Pacific recently came through Sacramento with its main track crew, Drew tells me, including some two hundred Native Americans, a fact that testifies to the industry's role as an entry-level catalyst in the melting pot. From the very beginning, however, the railroad has meant displacement, poverty, and violence for many who stood in the way, a subject even the best rail museums are mum about. As if the destruction of the buffalo herds weren't enough, some Indian tribes endured a further insult. "We finally agreed to let them build the railroad through our country, and they agreed to give us free transportation," remembered Crow chief Plenty Coups of the 1880s. "This was done at first but . . . since then we have had to pay for our own."

"Railroad history is filled with examples of danger, strife and discrimination," admits a signboard in the People Gallery, next to the Mexican American mannequins. Without skipping a beat, the sign goes on to add that "railroading has been and continues to be one of America's great industrial occupations." And so it has. But down the road in Bakersfield, for example, Mexican section hands at the turn of the twentieth century received a smaller wage than Greek or Japanese ones; the houses they lived in—single-room cabins of condemned rail ties built over a clay floor—are part of the story of western railroads as much as the fabled Chinese assault on the Sierras.

Similarly, railroads and women seem an uncomfortable mix, though they're acknowledged more in Sacramento than at many other museums. "It's not for lack of women being there [historically]," asserts Shirley Burman, former staff photographer for the museum, who explains that railroad history is still "a male-dominated area." Burman, who has designed traveling photographic exhibits on railroad women, has had to overcome a lot of inertia, both contemporary and historic. Although in recent years the museum has done much to promote her exhibits, she says, during her tenure as photographer in the early 1980s they did little to advance the profile of railroad women, remaining instead part of a stolid "old boys' network" she thinks is slowly changing.

The historic record is more intransigent. Burman has seen evidence of women's names mysteriously expunged from company payroll records, even though photographs show their presence in the early labor force. Native women in Oklahoma and Asian ones in California were telegraphers, for example. By 1910, some women were doing manual labor in the industry, Burman notes, though they had a hard time joining the unions, and equal pay was considered a dubious principle at best. Not everyone in the field, however, is so enamored of her research. "A lot of the men refer to us as revisionists," she complains, impatient with being accused of having "changed" the record she's spent so much of her time trying to illumine. "What it is, is that they didn't put us there in the first place."

Women were there from the beginning, of course, though not always on the company payroll. The nature of construction work created a masculine environment on the frontier with a lively economy in tow. Not least of the trades that followed the railroad was prostitution, a subject usually ignored at historic sites in spite of its considerable role. If there ever were a story of melting pot metaphysics, it's that of commercial sex on the frontier: white, black, Native, Oriental, and Mexican women procured customers all over the post–Civil War West, one historian estimating that some fifty thousand practiced the profession of "soiled doves" during the second half of the nineteenth century. Many of the houses were racially segregated, an ironic testament to the society that prostitution served while being officially condemned as a moral abomination.

The railroad didn't create prostitution, of course, but the urbanized settlement pattern it encouraged made for a booming trade in the West. The women—mostly young and poor—came first with the graders and the anvil chorus, inhabiting the temporary camps—such as Promontory—collectively known as "Hell on Wheels." As towns such as Virginia City, Nevada, or Cheyenne, Wyoming, blossomed into mining and commercial centers served by the iron rails, the bordellos, saloons, and one-room crib-houses multiplied to serve a burgeoning clientele. Prostitution is as much a part of the railroad story as were respectable institutions such as the cattle market or the U.S. Army. "In broad daylight they may be seen gliding through the sandy streets in Black Crook dresses," wrote Henry Stanley of women in Julesburg, Colorado, "carrying fancy derringers strung to their waists, with which tools they are dangerously expert. Should they get into a fuss, western chivalry will not allow them to be abused by any man whom they may have robbed."

Although rail museums such as those in Sacramento or Omaha tender a nostalgic hand to the hobo or armed bandit, they rarely touch the subject of the prostitute, another social outcast who made a living off the rails. It's estimated that some six thousand Chinese women were imported to America to become prostitutes between 1852 and 1873, an import trade controlled by the Chinese themselves. Many of these women were destined for railroad and mine workers across the West. Though laborers loading a black powder charge in the Sierras is an inspiring image, that of a Chinese prostitute sold into virtual slavery—working for fifty cents a customer to pay off an indenture amounting to thousands of dollars—gives a different slant to the story of how America was built.

Forceful about what it brings to light, Sacramento is silent about a great deal: hatred of the railroad by Grange farmers; black workers used as scab labor; violence between tramps and trainmen; state militia encountering angry mobs in Sacramento during the national strike of 1894, begun by employees of the Pullman Company and organized by Eugene Debs; the industry's initial refusal to accept the air brake and automatic coupler as safety improvements because cost-cutting measures were more important than maimed employees. Aside from a few picket signs, there is little sense of the scope of tragedy that dogged the railroad. The claims of nostalgia can simply be overpowering.

"Museums are one of the few places where you're forced to learn standing up," says Drew, a fact that explains why so much of the Sacramento routine is just that—stand-up, person-to-person, and, in many ways, successful. Sacramento makes the story of Pegasus believable—a rare achievement for any site—tethering the fabled horse to earth. But like other rail museums, its narrative mimics the industry's very objective—to move "freight" across difficult terrain while encountering a minimum of resistance. Even its reformist rhetoric hearkens to "the glory days." In Sacramento, the cry of "All aboard!" still has the unmistakable echo of "Gee whiz!"

THE ONLY RURAL CHINATOWN IN AMERICA

When the transcontinental was finished in 1869, many of its builders found themselves without work. In the 1870s, unemployed Chinese workers joined the "wheelbarrow brigades" hired to build levees and reclaim orchards for Caucasian farmers in the Sacramento-San Joaquin Delta. Paid one dollar a day or thirteen cents per cubic yard, they moved piles of earth too muddy for draft animals to tread in. With their barely subsistence wages, the mostly male immigrants realized they would never meet their plan of leaving "gold mountain," (as America was called) and returning home, and so they settled into the area above San Francisco, living on the edge of a culture that endured them so long as they did its dirty work without a gripe.

A few of their descendants would build and settle Locke, California—the only town in America built by Chinese for Chinese, it is said, even if the town was hammered together by Caucasian carpenters beginning in 1915. When a fire destroyed the Chinatown in nearby Walnut Grove that year, some merchants—originally from Zhongshan district—sought a new town they wouldn't have to share with either whites or rival Chinese. Today a living, if crumbling, testament to the legacy of the Iron Horse, Locke has been listed on the National Register of Historic Places since 1971. But the fragile town is in danger of collapsing before it can be restored, a story of corporate profit scheming, restrictive zoning practices, sacred Indian burial grounds, the residue of cultural prejudice, and the general apathy that has settled into a town whose Chinese inhabitants, except for about a dozen, have been slowly replaced mostly by Anglo inhabitants.

Not a railroad town in the usual sense, Locke is still unthinkable without the steel rails. Railroad workers were among those who raised the levees and reclaimed the Delta, putting to use the methods of gang labor perfected on the Central Pacific. The Southern Pacific came through in 1909, the tracks laid in large part by Chinese. The SP spur, which followed the levee in front of town and whose warehouse stands today, was a boon to the area: the first buildings in Locke were put up to serve workers at the company packing house. In the 1970s as many as five hundred boxcars filled with local produce came out of the area every year, though the tracks have been torn up since.

Because the interpretation of historic sites is influenced by ownership, Locke, the only rural Chinatown in America, is a town that doesn't own its own story. In fact, the residents have never owned the land they live on. The Alien Land Act of 1913 prohibited them from owning real estate, and it wasn't ruled unconstitutional until 1952. In the meantime, the inhabitants had agreed with the family of landowner George Locke to pay rent for the town, though many owned the buildings they lived in. In 1977, the land on which Locke stood was purchased from the family for $700,000 by the Hong Kong–based Asian City Development, Inc.—the plan being to turn it into a recreational theme park for Sacramento urbanites. To a lot of people at the time, it sounded like a rural Disney, complete with condominiums and yacht marina.

Two years later, the state stepped in to thwart excessive commercial development, passing strict zoning laws that would encourage historic preservation more than yuppie pleasure. All in all, it seemed a classic impasse. A corporation buys land for rapid development, the state intercedes to preserve a historic property, a tight real-estate market precludes resale of the land, and in the meantime a financial crisis makes state ownership increasingly unlikely. Meanwhile, most of the Chinese families of Locke either died or moved away, the town in limbo between the familiar camps of corporate development and state preservation.

As visitors will testify, Locke is a hard town not to like. Its Main Street is ramshackle—neat but decayed—a line of buildings made of fragile, unpainted wood, some sagging from the sheer weight of years. At the corner stands the old Chinese school, where students went to

Cruising Main Street: Locke, California

redouble their studies after public lessons—open today as a courtesy to tourists, rest rooms in the rear. There's an art gallery, a grocery, a restaurant, a museum, a bar called "Al the Wop's." Along the back streets are simple gardens, a few with succulents growing in toilet bowls, near the place where the SP railroad used to pass. To come down the short hill to Main Street from Highway 160 is to go back in time a century.

"Being Chinese, we can make sure certain Chinese there never go away," says Clarence Chu, co-owner and general manager of the former Asian City Development. Tired of being labeled "overseas Chinese," he says, Asian City changed its name to Locke Property Development, now a California-registered company. Chu claims the corporation (whose majority owner lives in Hong Kong) has improved the town—restoring the buildings it owns, operating the local museum, granting easement to the county for installation of a needed water pump. Plans for residential units were scrapped, he explains, when Indian burial mounds were discovered near town and the county demanded expensive archaeological studies as a prerequisite for development.

Envisioning a "cultural village"—not a theme park that would charge admission—Chu foresees Locke as a center for arts and handiwork, even if fewer than twenty Chinese still remain. Admitting the town is "almost like a money pit," he seems confident that residents, most of whom rent rather than own buildings and depend on tourism, will welcome whatever the company can do. A joint venture with the state nearly worked at one point, he says; in 1985 they almost sold the town to another investor. Progress is slow, says Chu, as the company tries to restore the town section by section. "If it works our way," he claims, "there's a chance Chinese people will come."

As one businessman to another, Ping Kan Lee, a grocer in nearby Walnut Grove, isn't so sure. "He's looking for a profit," Lee says of Chu's Locke Development, but "for the price he's asking, he might sit there till doomsday." Though Clarence Chu is a personal friend, Lee doesn't think the company has done much to keep up the town. They don't want even to disturb a dilapidated sewer line, he exclaims, in order to keep Locke "historic." He thinks that if current trends continue, the place where he was born in 1917 won't be on the map much longer. In fact, it isn't even on many maps now. "Unless someone comes in with some money to shore it up," Lee says, "there won't be a town there for long."

Unofficial mayor of Locke for twenty-eight years, Lee has long argued that the town should be a living memorial. He founded the Dai Loy Museum on Main Street—one of the few museums I know of dedicated to the art of gambling—on the very site of his father's gambling house. Lee has thought a lot about what Locke deserves as a historic site, as one outsider discovered several years ago. After Lee had made a plea at a public meeting for town recognition, the man responded that perhaps the accomplishments of Locke didn't warrant such enthusiasm. This came as something of a surprise to Lee, whose father, Lee Bing, had founded Locke in 1915.

"That's when I says, 'Well, let's look at it this way,'" Lee remembers. "'Here's Humphrey the whale three or four years ago swims up the Sacramento River. Five hundred cars went to see what the poor old whale was doing. Finally they got him out of here, went back to the Bay area, and then you set a plaque right down there by the waterside. Well, [it says] Humphrey was here such and such a day and all that. [He] deserves a plaque and you tell me all the Chinese that die for building the levees, helped the economic situation here—doesn't [that] deserve something?'"

It takes a moment for the passion of the memory to recede. "They did a lot," Lee finally says of the workers, "but never got much credit. If a living town like Locke is there, I figure it's like a marker." For a railroad town, a turn of fortune is hardly unusual. Some, such as Sacramento, flourished and turned from campsites into cities; others were abandoned weeks after the line went through. Like the SP spur whose tracks were torn up, Locke seems to be at the end of a line.

The loss is everyone's. "New immigrants aren't even aware of this history," says Bruce Chin, president of the Chinese Historical Society of America, so "certain rights and privileges [now] are taken for granted." The society had to lobby hard to get even a plaque erected at Golden Spike, Chin remembers, and met initial resistance at the California State Rail Museum to a prominent display on the Chinese. To his knowledge, no one in Locke has approached the society— currently raising money to build a national Chinese American museum in San Francisco—for assistance.

The Locke area has known Hindu, Japanese, Filipino, and now Mexican workers, a classic story of American immigrant layers. But the group whose ancestors first came to shore up the Delta has moved on—at least most of those who inhabited Locke have, a living example of what happens when we do almost nothing to preserve the past. Meanwhile, the town goes about the business of living, perhaps a reminder that all markers, once upon a time, were flesh and blood.

6

Conclusion

THERE'S NO PLACE LIKE HOMESTEAD

I FIND MYSELF back on the prairie one last time, a breeze stirring under a cloudless sky in Indian summer. Paul Harvey chatters away on the car radio. The shadow of a hawk sweeps the pavement, signs of roadkill increasing since I left Omaha. The towns stop on an invisible edge—a Texaco station rubs shoulders with a stand of corn, a baseball field blends into a cluster of hills. The roads are so straight they would bore a crow. A glance at the atlas shows counties that look as though they've been cut from a jigsaw, the macro-image of the quarter-sections on land handed out to settlers by the federal government in the nineteenth century. There on the side of Highway 77 is a historic marker of the Homestead Movement, the migration that would make *Little House on the Prairie*—not to mention the Dust Bowl of the 1930s—symbols of the American West.

The words on the sign are as inspired as they are simple. "Abraham Lincoln was called the great emancipator because his proclamation of 1862 gave freedom to the slaves," it reads. "In that same year he signed another extremely important document that gave land to free men. No single act had more effect on the middle west and great plains than the Homestead Act of May 20, 1862," enthuses the marker, proudly adding that "millions of acres from the public domain became available." Filled with the history of women and people of color, I'd come to find out something about their nemesis—the dead white male of American legend.

The Nebraska state marker, it turns out, isn't quite as true as the two-lane road that led me to it. Lincoln didn't "free" all the slaves, of course—only those in the secessionist South. The land didn't always go to "free men"; women homesteaded in large numbers across the West. And the "public domain" had to be wrested from its previous occupants before those millions of acres became "available" to the sod-busting newcomers in the first place. Of course, there isn't much room for elaboration in a hundred and fifty words. My doubts seemed like mere quibbles by the mythic standards of homestead lore.

One of the first quarter-sections of land filed under the famous Act of 1862 has become Homestead National Monument, today a 195-acre parcel on Highway 4 near Beatrice, Nebraska. U.S. House resolution 71-3572 identifies the original claim as "quarter section 26, township 4 north, range 5 east, of the sixth principal meridian in Gage County, Nebraska"—a platting so precise that there could be no doubt as to its rectitude. This was the plot given to one Daniel Freeman, reputedly the first claimant in January 1863 under the act earlier signed into law by President Lincoln.

Freeman's original house disappeared long ago. The Park Service acted to restore the vision of the early pioneers, however, when a nearby cabin, built in 1867, was moved to the site and restored in the 1950s. The ten-by-fourteen-foot structure sits behind the visitors' center and does permanent duty today as a tidy example of the homestead spirit. Set near a cozy stand of trees by Cub Creek, it has an almost fairy tale look. The wavy hardwood logs are tightly mortared; the roof above the brick loft is shingled; a picture of Mr. Lincoln hangs by the door. Gone is the oppressive sense of isolation endured by Nebraska homesteaders, not to mention the sod hut or cave that many of Freeman's peers would have actually inhabited. The homestead mood has been airbrushed with a touch of prairie picturesque.

The park museum does what it can to trumpet the virtues of busting sod. As one panel puts it, "Free Lands in the Wilderness"—a rather dubious view of the matter if one happened to be Ponca or Pawnee. But the complaints of many a white homesteader are just as studiously ignored. That speculators profited by buying out claimants and consolidating large amounts of acreage; that almost 20 percent of Nebraska's land was allotted to railroads, not homesteaders; that farming beyond the 100th meridian on a quarter-section of prairie was near impossible for a subsistence farmer—these stories go untold. "Like any public measure," admits a sign at the exhibit's end, "the Homestead Law was not all it promised to be," though the text doesn't bother to enlighten us with details. At a national monument in Nebraska, pioneer hardship is an easier story to sell than pioneer failure.

Failure, in fact, was depressingly common on public land. Barely half the people who filed homestead entries in nineteenth-century Nebraska stayed for the required five years to receive a deed for their 160 acres. By the early twentieth century, only half the acres of public domain in the state had been parceled out to settlers rather than ranching, railroad, timber, and other business interests. Although the park slide show brags that "most" homesteaders didn't leave their claims, it's a boast that, for Nebraska, is only barely true. The visitors' film, *The Settling of the Plains,* is more honest on the matter: a homesteader descendant recounts difficulties his grandparents had with drought, ill-preparedness, and the grasping railroads. Homestead reminds one a little of the proverbial jug—half full or half empty, it depends on how you look at it. After all, the "typical" filer would have just as likely jumped claim before five years were out as he would have become an upstanding citizen like Daniel Freeman.

How the Freeman claim came to become the Homestead National Monument isn't as upright a tale as the yeoman virtues it tries to uphold. Freeman long insisted he was the first to file under the Homestead Act on 1 January 1863, a claim that—subsequent investigation has borne out—any number of other filers at offices across the country could also have justly made. Convinced nonetheless of the priority of his claim, he was lobbying to have a homestead monument placed on his farm as early as 1884. Claiming to have once been an "Indian fighter," Freeman welcomed a battle with rival claimants for national recognition, even if, as it turns out, he never lived to see his niche in history confirmed.

A Freeman Daniel was; an Everyman he wasn't. Daniel Freeman, in fact, did so well in Gage County that he eventually came to own 840 acres with his wife, Agnes Suiter. Moving from his log cabin into a brick house by the creek (neither of them still standing), he was to become a doctor, sheriff, and justice of the peace, a prosperous Nebraska burgher who made a name for himself through a mix of community service and canny self-promotion. He said that he was a scout in the Union Army during the Civil War and a member of the "secret service"—claims that the Park Service has never been able to verify from extant muster rolls or other records.

Of course, a name like "Freeman" was a good advertisement for the Homestead spirit. When Daniel Freeman died in 1908, the citizens of Beatrice took up the fight for national recognition. Though many legislative defeats ensued, the effort coalesced in 1934 around the Beatrice Chamber of Commerce, the Homestead National Park Association, and U.S. Senator George Norris, who had fathered the bills creating the Tennessee Valley Authority. "If the park is created thousands of people will visit the city annually," gushed the *Beatrice Daily Sun* in 1934. "The sightseers of course spend considerable sums of money." When the Daughters of the American Revolution joined hands with the Secretary of the Interior to support the effort, the long decades of waiting had come to an end. It was as if the whole story had been scripted: the free land of the Homestead Act would be memorialized on a claim taken out by a man named Freeman.

Franklin Roosevelt signed public law 74-480 in 1936 authorizing Homestead as a national monument. But the government was ahead of itself: the original claim was still owned by Freeman family heirs. Before it could develop, Washington had first to reacquire the 160 acres, land it had once gladly given away for a nominal filing fee. Not inclined to give the property outright, the owners rejected all government bids as being under market value. Only when Washington instituted condemnation proceedings in 1938 did the heirs accept $18,000 for 162 acres. After all that had transpired, it was the antithesis of the Homestead spirit. The government had "given away" land in 1863 it could get back only with a threat—all to make a prairie memorial to the independent yeoman farmer.

A tour of the old Freeman claim today is a lesson in restoring the lush ecosystem of the American prairie. Most of the 160 acres have been replanted in big and little blue stem, cheatgrass, gramma grass, buffalo grass, switchgrass—who would have guessed the sheer variety of the native tallgrass prairie in Nebraska? A path leads past the graves where Daniel and Agnes are buried, winds along a hedge of osage oranges, and follows Cub Creek, circling the large swath of prairie the Park Service has painstakingly restored. In a warm October, at least, the crickets are so loud it's hard to think.

The land didn't look anything like this in 1938 when the Park Service bought it. In the seventy-five years after Freeman had filed his claim, the original quarter-section had badly deteriorated. On the Freeman homestead the Park Service found eroded slopes thick with silt, overcut woodlands, heavily grazed pasture—none of it a tribute to the conservation skills of the pioneers. In the following years, the Park Service would use a variety of herbicides (sodium chlorate; 2,4-D; and Dalapon) to control weed growth, a strategy later abandoned in favor of, ironically, the old Indian trick of prescribed burning. Daniel Freeman had gotten the land for nothing in 1863; its stewardship later incurred a substantial cost for the American taxpayer.

Set up to depict the hardships of the early pioneers, the plot has been restored to "pristine" condition, the land seeded to look the way it would have looked when Daniel and Agnes Freeman first settled on it. But the public should be thankful the park is a tribute to what the homesteaders acquired, not to what they left behind. Although Homestead claims to be a celebration of the "typical" pioneer, one can only hope it represents an exception to what happened on public land, not the rule. The family knack for development didn't end with Daniel Freeman, by the way—his son James went on to become one of the leading real estate developers in Beatrice.

Women and people of color should not have a monopoly on the concerns of social history. But even when we honor that most familiar figure—the dead white yeoman male—our understanding of what made him a national symbol is naive. Erecting a monument to his labors in the heartland, we suppress the memory of widespread failure, ignore the role of profiteering big business, bow before the efforts of a self-styled hero, and are forced to completely restore his legacy of land, not merely preserve it. The monument couldn't have happened in a nicer place. It's just that in Gage County, Nebraska, you'd think the truth would be a simple thing to get at.

THE NATIONAL PARK SERVICE: AN APPRAISAL

The National Park Service administers over two hundred historic and cultural sites in addition to Homestead National Monument. Where public history was once the domain of local bodies, the federal government, in fact, has become central to historic preservation efforts since the Great Depression. This development has been advantageous in marshaling resources to preserve sites that would have otherwise felt the wrath of the wrecking ball. It has also been problematic in that America has come to be "explained" more and more by a bureau of the government—one of the players in the story it purports to tell. A question arises: How well can government—any government, for that matter—tell the truth about itself and maintain the authority required to exercise stewardship of historic properties?

Since its establishment, the Park Service has been pledged to provide a public history that is patriotic in tenor. The Historic Sites Act of 1935 declares that national policy will preserve sites "for the inspiration and benefit of the people of the United States," language repeated in the National Historic Preservation Act of 1966. Such a sentiment, by no means unique to this country, reveals several assumptions about the past: that it's supposed to be "good"; that it should offer beneficent examples to the public; and that the lessons it provides are, by and large, worthy of emulation. These are excellent assumptions—provided, of course, one agrees that the American saga has largely been a happy and profitable one.

Because of its original mandate to protect natural and prehistoric sites, the Park Service was invested early with the role of "benevolent caretaker," a pose it has never relinquished. In fact, the gee-whiz school of explaining Yellowstone's Old Faithful isn't far removed from the celebration of nationhood at the Museum of Westward Expansion in St. Louis or the occasion of European "discovery" at Cabrillo National Monument in San Diego. The Park Service has been a perfect vehicle for the historical school that teaches that "geography and destiny are one." Cumberland Gap National Historical Park (Kentucky) and Natchez Trace National Scenic Trail (Mississippi) are explained as nature-made conduits that led to the Anglo settling of the West. As if by magic, the national mission and the natural terrain are one, a leftover of Manifest Destiny rhetoric that has become one of the most revered assumptions of the Service, borne out by rangers who might just as well be asked to explain a geologic formation at Yosemite as to outline the tactical shortcomings of Pickett's Charge.

By its own admission, the Park Service doesn't tell every facet of our history equally well. For instance, nearly one-quarter of its historic sites are forts and battlefields, giving the system a pronounced emphasis on the military. In part, this is a legacy of the sites the Park Service inherited from the War Department in 1933—including Antietam,

Shiloh, Vicksburg, Fort McHenry, Castillo de San Marcos, and others—when government administration was reorganized. In effect, the early emphasis on the military was the result of a bureaucratic dowry.

In another sense, however, this trend reflects an ongoing commitment to a portion of the American public that is drawn to battlefields. In fact, many sites were authorized long after the War Department had relinquished its properties: Horseshoe Bend and Pea Ridge (1956); Fort Davis and Fort Smith (1961); Andersonville (1970); Palo Alto (1978); War in the Pacific Historical Park (1978). It's no coincidence that of the last four chief historians of the Park Service—serving from the early 1960s to 1994—all professed research specialties of either the Western frontier or the Civil War.

Battles are grounded in sacrifice and tragedy. And tragedy is a common coin of the Park Service—provided, of course, the context is war and the battle itself is prideworthy. If victims are noted, it's to recall their sacrifice to patriotic ideals. George Custer was killed at the Little Bighorn—may we never forget. But Mystic, Connecticut; Bear River, Utah; Sand Creek, Colorado; even the Chinese disaster at Rock Springs, Wyoming, are scuffles of a different order: they are too uncomfortable to memorialize as national monuments, even if the losses involved were sometimes comparable to what passes as a major battle in American history.

Whether military or not, the Park Service's most cherished sites are intended as ennobling examples: here is the home of a president; here stands the residence of an inventor; here was born the slave who made good; here is the fort at the edge of civilization; here the battlefield where ideals were forged in blood. Let local bodies deal with stories of parochial interest or mine the exploits of the notorious. Above all, Park Service interpretation is marked by the ringing echo of the testimonial.

Sometimes the need to commemorate gets out of hand. The national monument in North Dakota remembering explorer Pierre de la Vérendrye was abolished in 1956 when it was concluded the site couldn't be verified as part of the Frenchman's eighteenth-century itinerary through the West. Still more noticeable names have been involved with official retractions. The NPS now admits in its promotional literature that the memorial home at George Washington's birthplace in Virginia doesn't even stand on the site of the original house. And the brochure for the site at Sinking Spring Farm in Kentucky allows that "the cabin displayed in the Memorial Building is probably not the birthplace cabin of Abraham Lincoln," earlier claims to the contrary.

More quiet alterations have also been made. When research in the 1960s failed to substantiate some of George Washington Carver's scientific discoveries, the bureau decided to focus on his humanitarian efforts instead. So it was that interpretation at the Carver birthplace in Missouri was subtly changed in order to avoid bruising racial sensitivities. The current brochure congratulates Carver for no discovery in particular, offering instead that "perhaps his greatest gift was a talent for drawing others into the spirit of his research."

Few people would question Carver's importance in American history—born a slave, he eventually committed his life to practical research and teaching people who had been systematically denied an education. What's more, his birthplace was the first specifically African American site to be included in the Park Service system (1943). His inclusion, however, is a reminder of how the bureau, ever conservative by nature, endorses a very traditional version of the role model. Booker T. Washington is memorialized with a monument, for example, but not Nat Turner or Charles Deslondes, leaders of slave rebellions. In fact, the NPS has specific sites dedicated to four former slaves (Washington, Carver, Douglass, and William Johnson), all of them male and all symbols of the national ethos of upward mobility, having pulled themselves up by their bootstraps to get a piece of the American Dream.

Even the most vocal critics will concede that the Park Service, largely funded through taxpayer revenues, isn't the master of its own fate. It can't create sites on its own, for example, nor can it appropriate money to administer them—both of these acts are the business of Congress. With some 20,000 total employees (only about 3500 are in uniform in the field), the bureau has had a hard time maintaining the sites under its current jurisdiction since the retrenchment of the Reagan years. Nonetheless, for a federal bureau mandated to administer sites that have "national significance," even the most cursory glance reveals that the Park Service map—whoever is responsible for drawing it—is characterized by an extremely narrow perspective.

Nowhere is this more evident than in the ethnic history of the Far West. Not until 1992, for example, did any national site tell the history of Japanese Americans. After some resistance within the NPS, Manzanar (California), a relocation camp during World War II, was finally included in the system. Such a long omission is perhaps explained by anti-Japanese feeling engendered by World War II, not to mention that a policy of interning part of the native-born population was not in the tradition of celebratory Park Service sites. But only one property (Golden Spike) pretends to treat the history of another group— Chinese Americans—and this, as noted earlier, is accomplished in a most perfunctory manner. It's not as though the Chinese are recent arrivals in America. It's also not as though their presence wasn't integral to the process of nation building during the nineteenth century. Their exclusion from the Park Service system is symbolic of at least two depressing trends.

First of all, since the Chinese were largely employed as agricultural and industrial laborers, the Park Service (and Congress) passed them over in favor of more "dramatic"—often military—sites. Second, the early experience of the Chinese makes for an embarrassing historic chapter, an important fact given the Park Service penchant for the testimonial. From Los Angeles to Rock Springs, Wyoming, from local labor unions to the halls of Congress, the Chinese were the object of organized mob violence and a series of discriminatory laws. If large immigrant numbers were decisive in making Ellis Island (New York) a national site while Angel Island (California) is not, it's a fortunate co-incidence for those who believe in an upbeat national narrative. The latter island, where immigrant Chinese were sometimes detained for years at a time, gives a less inspired context for America's huddled masses than does the Statue of Liberty National Monument.

The most prominent national events also seem arbitrarily weighted. Why, for example, is the Louisiana Purchase celebrated at the Jefferson National Expansion Memorial in St. Louis (by common admission one of the bureau's crown jewels), while the treaty of Guadalupe Hidalgo, which concluded the Mexican War, is nearly for-gotten? Neither "acquisition," so to speak, was formalized on Ameri-can soil. But both legally opened up large tracts of land to Anglo-American settlement and were crucial in the development of the West. (They also each cost $15 million). Rather than mark Guadalupe Hidalgo, however, the bureau celebrates the Chamizal Treaty of 1963, a happy end to a much less significant dispute. It remains to be seen whether, notwithstanding its sincere, though somewhat belated, in-

*Arch of triumph: Gateway Arch, part of the Jefferson
National Expansion Memorial, St. Louis, Missouri*

tentions, the Palo Alto battlefield will deal honestly with the legacy of
disputed borders.

The fact is, most Americans have a more romantic attachment to
Lewis and Clark (symbols of the Louisiana Purchase) than they do to
the Mexican War. The former pair is imbued with an impeccable reputation, having accomplished their expedition to great public acclaim
and incurred almost no losses in the doing. But there are other reasons for having a Museum of Westward Expansion in St. Louis rather
than, say, in Tucson or Albuquerque. In public history, as elsewhere,
there is safety in numbers. An occupational hazard of historic preservation is trying to avoid offending large constituencies, and it doesn't

take a demographer to realize that there are more Mexicans living in the Rio Grande Valley than there are Native Americans in St. Louis. The issue of historic ownership of land was easier to broach on the Mississippi than it was—and still is—on the Rio Grande.

Within the bureau, officials employ a company line to deflect criticism about site selection. "If we are a democracy," says Edwin Bearss, former chief historian of the bureau, "the creation of [sites] is reflected in Congress." In other words, the NPS is "given" sites to administer by the political process, a defense that echoes through the upper echelons of the service. There is truth in this: without solid congressional support, a bill proposing a new park would never even come to have a hearing. But given that the bureau considers potential sites years before they reach the legislative stage, such an argument is, at best, a half-truth. Although the Park Service doesn't handpick the sites it administers, it often nominates them very early for consideration and, in some circumstances, can block a potential one in the selection process.

The argument for congressional responsibility is repeated at the highest bureau levels. "When the Congress gets more Hispanic—people with Hispanic surnames in it—we're going to have . . . a larger recognition of these kinds of sites," adds Roger Kennedy, Park Service director since 1993. Enthusiastic about the New History, Kennedy emphasizes that the creation of sites is linked to congressional power, and therefore to population. Given their rising demographics, many Hispanics will no doubt find his prognosis a heartening one.

But the arithmetic of inclusion has a depressing side. If choosing historic sites is largely a reflection of demographics, what are we to say of those groups—Native Americans, Slovenes, Vietnamese, Amish —who comprise a small percentage of the population and whose numbers may be scattered across the country in even smaller pockets? Even if Hispanic numbers are on the rise, are they large enough to create change in the southeast, for example, where their history has been either ignored or romanticized beyond recognition? Still more troubling, if the selection of public sites is a function of numbers, historic preservation is a more self-serving pursuit than many citizens would have ever suspected.

Kennedy is still anxious to put the New History to work. "It isn't revisionist," he insists, "it's just more inclusive. . . . People keep dismissing anything they didn't know when they were twelve as revisionist." He shrugs, able to trade hats of the revisionist/traditional schools with the practiced hand of someone who's spent years in the spotlight. "I believe in teaching history through heroes. It's just you have to get a little broader reach of heroes," he allows, explaining that he'd like to see a W. E. B. Du Bois park and a Duke Ellington trail, or bring in a site such as Sand Creek to give balance to other "cannonball parks" in the system.

"The only way that large institutions get altered over time," says Kennedy, "is by staying optimistic." Indeed, the NPS mandate of national chest-thumping has started to change in the past fifteen years. Wounded Knee, South Dakota, where two hundred Sioux men, women, and children were killed by the Army in 1890, is currently being considered for admission into the system as the first tribally controlled park in the country. What's more, a number of parks established since the late 1970s—Lowell, Women's Rights, Manzanar—suggest that the Park Service is willing to acknowledge "casualties" other than military ones in the national narrative. Perhaps women did wait a long time to get the vote. Perhaps Japanese Americans were discriminated against during the war. Perhaps the mills that made us an industrial giant were unbearable sweatshops for some. To acknowledge such people is not to bow to the fad of victimology. Much at Lowell and Women's Rights, whatever their shortcomings, is about the active agency of people seeking to change their lives through organized reform.

The new sites reflect another change in attitude that may or may not indicate things to come. In preserving places that recall integral communities (not just battlefields or presidential homes) the bureau better reflects the perspective of social history. At the few earlier sites given to populist movements—Homestead National Monument, for example—little sense is given of the human cost, the ethnic rivalries, and the powerful business forces that made any such endeavor precarious. Current plans for remembering the Underground Railroad and the western settlement of Nicodemus, Kansas, for example, may be representative of a new vision in the Park Service.

Kennedy isn't cowed by bureau shortcomings, real or imagined. While he concedes that the criteria for site acceptance (that is, "national significance") may be skewed against some groups, he also says that "it's giving up the game before the game gets started" to let that stop anyone from reinterpreting the rules. As he puts it, Women's Rights park "is there because it represents a forced alteration of the criteria for significance"—not because the convention of 1848 had any immediate political fallout. Sometimes an event becomes significant in retrospect, Kennedy explains, a call for continually redefining the bureau's turf.

Such a principle works both ways, however. If some sites gain in symbolic importance, others may erode. The NPS brochure for the DeSoto Memorial in Florida, for example, reflects how hard it is to rationalize the existence of some sites in changing interpretive terrain. DeSoto's mission, the brochure confesses, was a "futile" one that was "inconsequential" for Spain and "disastrous" for Indian peoples. The operating budget for 1993 was a quarter of a million dollars, another reminder that while books go in and out of print, monuments are (more or less) permanent alterations of the landscape. Worse still could be said for many "park barrel" projects over the years, pushed through more as a means of economic development than as sites of genuine importance. One of these—Steamtown National Historic Site in Scranton, Pennsylvania—has generated considerable doubt even among railroad scholars about its historic significance. With few exceptions, "once a park, always a park"—a tribute to the obdurate nature of memorials as much as to any notions of historical permanence.

A proposed structural realignment for the NPS is yet another sign that times may be changing. Kennedy believes that the restructuring will give park superintendents more control over interpretation and less accountability to the Washington bureaucracy, a blunt and unwieldy instrument. But such a realignment won't significantly change the way sites are chosen. Nor will it alter appropriations to the various parks, based as they are, in large part, on raw visitation numbers. (The more people who visit a site, the more money is appropriated— a self-fulfilling prophecy for park development.) Almost eighty years old, the Park Service has learned, like any self-respecting bureaucracy, to look after its own. The tendency of any large organization to harden and ossify is its greatest enemy in promoting a narrative that will reach out to people who do not see themselves reflected at national sites.

THE HISTORIC ROAD MARKER: A CASE STUDY

Emphasized at federal sites, military history is also a favorite at the state level. Virginia, for one, lays claim to being the field of battle for two major wars, a fact evident to any tourist who bothers to travel its byways for long. The state instituted one of the nation's first historical highway marker programs in the 1920s, and had twelve hundred signs in place by the following decade. The first markers were meant to be read by people puttering by in an age when automobile speeds weren't much more than a sprightly crawl. Later the state added pull-offs where people could get a longer look at the story without fear of being rear-ended in mid-sentence. Today's travelers might even find a shade tree and a picnic table for their trouble.

Although a local tourist motto has it that "Virginia is for lovers," it's a claim hardly borne out by the Commonwealth road markers. Of some sixteen hundred signs installed since the 1920s, hundreds detail the campaigns of the American Revolution and Civil War. Many, to be sure, explain encounters crucial to the fate of the nation: the siege of Richmond, the battles of Petersburg and Yorktown. But others concern matters a little less pressing: the place where Stonewall Jackson's army halted to rest one morning in 1862; the site where Jubal Early's troops crossed the road before the battle of Winchester; the road where the Marquis de Lafayette passed on his way to protect the stores of Albemarle from the devious Colonel Tarleton. Spared the usual cliché of "George Washington slept here," tourists in the Old Dominion find a marker program that details the minutiae of military tactics.

Once the major wars are exhausted, there are plenty of others to draw from. On Route 16, near Tazewell, I find a marker titled "Indian Outrages"—a tabloid headline likely to entice bored or weary drivers to pull over for the rest of the story. "Four miles south the first Indian attack in the Upper Clinch Valley took place, September 8, 1774," it reads. "John Henry was wounded and his wife and children were carried into captivity. In 1781, Indians attacked the house of Robert Maxwell, near here, and killed two girls." In three sentences is compressed all the woe of Old Deerfield. White settlement was impeded, a woman abducted, children captured and killed. The cast-iron marker I saw had the plaint of a roadside tombstone.

I came to find that the outrage in the Clinch Valley was no exception. There were other signs like the one near Tazewell: "Indian Massacre," "First Indian Fight," another "Indian Massacre," "Last Indian Raid," another "Indian Massacre," another "Indian Outrage," and, for good measure, "Last Indian Outrage." Obviously, Virginia had had a bloody time of it with the natives. Of the roughly 130 signs in the state system mentioning Native Americans, two-thirds of them describe or allude to violent attacks. Samuel Cowan was killed and scalped by Cherokees. Eight people were killed by the Piscataways at the Thomas Barton home. Unidentified Indians massacred the family of Archibald Scott. If you think television is violent, try traveling America's blue highways.

Numerous signs record the mounting toll of settlers who perished in Indian massacres—hundreds, if one bothers to do a body count. In the entire marker system of the Commonwealth, however, only two signs (one no longer standing) mention Indians being killed by white settlers. One notes that "many" died at the hands of rebel Nathaniel Bacon in 1676; the other allows that an Indian war party, having led an attack on settlers, later came to be "exterminated"—a word with rather unfortunate connotations. Although many signs take pride in Virginia's "Indian fighters," the fruit of their labors isn't described with anything near the relish accorded the work of their capable enemies.

From my study of Virginia markers, I began to fashion a hypothesis: although some kinds of violence are exemplary, others are unfit for public consumption. One can drive a long way in the Old Dominion, for example, without ever seeing a sign that recalls a lynching. Indeed, Commonwealth markers admit only two such examples, and those are chosen with considerable care. One notes that Tories were summarily punished in 1780 by patriot Charles Lynch, who thus lent his name to the infamous word for mob justice; in the other, a "Negro" guide was hanged during the 1864 campaign for Richmond for allegedly betraying his army. Worth noting is that the "army" in question was the federal, not the Confederate, one. In Virginia, where over sixty lynchings—with both black victims and white—took place between 1880 and 1900 alone, the only summary execution of the century worthy of mention was ordered by a Yankee colonel named Dahlgren.

The lynching examples, of course, are "safe" by design. No one is likely to be offended by the memory of Tories being whipped by a colonial martinet, nor is the hanging of a "Negro" likely to stir up explosive memories when, after all, it was ordered in wartime by an unscrupulous invader. In sum, the casualties of cruel Indian raids in the Clinch Valley are remembered as martyrs; those of kangaroo courts convened by white-sheeted posses are forgotten as the unfortunate victims of a bygone era. Although regrettable, the conclusion is no less obvious: not all victims of violence are created equal in the public marker system of Virginia.

What value could there be in remembering such awful events? Perhaps none. The only thing worse than stringing up someone from a tree may be to accord the incident a place in our public memory. But why should we memorialize the killing of David Musick by Indians in 1792, and fail to note that George Towler of Pittsylvania County was murdered by a mob in January 1892 for the crime of—miscegenation? In short, why recall the outrages of one culture while suppressing those of another? Whatever its fascination with pitched battles, the Commonwealth has bowdlerized the story of statewide violence to exclude incidents now deemed inflammatory or embarrassing.

The massacre signs went up in the 1920s and 1930s, says John Salmon, staff historian and manager of the state marker system for the Department of Historic Resources in Richmond. Although Salmon regards the signs as "indecent," he adds reluctantly that "we haven't really done much of anything" to change them, either. "They make it sound like a drive-by shooting," he says, explaining that context for the "massacres" is rarely given. But Salmon cautions that the signs are of historic value to the communities near them, and that, what's more, he's never had a complaint about one from a native person. He doesn't like the idea of balancing history by adding markers with the opposite slant—"Indian Village Massacred Here"—but believes that existing signs could be changed to reflect new sensibilities. The only question is, as always, who will pay for it?

In 1976, the state ended its funding for highway markers, turning over financial responsibility to the private and local public sectors. Today signs are proposed and funded by, among others, private citizens, churches, historic societies, and local governments. Now, Salmon says, "the whole program is much more inclusive and open to the public," a system that "forces a partnership" between the Commonwealth and the public at large. But correcting the omissions of history can be an expensive task. Salmon says it costs $1,050 to have a sign cast in aluminum and erected at a safe spot on the road, not exactly pocket change for the average citizen. Virginia's marker system is thus a kind of public history by auction.

Aside from money, there are few obstacles. Salmon, who screens and edits proposals, says the vast majority are approved by the Board of Historic Resources, provided the building or event can be shown to have had state or national significance and is at least fifty years old. The system, in fact, is tailor-made for organizations that can raise contributions from a large member base. The Harriet Tubman Historic Society of Delaware, for example, sponsored a sign marking the arrival of the first Africans in Jamestown. But the Indian population of the area is very small. The "outrages" of Indians, as a result, have stayed put. The only Indian marker that's been removed by order of the board, Salmon adds, described an ancient burial mound that turned out to be a natural formation.

Since most of the markers were put up in the first two decades of the system, however, the heavy hand of public morality is apparent. Although military campaigns are intricately detailed, mob violence isn't even worthy of mention—except, it turns out, when the state itself is threatened. Several markers denote failed insurrections—the Nat Turner revolt (1831), the Gabriel revolt (1800), the indentured servants' plot (1663), the Powhatan massacre (1622), most of these alleging that greater violence was averted when a loyal slave, servant, or Indian revealed the treachery to neighbors just in time. In short, the depiction of violence in the Commonwealth depends on who's doing the giving and the getting. When the state is threatened, mob justice—otherwise ignored—becomes worthy of contemplation as a parable on public law and order.

No doubt charges of political correctness will fill the air. But Virginia should take solace in the fact that it hasn't even begun to explore the ironies of its own past. If Indian fighters are a favorite theme, why not give the ladies a chance? There's Mad Ann Bailey of Staunton, an indentured servant who avenged the murder of her husband by dressing in men's clothes, taking up the hatchet, and killing any number of local natives before she died at the ripe old age of eighty-three. If the state is so keen on marking Indian outrages, it should at least do us the favor of remembering the most significant ones—such as Big Springs (1764), where between fifty and sixty white settlers lost their lives. If the state should fully own up to an embarrassment such as slaveholding, for example, it should consider the case of Anthony Johnson, the founder of one of the first black communities in Virginia who was himself a slaveholder and deserving of some mention as a colonial entrepreneur of color.

At present adding some twenty new signs every year, Virginia is still in search of its past—especially the African American variety. A new replacement marker noting the Turner slave revolt, for example, discreetly avoids the word "massacre," this time adding that not only white people but blacks as well were killed in the insurrection. What's more, many signs put up since the 1970s have noted places of importance in the history of black education, a welcome change from the usual roster of battlefield maneuvers. The black population of the area is making itself felt.

Adding new signs is easy; the markers are hard to change once they've been sunk in the ground. "They have value of their own as artifacts," admits Salmon of the older signs, noting that some communities are attached to the markers telling Indian stories that went up seventy years ago, by now certified antiques in their own right. In Virginia, as in other states, it's not, as George Orwell once imagined, the nightmare of statist history altered at will. In cast aluminum and iron, the stories of the past—right or wrong—can become almost impossible to revise.

OLD MODELS AND NEW

Just as the Great Depression was about to strike in 1929, Henry Ford opened the granddaddy of large-scale American preservation efforts near Detroit, Michigan. In the village of Greenfield, today surrounded by the concrete sprawl of auto factories in urban Dearborn, Ford imported everything from the Wright brothers' bicycle shop to Thomas Edison's Menlo Park laboratory in a small-town testimonial to America's "common man." Visitors to Greenfield can still amble by an antebellum plantation from Maryland set down next to a colonial New England dwelling just a few steps from a Greek Revival frame owned by Noah Webster. Girdled by railroad tracks (no additional charge for riding the trains), Greenfield resembles a life-size Monopoly Board for travel buffs tired of just reading about the good old days.

There's a little something for everyone at Greenfield. A gristmill. A millinery. A machine shop and foundry. A memorial home to George Washington Carver. Two brick slave quarters from Georgia that sit across the street from, of all things, the Stephen Foster Memorial Home, whose front plaque waxes poetic about "Camptown Races" and "My Old Kentucky Home." Meanwhile, horse-drawn buggies

*My old Kentucky home: transplanted slave cabins at
Greenfield Village, Dearborn, Michigan*

carry tourists down streets lined with antique lamps and shady hard-
woods. Chock full of real "artifacts," Greenfield is a complete fabrication, a piece of depression-era social history concocted by one of
America's favorite sons in the guise of a small New England town.
Spanning centuries in its exhibits, Greenfield celebrates America's
spirit of invention, embodied by men like Ford who, in spite of modest origins, used their native genius for the benefit of humankind.

Much of our public history is driven by the notion of models such
as Greenfield. These models take many forms, from the H&O trains of
railroad buffs to the full-scale replica of a pre-industrial New England
village such as Old Sturbridge; from pioneer museums with log cabin
reproductions to restored Southern antebellum estates. Whatever
their scale, the models serve to entertain and reassure us. Their purpose isn't so much to mirror the past as it is to consciously rebuild
it—a feat that requires, at the very least, an act of feigned omni-
science. From Williamsburg to Deerfield to Plimoth Plantation, to "restore" has often meant to recreate an entire ambiance, not just a
patch of garden or an isolated home. In offering such communities for
scrutiny, we argue, implicitly, that we understand them—which demands a large leap of faith on the part of the visiting public.

Too often the implication has been that the model (reconstruction) should serve as a model (ideal) for public beliefs or behavior. It seems difficult to reconstruct what a place was like without somehow imposing a sense of what we wish it had been like at the same time. Confusion, dissent, aberrance, decay, and death are not in the blueprints of most public curators as a result. The upshot is that many aspects of social history are eclipsed in the places specifically designed to tell us about them. Reimagined for the general public, the historic community becomes sanitized and idyllic, a haven from doubt and controversy to a degree that would probably have baffled its original inhabitants.

But rather than tell the history of the unskilled, the immigrant, the servant, the miner, the mechanic, or the field slave, we've mounted a selective national narrative of the "typical." The replicas of a few chosen communities—from Williamsburg to New Harmony to Sturbridge to Pleasant Hill—are perhaps "typical" in their approximation of daily life for a given locale—usually inhabited by a middle-class population. But in their sum, they offer a poor reflection of the mass of people who built America. Although one can find an occasional reconstructed Indian village, for example, it would almost come as a shock to find a living Freedman's Village from the 1860s, a Spanish frontier community, a Chinese railroad camp, or a New England factory town with spinning looms and a hunkered-down proletariat.

The rationale for the public site has changed little since Greenfield opened. Our monuments are still intended to be "inspiring"; to revere heroic ancestors more than understand their complexity; to forget the invisible labor of those who built much of the environment; to anchor us in a comfortable past, even if that past requires a carefully scaled replica to hide its flaws. Our desire is to have heroes who, though imperfect, are tragic because of the circumstances that crushed them, not because of personal shortcomings or the usual tonic of hubris. This is as true in our appraisal of George Washington as it is of Crazy Horse, Frederick Douglass, Junípero Serra, or Elizabeth Cady Stanton.

The devoted visitor to public sites may confront, over time, a baffling question: If our ancestors were so worthy, how did we ever come to find ourselves in such a mess? For all the rewards of nostalgia, this is its most damaging legacy—it keeps the humanity of our ancestors a secret. As a result, certain subjects at historic sites are driven underground, if not forbidden outright: venereal disease; the sexual mixing of races; domestic violence; state-supported persecution; dissent from cultural norms; and your common, everyday garden variety of human failure. I think of how much in our past, as a result, is untold. Issues that remain virtually off limits include the immense toll of disease, even on the battlefield; changing attitudes toward death; the use of contraceptives; and the virtual invention of childhood as a stage of human life. We've restored countless forts and towns and mansions across the country; is it within our grasp to rebuild a line of shacks and tell about the people who inhabited them, whether they lived on a plantation, in a railroad yard, on a mission ranch, or a factory community?

In the end, our public history subsists on a teetering irony. With few exceptions, it is a profession dedicated to the history of the Few (the material culture of the middle and upper classes), as told by the Few (the curatorial establishment, recruited from the same groups), for the betterment of the Many. Told by the Park Service or various states, it's the ultimate example of engineered mass consumption—a form of popular culture created by the government and consumed by a largely captive audience. Public history has, however, this difference: advanced as "official" culture, it has a status denied most images that fill the mass media. It's easy to distrust the manipulations of Madison Avenue; harder to visit James Madison's mansion at Montpelier (Virginia) and begin to inquire systemically why hardly a scrap of evidence is present about the people who built and ran the house where the fourth president retired.

Simply put, preservation is *for* the average middle-class visitor— not *about* the average historical subject. Ours is a kind of consumer social history, where the lowest common denominator (an eighth-grade education) is judged to be the locus of discussion. Most curators (and the organizations that employ them) would like to reach the broadest possible audience while confining their efforts to the lives of people who owned artifacts of scale (houses, furniture, weapons) intended to overwhelm visitors with feelings of awe and envy. Manual laborers—of any race or ethnicity—although present in spirit through the mansions, gardens, churches, and machines they built, are an embarrassment, both to preservationists and to the well-heeled public to whom they traditionally cater, because of the dim memory of the conditions under which they labored. Although their descendants may be welcome to visit such sites, their historic presence is still laden with guilt and fear for many public historians, bent as they are on maintaining the venerable preserve of "culture."

THE PROBLEM WITH DISNEY'S CRITICS

Once upon a time, the many pasts of America were to be assembled into a theme park in northern Virginia owned and operated by the beloved Walt Disney Company. Plans announced in late 1993 allowed for the ultimate historical theme park—Disney's America—complete with Lewis and Clark raft ride, Native American village, Civil War battle reenactments, and antique steam trains that would deposit thirty thousand visitors a day at the hundred-acre core site. The company that brought you Fess Parker as Davy Crockett promised that the story of America's native peoples would be told with sensitivity; the creators of *Song of the South* assured us the saga of African Americans could faithfully unfold in an atmosphere of family entertainment. Cynical culture critics, many with good reason, took to Disney-bashing with near cartoonish delight.

Many questions arose after a perusal of the preliminary park plan. Would the Presidents' Square, for example, remind us that Jefferson and Washington were plagued by runaway slaves? Would the Victory Field honoring our military past bother to mention the Mexican War? Would the factory town complete with roller-coaster ride also give us a bird's eye view of a labor strike—and a group of black or Chinese workers called in to cross picket lines? Would the Civil War battle reenactments remind us that over half the casualties of the war were caused by disease, not gunfire? The site, in Prince William County, was eventually killed by organized opposition in 1994, but more for environmental than ideological reasons. As the Disney people scout Virginia for another choice piece of land, the issue of a historic theme park is still alive.

Although professional reactions ranged from the dubious to the derisory, there are those who think Disney may offer a credible vehicle for popularizing social history. "Historians, I am afraid, have often abdicated their responsibility to the public," charges James Horton, a professor of history at George Washington University and a Disney theme-park consultant. "We only—in many cases—provide history to those who are willing to pay big prices for it," he says. Although

Disney tickets aren't a cheap day for a vacationing family of six, Horton points out that the academy, with skyrocketing tuition rates, has made history a high-priced commodity. For him, the separate worlds of academia and public history might find a plausible fusion in, of all things, the company that brought us *Spin and Marty, Bambi,* and *Pollyana.*

"I think Disney has a golden opportunity here to redefine the way that public history is presented," says Horton, excited by the prospects of commercial history but no less cognizant of the ironies involved. "Nixon was able to open China because he was Nixon," he notes confidently. "Disney might be able to do this because they're Disney." Horton concedes that Disney's track record with historical subjects is far from exemplary, but he's heartened by signs of change, citing as examples the refurbished Hall of Presidents at Disney World and the more mature scope of films the company has produced in recent years.

It will take more than one man's enthusiasm to convince skeptics that Disney should be doing American history on a grand scale. But Horton's boosterism contrasts with the usual reaction: it's become very fashionable to mock the Disneyfication of history. Many people in preservation circles expressed doubts to me about Disney even proposing such a project. But the more I visited historic sites, the more the Disney idea didn't seem to contradict public history trends so much as it merely exaggerated them. If the theme park's format seemed a commercial parody, it was still drawing on the same fund of myths that the Park Service, the Smithsonian, and many nonprofit corporations have subsisted on for decades. Pointing the finger at Disney in the historic preservation community seemed, the more I thought about it, a decisive act of self-preservation.

After all, the Disney dream didn't materialize out of nothing. From the beginning, Disney has capitalized—in every sense of the word— on our most naive national myths. "Frontierland" in Anaheim is unthinkable without the siege mentality that consecrated shrines such as the Alamo and the Little Bighorn. The idea of including slavery at a theme park, while potentially callous, is at least more honest than the benign indifference displayed to it at popular sites such as the Hermitage and Mount Vernon. Using a steam railroad as a time-travel machine may be lightweight history, but it doesn't contradict the romantic Iron Horse depicted in most of our museums. Disney's was an idea in the tradition of Greenfield Village, the railroad surrounding the mythical small town that all Americans could momentarily possess—for a price.

The world of historic preservation pretended to be horrified at the thought of so commercializing history. But their desire to distance themselves from Disney was a way to occlude many of the similarities their organizations share with the for-profit sector. First, many nonprofits are admission-driven, and therefore sensitive to the specialized public they serve, whether at Williamsburg or Plimoth Plantation. Not scaring away a middle-class audience (largely white) is uppermost in the minds of people responsible for interpretation, though Plimoth is much bolder than most. At numerous private sites I visited, I was matter-of-factly told that when ethnic groups had sufficient disposable income to visit, they would probably come to have a higher interpretive profile—evidence, if any were needed, of the marketplace at work in the nonprofit sector.

Second, the independence of nonprofits is not to be confused with neutrality. Many have innocuous-sounding mission statements that conceal the most traditional of vested interests. In fact, large nonprofits operate with budget surpluses that would be the envy of many a private corporation. The Mount Vernon Ladies' Association, blessed with a thirty-million-dollar endowment, earned over two million dollars from investments and capital gains alone during fiscal year 1993. While the Ladies expand interpretive programs rather than distribute profits, they have the investment portfolio of a prosperous business. It seems a crowning irony that exemption from state and federal income taxes ("public" monies) has inured so many nonprofits from discussing what would have been the "public" at many a historic site—whether in a cloister, cotton field, or utopian community.

Third, a reliance on corporate funding has made it hard to discuss elements that may be sensitive to sponsors, as in the case of rail museums telling industrial history. Even when a benefactor has no obvious motives in giving money, it's worth considering the ironies of largesse. Mount Vernon, for example, recently received its largest individual cash donation in history, a million-dollar pledge from entrepreneur Alfred Taubman. The owner of A&W restaurants and Sotheby's art auctioneers, Taubman is also a major developer of shopping malls across the country. In fact, the pleasant, bucolic retreat of

Washington's home has a benefactor who made part of his fortune through fast-food and shopping malls—two icons of popular culture that Disney itself has come to exemplify, and just the kind of places one goes to Mount Vernon to escape.

Fourth, even sacred shrines—from Washington's tomb to the chapel of the Alamo heroes—thrive on a whopping souvenir trade. There may be nothing wrong with "history by souvenir," but the employers of public historians have become expert at hawking them. It's not just the odd Freedom rifle or coonskin cap, but the Winkin' George Washington banks, the Southern-belle dolls, the glow-in-the-dark rosaries, and the mock tombstones of the Seventh Cavalry sold to help enlarge Little Bighorn battlefield under the auspices of the Department of the Interior. The nonprofit and public sectors stay afloat from the most tried-and-true commercial ploys—not a damnable fact in itself, but a reminder that they are less lofty and disinterested than one might assume. If there are problems with the Walt Disney Company, at least we are not in any doubt about its motive.

While most are billed as nonprofit, nondenominational, or state organizations, the choice of sites these entities develop and the manner in which they do so suggest an exclusive clientele. Most of all, they appeal to a moneyed class; even those who don't charge admission preserve the lifestyles of those who, regardless of the time and place, were to the manor born. Of course, Disney World itself is too expensive an entertainment for many working people to indulge. But poorer folk, whether or not they're charged admission, have never been the main public of the Smithsonian, the Park Service, Monticello, or Williamsburg. The real Disneyfication of our history began many decades ago.

The melting pot, the mosaic, the salad bowl—old metaphors used to describe the American experience—may fall like dominoes before the one Disney wants to edify in Virginia: the shopping mall as history. The mall, like the mosaic, is rife with variety and choice, but it comes with a commercial twist that portends, if nothing else, a kind of social history of the marketplace, perhaps a unique American contribution to the field of public history. Although I don't welcome such a development with open arms, the narrow self-interest of many professionally curated sites has made the transgressions of Disney even more likely to dominate. However sterile and two-dimensional,

Disney's proposed reinvention of the past is a response, in part, to the failures of the public museum to democratize history and engage a broader audience.

EPILOGUE

There are ways in which paying homage is a selfish act. Ancestor worship has, for all its virtues, a vampish streak of self-aggrandizement. The line between traditional filiopiety and the new culturally affirming "roots" can, at times, be a fine one. Although genealogy has long been seen as an affirmative pursuit, logic will tell us that there's a Cain in the closet for every portrait of Abel we hang in the front hall. We rarely stop to consider how tangled our roots really are.

This has never been more true than today, when categories of race and gender in America seem to be permanent badges of identity. But the Indian battle, we know, encouraged strange alliances wherever the frontier shifted. The blend of black and white on the plantation, further confusing our identities, is still too painful a memory for many of us to discuss. The mission was a melding of people so thorough that, in some places, the different strands can hardly be separated any longer. There is little of race and culture that is "pure" in our story, from the descendants of Uncas and Somerset Place to the dreamers of New Harmony and the San Antonio missions.

Our past has always been multicultural, even if some sites have been slow to admit it. As minorities increase in number, we can expect their stories to be better represented. But such an improvement still seems a timid concession to the pull of demography and disposable income, the invisible hands that guide our most dedicated public historians. In its most literal sense, the change in numbers may bear out an old saw: maybe the "winner" does write history after all. But from the Capitol building in Washington to Castillo San Marcos to Mount Vernon and Monticello—put up, in large part, by gangs of forced labor—the reminders are everywhere that the loser builds it, a fact that most sites are happy to have us forget when we check our hats at the door.

Finding a way to retell our history won't be easy. Much of the critique denouncing the excesses of "Western culture" has attempted to repossess certain of its accomplishments, presumably for safekeeping. The "paternity suits" that mark many such challenges only deepen an already outworn tradition. A woman, not Eli Whitney, is now said to have invented the cotton gin; a black man, I learn at one museum, actually invented the golf tee; in a more substantive case, the Iroquois Confederacy is credited with having founded the principles of American democracy. Perhaps. All, to varying degrees, are worthy of consideration. But true or false, they suggest that "alternative" perspectives can become stuck in the very assumptions they set out to question in the first place, not an auspicious sign for the broader concerns of social history.

Telling minority history is full of irony—in many cases, the group involved was not a minority at all, whether in a local or regional sense. Only historic circumstance has made the Pequots a tiny group in Connecticut; Mexican Americans, while a minority nationwide, are a majority in San Antonio. Our conception of minorities seems shallow as a result. Nowhere is this more apparent than in our failure to plumb the variety within such groups, the stories of "unconventional minorities," if you will—blacks who owned slaves or fought to subdue Indians on the frontier; Spanish settlers who resented the power of the missions; Native people who fought other tribes for gain and glory. It is also apparent even in the case of the "majority"—white women, for example, who gladly homesteaded land in Indian Territory. Our history is filled with loners and strange bedfellows, many acting out of motives more complex than the usual excuse of "cultural oppression."

There are whole groups of people—of all colors—missing in action from the landscape of public history. The harsh lot of white indentured servants, for example, is rarely mentioned on the plantation. The phenomenon of child labor, commonplace through most of our history, is only reluctantly noted. The close rapport between prostitution and the U.S. Army in the winning of the trans–Mississippi West might as well have the censor's stamp on it at most restored fortifications.

For all its rewards, social history makes for a difficult task. People have to pass beyond the usual house tour to ask the simple but demanding question, "Who did the work here, and under what conditions?" Our curiosity about who may have inhabited the White House in 1820 should also include an appreciation of those who built it. In the end, any object, in addition to being enjoyed for its function or beauty, can reveal a whole world to us if we ask the right questions. Even a simple cupboard can lead us to talk about the craftspeople who built it; the kind of community they lived in; where the raw materials were found; how the object was transported for sale; who moved the piece up from the dock; what kind of god their children believed in; and how the owner accumulated the wealth that permitted him (or her) to buy it in the first place. In so doing, how the other half lived may one day truly come to be a part of the public domain.

Acknowledgments

In writing this book, I owe a debt to scores of people. Many of those generous enough to grant me interviews appear in the course of these pages. Whether or not they agree with my assessment of public history, I want to thank them again for their cooperation.

Many others with whom I spoke and corresponded do not appear in the book, though their contributions were significant. Not surprisingly, a number are employed by the National Park Service. Among my valuable sources were Barry Mackintosh, Dwight Pitcaithley, Corky Mayo, and Sandra Webber in Washington; Martin Blatt and Kelly Fellner at Lowell NHP; Hovey Cowles at San Antonio Missions NHP; Doug Murphy and Aaron Mahr at Palo Alto Battlefield NHS; John Reid, Horseshoe Bend NMP; Rick Wilson, Golden Spike NHS; Doug McChristian, Little Bighorn NM; Laura Appler, Homestead NM; Brian Peters, Kingsley Plantation; Art Gomez, Glenn Kaye, and Neil Mangum, Southwest Regional Office. Without them, my task would have been immensely more difficult.

My gratitude extends beyond the Park Service to the following people as well: Walter Gray, the California State Railroad Museum; James Dilts and Herb Harwood, associates of the B&O Railroad Museum, and John Hankey, formerly of the same; Don Snoddy, the Union Pacific Museum; Jean Lee, Historic New Harmony, Inc.; Sister Barbara Jackson, San Antonio de Pala mission; Mary Whalen, San Luis Rey mission; Melinda Plourde-Cole, Southeastern Connecticut Peace and Justice Coalition; Richard Clifford, Connecticut Depart-

215

ment of Environmental Protection; Elizabeth Lodge, Plimoth Plantation; Gary Thompson, Springfield Center, New York; Rayna Green, the American Indian Program at the Smithsonian Institution; Susan Parker, Historic St. Augustine Preservation Board; Charles Albi, Colorado Railroad Museum; Thomas Davidson, Jamestown Settlement; Richard Curilla, Alamo Village; and Jim McBride, Rancho de las Golondrinas in New Mexico.

I thank Fiona McCrae for her encouragement in starting me on this project, and my editor, Betsy Uhrig, for her many suggestions that improved the manuscript. I also thank Gregory Burnham, Rosemarie Scharfe, and Sam Girgus for their critical commentary, and the steady work of my correspondents, Alan and Richard Drover. The staff and holdings of the Library of Congress were also critical to my research from the beginning.

Finally, I extend a warm thanks to friends and family who put me up on my many journeys. The greatest debt I owe to my parents, whose own love of writing and history enabled me to imagine this book.

Endnotes

to tell the story. Custer Battlefield: A History and Guide to the Battle of the Little Bighorn, Robert Utley (Washington, D.C.: U.S. Department of Interior, 1988), p. 9.

For a detailed discussion of recent changes at the battlefield, see *Sacred Ground: Americans and Their Battlefields,* Edward Linenthal (Urbana, Illinois: University of Illinois Press, 1991).

simply wild, open land. Congressional Record, Volume LXXII-part 3 (Washington, D.C.: U.S. Government Printing Office, 1930), p. 2962.

the Indians herein named. Indian Affairs: Laws and Treaties, Volume 2. Compiled by Charles Kappler. Senate Document No. 452, 57th Congress, 1903, p. 776.

For a further discussion of land issues in Crow country, see *Apsaalooka: The Crow Nation Then and Now,* Lloyd Mickey Old Coyote and Helene Smith (Greensburg, Pennsylvania: MacDonald/Sward, 1993).

unsettled country in America. From original text at Horseshoe Bend museum.

For a recent reading of Fort Mims, see *Creeks and Seminoles: The Destruction and Regeneration of the Muscogulge People,* J. Leitch Wright, Jr. (Lincoln: University of Nebraska Press, 1986). On the Creek War, see *Struggle for the Gulf Borderlands: The Creek War and the Battle of New Orleans 1812–1815,* Frank Owsly, Jr. (Gainesville: University Presses of Florida, 1981).

sickness of his hands. The Papers of Andrew Jackson, Volume 3, 1814–1815, Harold Moser et al., editors (Knoxville: University of Tennessee Press, 1991), p. 71.

For U.S. Army casualties, see "Indian-United States Military Situation, 1848-1891," Robert Utley. In Volume 4, ("History of Indian-White Relations") in *Handbook of North American Indians*, (Washington, D.C.: Smithsonian Institution, 1988), p. 174.

of its early history. Historic Deerfield: An Introduction, (Deerfield: 1992), p. 2.

local history and preservation. Visitor Orientation Program, video, Historic Deerfield.

killed my Negro man. The Redeemed Captive, John Williams. Edward Clark, editor (Amherst: University of Massachusetts Press, 1976), p. 48.

For an account of slavery in Deerfield, see *A History of Deerfield, Massachusetts,* George Sheldon (Deerfield: New Hampshire Publishing Company, 1972), Volume 2, pp. 888–905.

to forget their past. Historic Deerfield, p. 3.

For a detailed discussion of Frances Slocum, see *The Lost Sister Among the Miamis,* Otho Winger (Elgin, Illinois: The Elgin Press, 1936).

him, than to Massasoit. Of Plymouth Plantation, William Bradford (Franklin Center, Pennsylvania: The Franklin Library, 1983), p. 96. Bradford's account of Plymouth is among the most detailed, along with *Mourt's Relation,* William Bradford and Edward Winslow (New York: Garrett Press, 1969). See also "Squanto: Last of the Patuxets," in *Struggle and Survival in Colonial America,* David Sweet and Gary Nash, editors (Berkeley: University of California Press, 1981).

could hardly passe along. Newes From America. John Underhill (New York: Da Capo Press, 1971) p. 40.

to Hell that day. A Relation of the Troubles Which Have Hapned in New England, Increase Mather (New York: Arno Press, 1972), p. 47.

and did great Service. A Brief History of the Pequot War, John Mason (Freeport, New York: Books for Libraries Press, 1971), p. 5. For a good secondary source, see *Manitou and Providence,* Neal Salisbury (New York: Oxford University Press, 1982).

Chapter 2

For comparison of immigrant numbers, see *Who Built America?: Working People and the Nation's Economy, Politics, Culture, and Society,* Bruce Levine et al. (New York: Pantheon Books, 1989), Volume 1, p. 19. For figures on black population, see *American Slavery: 1619–1877,* Peter Kolchin (New York: Hill and Wang, 1993), pp. 240–245.

answered the final summons. Mount Vernon: A Handbook (Mount Vernon, Virginia: The Mount Vernon Ladies' Association, 1985), p. 76.

Ibid., p. 21.

it can be avoided. The Writings of George Washington, John Fitzpatrick, editor (Washington, D.C.: U.S. Government Printing Office, 1940), Volume 35, p. 202.

talks pretty broad. Fitzpatrick, Volume 3, p. 289.

remained in Washington's family. Slave Testimony: Two Centuries of Letters, Speeches, Interviews, and Autobiographies, John Blassingame, editor (Baton Rouge: Louisiana State University Press, 1977), p. 249.

measure, leading to it. Fitzpatrick, Volume 34, p. 154.

finest in the world. Arlington House. National Park Service brochure, Department of the Interior (Washington, D.C.: U.S. Government Printing Office).

the heathen around us. Slaves No More: Letters From Liberia, 1833–1869, Bell Wiley, editor (Lexington: University Press of Kentucky, 1980), p. 199.

as model lodging houses. Letters From Canada and the United States, George Tuthill Borrett (London: J. E. Adlard, Bartholomew Close, 1865), p. 233.

at the gardener's house. Monmouth Plantation: A Dream in Time (Los Angeles: Timothy Perior, 1989), p. 43.

is still in him. The Papers of Andrew Jackson, Harold Moser et al., editors (Knoxville: University of Tennessee Press, 1991), Volume 3, p. 213.

weak and less privileged. Andrew Jackson's Hermitage, (Hermitage, Tennessee: The Ladies' Hermitage Association, 1987), p. 9.

amount of three hundred. Moser et al., Volume 2, p. 41.

answer I pity him. Moser et al., Volume 3, p. 213.

place to call home. "Andrew Jackson: His Story is History," film production, The Hermitage.

settlement of free men. This is Your Heritage, Mabe "Doc" Kountze (Medford, Massachusetts: Pothier Brothers, 1969), p. 109.

For a fine account of plantation architecture, see Back of the Big House: The Architecture of Plantation Slavery, John Michael Vlach (Chapel Hill: University of North Carolina Press, 1993).

gentlemen and demure ladies. Florewood River Plantation: The 1850s Recreated, site pamphlet, unpaginated.

stars through the cracks. Lay My Burden Down: A Folk History of Slavery, B. A. Botkin, editor (Athens: University of Georgia Press, 1989), p. 139. For another fine collection of slave reminiscences, see Voices From Slavery, Norman Yetman, editor (New York: Holt, Rinehart, Winston, 1970).

two rooms lak dis. *The American Slave: A Composite Autobiography,* George Rawick, editor (Westport, Connecticut: Greenwood Press, 1977), Volume 7, (Mississippi Narratives, Part 2), p. 350.

an' feed us good. Ibid., p. 356.

intrigue of romantic interludes. *Florewood River Plantation.*

the difficult post-war years. "Eliza's House," pamphlet, (Charleston: Middleton Place Foundation), unpaginated.

kindly master. *Monmouth,* p. 9.

There are several excellent studies of slave life. See, for example, *Roll, Jordan, Roll: The World the Slaves Made,* Eugene Genovese (New York: Vintage, 1976); *The Slave Community: Plantation Life in the Antebellum South,* John Blassingame (New York: Oxford University Press, 1979); and for a broader view, *Red, White, and Black: The Peoples of Early America,* Gary Nash (Englewood Cliffs, New Jersey: Prentice Hall, 1982).

For a good study on slaveholders, see *The Ruling Race: A History of American Slaveholders,* James Oakes (New York: Vintage Books, 1983).

A compelling account of Dorothy Redford's saga is to be found in *Somerset Homecoming: Recovering A Lost Heritage,* Dorothy Spruill Redford with Michael D'Orso (New York: Doubleday, 1988).

The Uriah Bennett account is from an interview transcript provided to the author by Dorothy Redford in 1994. From the Scuppernong Farms Project, Farm Security Administration Papers, North Carolina State Archives.

wax and food spatters. *Somerset Place: An Antebellum Plantation Community,* brochure, unpaginated.

of white persons only. Quoted in *Frederick Douglass Home, Cedar Hill: Historic Structures Report,* Part II, James Hinds (Washington, D.C.: National Park Service Division of History, 1968), p. 2.

CHAPTER 3

For an overview of Anglo attitudes toward Hispanic cultures, see *Tree of Hate: Propaganda and Prejudices Affecting United States Relations with the Hispanic World,* Philip Wayne Powell (New York: Basic Books, 1971). For an excellent discussion of Hispanic culture in the United States, see *The Spanish Frontier in North America*, David Weber (New Haven, Connecticut: Yale University Press, 1992). See also *New Spain's Far Northern Frontier*, David Weber, editor (Albuquerque, University of New Mexico Press, 1979).

paid, not slave. *St. Augustine's Historical Heritage,* John Vollbrecht (Jacksonville, Florida: Awo Printing, 1992), unpaginated. See also *The Building of*

Castillo de San Marcos, Luis Rafael Arana and Albert Manucy, (Eastern National Park and Monument Association, 1977).

look at wild animals. Indeh: An Apache Odyssey, Eve Ball (Provo, Utah: Brigham Young University Press, 1980), p. 137.

of simple military expediency. Vollbrecht.

For an excellent background on the San Antonio missions, see *San Antonio Missions National Historical Park,* Louis Torres (Tucson, Arizona: Southwest Parks and Monuments Association).

of lack of natives. Guidelines for a Texas Mission, Fr. Benedict Leutenegger, editor (San Antonio, Texas: Old Spanish Missions Historical Research Library, 1976), pp. 47–48.

men in the kitchen. Ibid., p. 18.

For San Antonio census, see *History of Texas, 1673–1779,* Fray Juan Agustín Morfi (Albuquerque, New Mexico: The Quivira Society, 1935), Part 1, p. 99.

For the early history of the Alamo, see *The Alamo Chain of Missions,* Marion Habig (Chicago: Franciscan Herald Press, 1976).

For much of the background information regarding the Alamo controversy, I'm indebted to the series of articles "Remember the Alamo," published in the *San Antonio Express-News* between February 27 and March 2, 1994, by Robert Rivard et al.

A good account of recent visitors to the Alamo—and some of the controversy surrounding it—can be found in Linenthal's *Sacred Ground* (see above, Chapter 1).

we did not understand. With Santa Anna in Texas: A Personal Narrative of the Revolution. José Enrique de la Peña (College Station: Texas A&M University Press, 1975), p. 49. There has been some controversy of late over whether the de la Peña source is authentic. A consensus in academic circles had not been reached by early 1995.

a Spanish frontier fort. Presidio La Bahia brochure.

Silence prevailed. "Diary of the Military Operations," General José Urrea, in *The Mexican Side of the Texan Revolution,* Carlos Castaneda, editor (Austin, Texas: Graphic Ideas, 1970), p. 244.

a war of extermination. Presidio La Bahia brochure, unpaginated.

weigh over 160 pounds. Readings on the Alamo, John Rios, editor (New York: Vantage Press, 1987), p. 319.

sought to save them. "Old Mission San Luis Rey," brochure, unpaginated.

doors of the sanctuary. Life in California, Alfred Robinson (Santa Barbara, California: Peregrine Publishers, 1970), p. 18.

by three to one. *As the Padres Saw Them: California Indian Life and Customs*, Maynard Geiger, editor (Santa Barbara, California: Santa Barbara Mission Archive Library, 1976), p. 74.

keep them securely hid. Ibid., p. 89.

benefit of the Indians. "Old Mission Santa Barbara, Queen of the Missions," brochure, unpaginated.

The valuable guidebook for Purísima is called *La Purísima Mission: A Pictorial History,* Joseph Engbeck Jr. (Sacramento: California Department of Parks and Recreation, 1987).

to drown their sorrow. Geiger, p. 99.

For a detailed and critical appraisal of life in the missions, see *The Conflict Between the California Indian and White Civilization,* Sherburne Cook (Berkeley: University of California Press, 1976).

to a pagan race. "Welcome to the Basilica of Mission San Carlos Borromeo del Rio Carmelo," brochure, unpaginated.

the pueblos they wish. *Narratives of the Coronado Expedition, 1540–1542,* George Hammond and Agapito Rey, editors (Albuquerque: University of New Mexico Press, 1940), p. 257.

frightfully wounded and dead. *Our Army on the Rio Grande,* T. B. Thorpe (Philadelphia: Carey and Hart, 1846), p. 83.

as if of paper. Ibid., p. 83.

CHAPTER 4

For two valuable sources listing public monuments to women, see *Women Remembered: A Guide to Landmarks of Women's History,* Marion Tinling (New York: Greenwood Press, 1986) and *Susan B. Anthony Slept Here: A Guide to American Women's Landmarks,* Lynn Sherr and Jurate Kazickas (New York: Times Books, 1994).

in crossing Contocook River. Quoted in "Hannah Dustin: The Judgement of History," by Kathryn Whitford, in *Essex Institute Historical Collections* Volume 108 (October 1972), p. 320.

For Mather quotes, see *The Garland Library of Narratives of North American Indian Captivities,* Wilcomb Washburn, editor (Garland Publishing, 1977), Volume 1, pp. 41–47.

American science and education. *New Harmony, Indiana, Visitors' Guide.*

For developing a critical perspective on utopian communities, I am indebted to Thomas Schlereth's *Cultural History and Material Culture* (Charlottesville: University of Virginia Press, 1992).

Zundel he and she. A Documentary History of the Indiana Decade of the Harmony Society *1814–1824*, Karl Arndt, editor (Indianapolis: Indiana Historical Society, 1978), Volume 2, pp. 920–921.

dark and took $115. Ibid., p. 841.

pass into the world. The Communistic Societies of the United States, Charles Nordhoff (New York: Dover Publications, 1966), p. 89.

and mistery of Housekeeping. Arndt, Volume 2, p. 25.

term of forty years. Arndt, Volume 1, p. 409.

condition in all adults. The New Harmony Story, Don Blair (New Harmony, Indiana: New Harmony Publications Committee, 1993), p. 50.

she can go through. New Harmony: An Adventure in Happiness, Thomas Pears Jr., editor (Clifton, New Jersey: Augustus Kelley Publishers, 1973), pp. 81–82. For an excellent account of women's roles in the Owen community, see Women in Utopia: The Ideology of Gender in the American Owenite Communities, Carol Kolmerten (Bloomington: Indiana University Press, 1990).

contempt for their teachers. Ibid., p. 74.

belonged to an army. Twelve Months in New Harmony, Paul Brown (Philadelphia: Porcupine Press, 1972), p. 87.

that are positively usefull. Education and Reform at New Harmony, Arthur Bestor Jr., editor (Clifton, New Jersey: Augustus Kelley Publishers, 1973), p. 380.

all their characteristic grandeur. New Harmony Gazette, January 16, 1828, pp. 106–107.

ranged at pleasure throughout. Brown, p. 36.

mother, or the community. Arndt, Volume 2, p. 671.

depletion of their stores. A Map and Guide to the Shaker Village of Pleasant Hill, unpaginated.

the pretty general sense. Letters From a Young Shaker: William S. Byrd at Pleasant Hill, Stephen Stein, editor (Lexington: University Press of Kentucky, 1985), p. 121.

they can consistently help it. "The Millenial Laws of 1821," Theodore Johnson, editor, in The Shaker Quarterly, Volume 7, No. 2 (Summer 1967), pp. 45–58.

the work of God. Stein, pp. 73–74.

still their poison behind. Ibid., p. 121.

successful type of society. "Map and Guide."

which caused a separation. *An Account of the People Called Shakers,* Thomas Brown (New York: AMS Press, 1972), p. 287.

left desolate and destitute. Ibid.

are forbidden among Believers. Johnson, p. 46. For a fine overview of Shaker women, see *Women, Family, and Utopia,* Lawrence Foster (Syracuse, New York: Syracuse University Press, 1991). For Shaker life as a whole, see *Shaker Experience in America,* Stephen Stein (New Haven, Connecticut: Yale University Press, 1992).

unique yet universal journey. *Monument to Women* (Church of Jesus Christ of Latter-Day Saints, 1978), unpaginated.

a garden in Nauvoo. Ibid.

it all on paper. "Remembering Nauvoo," film production, Nauvoo Visitors' Center.

it to someone else. Quoted in Foster, p. 142. *Women, Family, and Utopia* offers an excellent overview of Mormon plural marriage.

will take you on. *The History of the Saints; Or, An Exposé of Joe Smith and Mormonism,* John Bennett (Boston: Leland and Whiting, 1842), pp. 236–239.

literally a wilderness. "Remembering Nauvoo."

children of the Puritans. *A New England Girlhood,* Lucy Larcom (New York: Corinth Books, 1961), p. 252.

me a painful impression. *American Notes: A Journey,* Charles Dickens (New York: Fromm International, 1985), p. 66.

uninteresting, when separately known. Larcom, p. 183.

but white lowell cloth. Yetman, p. 331.

slips made of Lowell. See Botkin, p. 90.

operatives and colored slaves. *Factory Life as It Is: Factory Tracts Numbers 1 and 2* (Lowell, Massachusetts: Lowell Publishing Company, 1982), p. 4.

subscribers would 'please discontinue.' *The Lowell Offering and Magazine,* 1844, p. 240.

factories was made possible. *Loom and Spindle: Or, Life Among the Early Mill Girls,* Harriet Robinson (Kailua, Hawaii: Press Pacifica, 1976), p. 9.

better for the future. Quoted in *Aspirations and Anxieties: New England Workers and the Mechanized Factory System,* David Zonderman (New York: Oxford University Press, 1992), p. 142.

Tuesday we were paid. *Farm to Factory: Women's Letters, 1830–1860,* Thomas Dublin, editor (New York: Columbia University Press, 1993), p. 126. An excellent overview of Lowell history is provided in Dublin's *Lowell: The*

Story of an Industrial City (Washington, D.C.: U.S. Department of the Interior, 1992).

their bitterness against us. *A Diary from Dixie,* Mary Boykin Chesnut (Cambridge, Massachusetts: Harvard University Press, 1980), p. 163.

for her to obey. *History of Woman Suffrage,* Elizabeth Cady Stanton et al., editors (New York: Arno Press, 1969) Volume 2, p. 391.

Yankee children of light. Chesnut, p. 138.

For a good discussion of women in public history, see *Reclaiming the Past: Landmarks of Women's History,* Page Putnam Miller, editor (Bloomington: Indiana University Press, 1992).

CHAPTER 5

For background on the John Henry story, see *John Henry: A Bio-Bibliography,* Brett Williams (Westport, Connecticut: Greenwood Press, 1983).

One of the best general histories of the railroad in this country is *The Story of American Railroads,* Stewart Holbrook (New York: Crown Publishers, 1947). Histories that touch specifically on labor issues in the nineteenth century include *Working for the Railroad: The Organization of Work in the Nineteenth Century,* Walter Licht (Princeton, New Jersey: Princeton University Press, 1983) and *Men of the Steel Rails: Workers on the Atchison, Topeka & Santa Fe Railroad, 1869–1900,* James Ducker (Lincoln: University of Nebraska Press, 1983).

man in the world. Yetman (see above, Chapter 2), p. 28.

good on his trains. Botkin (see above, Chapter 2), p. 58.

the way to work. *Workin' on the Railroad: Reminiscences from the Age of Steam,* Richard Reinhardt, editor (Palo Alto, California: American West Publishing, 1970), p. 156.

barbarous to require more. *The Register Inquirer,* Hollidaysburg, Pennsylvania, June 2, 1852.

these diminutive Chinese. *The Golden Spike,* Promontory visitors' film.

immense basket-hats, like umbrellas. *Beyond the Mississippi: From the Great River to the Great Ocean,* Albert Richardson (Hartford, Connecticut: American Publishing Company, 1867), p. 462.

travel across the plains. Reinhardt, p. 49.

division of Longstreet's rebels. *Alta California,* May 8, 1869.

generally commands and directs. Reinhardt, p. 50. The story of the transcontinental has been told many times. For a good recent version, see *A*

Great and Shining Road: The Epic Story of the Transcontinental Railroad, John Hoyt Williams (New York: Times Books, 1988).

were frozen to death. Quoted in "Chinese Laborers and the Construction of the Central Pacific," George Kraus, from *Utah Historical Quarterly,* Volume 37, No. 1 (Winter 1969), p. 49. For more on the early history of Chinese in America, see *A History of the Chinese in California: A Syllabus,* Thomas Chinn, editor (San Francisco: Chinese Historical Society, 1969) and *Bitter Strength: A History of the Chinese in the United States,* (Cambridge, Massachusetts: Harvard University Press, 1964).

to do the same. "Evidence of a Dream," visitors' film, California State Railroad Museum.

pay for our own. Native American Testimony: A Chronicle of Indian-White Relations From Prophecy to the Present, Peter Nabokov, editor (New York: Viking, 1991), p. 144.

they may have robbed. My Early Travels and Adventures in America, Henry M. Stanley (Lincoln: University of Nebraska Press, 1982), p. 166. Also see *Daughters of Joy, Sisters of Misery: Prostitutes in the American West,* Anne Butler (Urbana: University of Illinois Press, 1985) and "Red Light Ladies," Alexy Simmons, *Anthropology Northwest,* Number 4 (1989), pp. 13–21.

For the story of Locke, see *Bitter Melon: Inside America's Last Rural Chinese Town,* Jeff Gillenkirk and James Motlow (Berkeley, California: Heyday Books, 1987) and *One Day, One Dollar: Locke, California and the Chinese Farming Experience in the Sacramento Delta,* Peter Leung (El Cerrito, California: Chinese/Chinese American History Project, 1984).

CHAPTER 6

For an introduction to the story of the first homestead claims, see "The 'First' Homestead," Charles Plante and Ray Mattison, from *Agricultural History,* Volume 36, Number 4, pp. 183–193.

For statistics on land ownership in Nebraska, see *History of Nebraska,* James Olson (Lincoln: University of Nebraska Press, 1966), pp. 159–163. For a more general history, see *The Lure of the Land: A Social History of the Public Lands from the Articles of Confederation to the New Deal,* Everett Dick (Lincoln: University of Nebraska Press, 1970).

considerable sums of money. Quoted in "Homestead National Monument: Its Establishment and Administration," Ray Mattison, from *Nebraska History,* Volume 43, Number 1 (March, 1962), p. 12. Mattison provides a detailed account of Freeman's claim to fame.

For an overview of environmental damage at Homestead, see "Prairie Restoration/Management at Homestead: A History," James Stubbendieck and Gary Willson, from *Park Science,* Volume 7, Number 4 (Summer, 1987).

of the United States. Federal Historic Preservation Laws (Washington, D.C.: U.S. Department of the Interior, 1990), p. 2.

For specific accounts of NPS interpretive changes, see *Interpretation in the National Park Service: A Historical Perspective,* Barry Mackintosh (Washington, D.C.: U.S. Department of the Interior, 1986).

For a complete listing of Virginia markers, see *A Guidebook to Virginia's Historical Markers,* John Salmon, editor (Charlottesville: University Press of Virginia, 1994). For lynching figures, see *Lynching in the New South,* W. Fitzhugh Brundage (Urbana: University of Illinois Press, 1993).

For details on the original plan proposed by Disney, see *The Washington Post,* November 12, 1993, Michelle Singletary and Spencer Hsu, pp. A1, A18.

Selected Bibliography on Public History

Anderson, Jay. *Time Machines: The World of Living History*. (Nashville: American Association for State and Local History, 1984).

Benson, Susan Porter, Stephen Brier, and Roy Rosenzweig, eds. *Presenting the Past: Essays on History and the Public*. (Philadelphia: Temple University Press, 1986).

Bodnar, John. *Remaking America: Public Memory, Commemoration, and Patriotism in the Twentieth Century*. (Princeton: Princeton University Press, 1992).

Deetz, James. *In Small Things Forgotten*. (Garden City, New York: Doubleday, 1977).

Gardner, James and George Rollie Adams, eds. *Ordinary People and Everyday Life: Perspectives on the New Social History*. (Nashville: American Association for State and Local History, 1983).

Hosmer, Charles, Jr. *Presence of the Past: A History of the Preservation Movement in the United States Before Williamsburg*. (New York: G.P. Putnam's Sons, 1965).

Kammen, Michael. *Mystic Chords of Memory*. (Alfred Knopf: New York, 1991).

Leon, Warren and Roy Rosenzweig. *History Museums in the United States: A Critical Assessment*. (Urbana: University of Illinois Press, 1989).

Lowenthal, David. *The Past Is a Foreign Country*. (Cambridge, England: Cambridge University Press, 1985).

Schlereth, Thomas J. *Cultural History and Material Culture*. (Charlottesville: University of Virginia Press, 1992).